Birthing the Nation

CALIFORNIA SERIES IN PUBLIC ANTHROPOLOGY

The California Series in Public Anthropology emphasizes the anthropologist's role as an engaged intellectual. It continues anthropology's commitment to being an ethnographic witness, to describing, in human terms, how life is lived beyond the borders of many readers' experiences. But it also adds a commitment, through ethnography, to reframing the terms of public debate—transforming received, accepted understandings of social issues with new insights, new framings.

Series Editor: Robert Borofsky (Hawaii Pacific University)
Contributing Editors: Philippe Bourgois (UC San Francisco),
    Paul Farmer (Partners in Health), Rayna Rapp (New York
    University), and Nancy Scheper-Hughes (UC Berkeley)
University of California Press Editor: Naomi Schneider

1. *Twice Dead: Organ Transplants and the Reinvention of Death,*
   by Margaret Lock
2. *Birthing the Nation: Strategies of Palestinian Women in Israel,*
   by Rhoda Ann Kanaaneh

Birthing the Nation

Strategies of Palestinian Women in Israel

Rhoda Ann Kanaaneh

with a Foreword by Hanan Ashrawi

UNIVERSITY OF CALIFORNIA PRESS
Berkeley · *Los Angeles* · *London*

University of California Press
Berkeley and Los Angeles, California

University of California Press, Ltd.
London, England

Grateful acknowledgment is made for reuse of
material from previously published articles by the
author: "New Reproductive Rights and Wrongs" in
*Contraception across Cultures: Technologies,
Choices, Constraints*, edited by Andrew Russell,
Elisa Sobo, and Mary Thompson (Oxford: Berg
Press, 2000), and "Conceiving Difference: Planning
Families for the Palestinian Nation," *Critical Public
Health* 7, nos. 3–4 (1997): 64–79.

Library of Congress Cataloging-in-Publication Data

Kanaaneh, Rhoda Ann.
   Birthing the nation : strategies of Palestinian
women in Israel / Rhoda Ann Kanaaneh ; with a
foreword by Hanan Ashrawi.
        p. cm. — (California series in public
anthropology ; 2) Includes bibliographical
references and index.
   ISBN 978-0-520-22944-0 (Paper : alk. paper)
      1. Birth control—Israel.   2. Women, Palestinian
Arab—Israel—Social conditions.   I. Title.
II. Series.
   HQ766.5.I75 K363 2002
   363.9′6′095694—dc21

                                            2002001244

Manufactured in the United States of America

16   15   14   13   12   11   10
11   10   9   8   7   6   5

The paper used in this publication meets the minimum
requirements of ANSI/NISO Z39.48-1992 (R 1997)
(*Permanence of Paper*). ∞

*To my mother, Dolores Agnes Kanaaneh,
and my father, Hatim Abdul-Kader
Kanaaneh, with love*

Contents

Illustrations

Foreword

Hanan Ashrawi

As I sit in my home in Ramallah, the sights, sounds, and smells of the Israeli attacks bombard my senses: helicopters, bombs, bullets, gas. The conflict that shapes this book is sadly alive and indeed booming louder than ever. News broadcasts around the world almost daily report the rising death toll. This sinister numerical game, whereby Palestinian victims of Israeli live fire are daily given as x numbers killed and y numbers wounded, reduce our humanity to a series of abstractions. The victims' names, identities, dashed hopes, and shattered dreams are nowhere mentioned. Absent too are the grief and anguish of their mothers, fathers, sisters, brothers, and other loved ones who will have to live with that tragic loss. This routinized reporting allows viewers to accept comfortably the continued killing of this "intransigent," "hard-line," "violent" people. Indeed, Palestinians' will to resist subjugation and oppression is spun by the media as proof of their culpability for their own victimization.

Only through the most sophisticated and approachable analyses can the layers of abstraction and dehumanization begin to be peeled away. Rhoda Kanaaneh's book, standing among the best of scholarship and still widely accessible, is an important model for such efforts. It gives voice to subjects that historically have been kept voiceless. In the array of diverse Palestinians she interviews, people otherwise thought of as "violent," "dictatorial" "terrorists" are humanized. The book gives readers a beautiful introduction to individuals who become complex reflexive creatures—in short, human beings. These Palestinians are capable of being subtle, introspective, witty, and playful as well as strategically blunt and dogmatic. These portrayals come as a welcome reprieve from the ubiquitous distortions of the Palestinian people. They will unsettle any reader's sense of complacency about the anonymity of Palestinians and thus the invisibility of their suffering and the meaninglessness of their deaths.

Significantly, one of the recent misrepresentations of Palestinians and perhaps the most blatantly racist slur against us is the Israeli and international media's theft of our humanity as parents. In an attempt to rob us of our most basic feelings for our children, we are accused of sending our children out to die for the sake of scoring media points. Even as 18-month-old Sara Abdil-Athim Hassan was shot in the back seat of her father's car and other child victims were killed in and around their own homes, their parents were blamed for putting their children "on the front lines," thus obstructing the free path of Israeli bullets. Rhoda's book is a highly appropriate antidote; Palestinian mothers and fathers reflect on their parental roles, responsibilities, affections, and strategies. They carefully consider and weigh the impact of national struggle on their families, as well as medicalization, consumerism, and other trends of globalization that many parents around the world increasingly face.

Birthing the Nation focuses on Palestinians living inside the borders of Israel established in 1948. Israeli propaganda would have us believe that these Palestinian citizens of the state are different creatures from Palestinians in the West Bank and Gaza Strip. We are told that these "Israeli Arabs" are happily integrated into the Jewish state. Despite such misleading claims, the current al-Aqsa intifada spilled beyond the borders of the West Bank and Gaza Strip. Palestinians living inside the so-called green line of Israel loudly and publicly demonstrated in solidarity with their compatriots in the Occupied Territories. In more than thirty towns and villages they protested the injustices of Israeli-imposed "peace." The Israeli response also erased the alleged dividing line between "Palestinian" and "Israeli Arab" when it shot thirteen of its Palestinian citizens dead. The same brutal military tactics are used on all Palestinians, regardless of citizenship. It seems Palestinians are subhuman no matter what passport they carry. Two of the citizen victims, 18-year-old A'laa Nassar and 17-year-old Asel Asli, were from 'Arrabi village, Rhoda's hometown.

Anyone who wishes to understand the connections within and across state borders must read Rhoda Kanaaneh's vivid analyses of the porousness of the green line in relation to Palestinian identity. The contracting and expanding zones of identification that nurture a Palestinian sense of community are elegantly illuminated. Variously partitioned, annexed, occupied, closed, and besieged, these territories and histories fragment Palestinian identity but are also transcended by it. In discussing vital issues of fertility, demography, and modernization, Rhoda's subjects use "Palestine" to refer to pre- and post-1948 entities, depending on the context. These linguistic switches and slippages highlight the limitations of the framework of the now collapsing peace process and the multiple forms Palestinian struggles take in varying locations.

Among those kept voiceless, women are often doubly silenced. The expressions, arguments, and analyses of Palestinian women collected in this book, including those of the author herself, are thus doubly important for undoing misrepresentations. In part, this book is significant simply because it is written by a mature and articulate Palestinian woman. We urgently need to hear more feminist perspectives (both male and female) that, like Rhoda's, seriously attend to the intersections of politics, "race," class, religion, and gender. In the case of this book, the results of such an approach are fresh insight, powerful arguments against Israeli domination, and much-needed internal criticism. This multifaceted framework is relevant well beyond Israel and Palestine. It is indispensable to anyone interested in struggles for justice and freedom, including those against racism and sexism, wherever they may occur.

March 8, 2001

Acknowledgments

This book has been shaped, nurtured, and supported by a great number of people. Elaine Combs-Schilling of Columbia University went well beyond the call of duty in supervising its first incarnation. She painstakingly read draft upon draft, providing a great deal of feedback, from "There should be a comma here" to deeply insightful criticisms of my arguments. I hope her remarkable capacity for nuance is evident in my text. In addition, she supplied me with a vital and constant flow of encouragement from the inception of this project to its current form. Roger Lancaster was also there for me from the start. I am indebted to him for his tremendous energies in vitalizing this project. His unfailing attention to political economy pushed me to recognize forms of power I had marginalized. Through their support, both Roger and Elaine have strongly influenced my thinking in this book and beyond. Brinkeley Messick, Rayna Rapp, and Jane Schneider provided important challenges. Linda Green's support at the earlier stages of the project was critical. Amitav Ghosh's comments on a paper I wrote ages ago (or so it seems) helped launch this project and stimulated my continued interest in studying nationalisms. Similarly, Talal Asad helped shape several chapters through his comments. Mervat Hatem also read that seed chapter and helped me set priorities for the work to come. More recently Dan Rabinowitz worked his way through the entire manuscript and offered insightful reflections. Philippe Fargues similarly provided significant feedback. Tania Ruth Forte raised questions that I continue to think about. Salim Tamari facilitated my research, its circulation, and its presentation for feedback, and in contacting Hanan Ashrawi to write the foreword. Sue Kahn, Mark Levine, Sandra Sufian, Judith Tucker, and Elia Zureik all made key interventions in this work.

The line often drawn between thanks to colleagues for their academic and intellectual contributions, on the one hand, and friends and family for their emotional support and morale boosting, on the other, is thoroughly blurred by so many people on my list. Moslih Kanaaneh, cousin and colleague, is to be thanked for his generous long-distance comments and support. I am grateful to Shiko Behar, Avram Bornstein, Marcial Godoy, Chauncy Lennon, Joseph Massad, Dana Sajdi, Corrina Schneider, and Huda Seif for their comments, encouragement, and the supportive sense of community they fostered when we were graduate students together. My friends Dina Abu-Ghaida, Peter Mitchell, and Aseel Rabie kindly allowed me to experiment with my language and style on nonanthropologists. My husband, Seth Tapper, has provided bountiful sustenance on all levels throughout this process. His wit, humor, and love enriched both the production process and its result. My father, Hatim Kanaaneh, was invaluable in his unwavering faith in me, in the long hours he spent poring over printed-out e-mails of my text, in his clipping of articles for me that proved central to the work, and in his deep connections and illuminating insights into the Galilee. My mother, Dolores Kanaaneh, made my fieldwork a pleasure. Her companionship and unquestioning love as well as her contacts, comments, and enthusiasm were essential. My friends Fadia Khury and ʿArin Khalil are to be singled out for special thanks. They introduced me to numerous contacts and evaluated my methods and ideas; their long friendship has made all my stays in the Galilee truly joyful. Sana Odeh made my writing struggles in New York much more tolerable. It is easy for acknowledgments to sound repetitive and formulaic, yet my sense of gratitude feels anything but. I am truly grateful for all the help I have received.

During my fieldwork the encouragement and assistance of Rita Giacaman, Rema Hammami, and Sharif Kanaana at Birzeit University were extremely helpful. Safaʾ Tamish, ʿAbla Jabaly, Muhammad Qaraqra, Nihaya Dawud, Siham Badarni, Renée Ballan, Fathiyyi Ighbariyyi, and Zaynab Khatib gave generously of their time, allowing me to learn from their wealth of professional knowledge and experiences. Two organizations, the Galilee Society for Health Research and Services and ʿArrabi al Mustaqbal, were important forums for debates from which I learned a great deal. The liveliness and frankness of my research assistant, Manhal Zoʻby, were invaluable to the work. I am grateful to the many friends and relatives who introduced me to their networks of friends and relatives. Finally, the many women and men whom Manhal and I interviewed generously allowed us into their private lives, sparing us their valuable time and thoughts. I thank them for that honor.

This research was made possible by a summer research grant from Columbia University's anthropology department, a Population Council Middle East Project Development Award and Research Award, a Fulbright Hays Doctoral Dissertation Award, a Bell Fellowship from the Harvard Center for Population and Development Studies, and a Faculty Fellowship at the New York University Center for the Study of Gender and Sexuality. Key individuals at each of these institutions showed special interest in my project. Seteney Shami at the Population Council in Cairo got me involved in projects and conferences that helped mature this work. At Harvard George Zeidenstein, Arachu Castro, Chu Junhong, and Elaine Gonçalves all read chunks of manuscript of varying sizes and shared their wisdom to improve it.

Finally, I cannot thank Naomi Schneider and Rob Borofsky of the University of California Press enough for their patience and persistence, faith and encouragement. I thank Julie Peteet, Rashid Khalidi, and a third, anonymous reviewer for their comments and support.

Introduction

Placing

Jamili gets pregnant. She is going to have a fourth child because "four is the perfect sized family." Her husband hopes for a new construction contract that will allow him to squeeze all of the child's "needs" into the budget. Jamili's friend and neighbor Latifi describes her as still "a bit primitive": "She still thinks the role of women is primarily as breeders." Jamili's nurse is upset with her because Jamili is over 35, and she warns her: "You better do all the tests I send you to, or else." Her mother hopes it's a boy who will "raise our heads high." This pregnancy puts Jamili well above the average birth rate for Jews in Israel and pushes her closer to the higher average birth rate of Arabs. "Another Arab baby for the [Jewish] state to contend with," she says defiantly.

In looking at family-planning processes among Palestinians in the Galilee (il-Jalil in local dialect), it is important to recognize "that reproduction, in its biological and social senses, is inextricably bound up with the production of culture" (Ginsburg and Rapp 1995: 2). The negotiation of reproductive decisions in the Galilee has recently become a struggle not only over women's bodies and lives but also over significant social concepts such as "the feminine," "the masculine," "the household," "our culture," "the nation," and "progress." Family planning is now part of the social processes in which these concepts are daily defined, changed, and redefined in people's lives; in which gender is configured, communities are imagined, and boundaries of the modern are drawn.

The five chapters of this book correspond roughly to five interrelated fields of meaning and power in which reproduction is caught up and constructed: nation, economy, difference, body, and gender. Jamili's pregnancy acquires various significances as it circulates in these realms of life. Jamili's remark that "we want to increase the Arabs" must be understood within the realm of the nation. Her concern that "if I thought we could provide more children with all the necessities of modern life, then I wouldn't hesitate to have more" must be understood within a new conceptualization of household economy. Her mother's preference for a male child who will make her proud must be understood as constructing a particular cosmology of gender. Her neighbor's mocking "What does she think in her simple mind, that if she has another son he's going to somehow make Palestine victorious [yunṣur falasṭīn]?" must be understood in light of the measures of difference that Palestinians are coming to use to evaluate each other. Her determination that "after I deliver I'm going on this new diet so I don't become like those fat women whose husbands neglect them" must be understood within a new discourse of the body (as well as economy, difference, and gender). These interwoven spheres of reproduction tell a new and interesting story of how babies, power, and culture are being made in this corner of the world.

INTRODUCTION TO (MY) PLACE

There are many ways to name the Galilee, its people, space, and place (see map). Growing up there, I identified at different moments with my nuclear family, parts of my extended family, my school district, my village, the triangle of three villages to which we belong, the neighboring village in which I went to high school, the Battuf valley area, the Acre district, the Nazareth region, the Tiberias vicinity, the Galilee, northern Israel, Palestine, "the people of 48," hapa-haoles (half whites) in Hawaii, internal diaspora, the homeland, the East, the West, the "developing" world, my father's religion, my mother's religion, people of the book, my essence, my hybridity . . . I belonged to each of these categories, but not equally and not all at once; or, as Ann Laura Stoler puts it, "in different measure and not all at the same time" (1991: 87). It is in the measure and time that different parts of my identity become salient in my own mind and in the minds of those around me that a fragmentary yet in some ways cohesive history of power can be traced. These various subjectivities emerge situationally, and one can trace the condi-

Galilee

tions and systematicities that allow them to do so. Power circulates, but not endlessly: it congeals at significant moments.

The many family members, friends, and acquaintances (and ene-mies?) whom I evoke in this study as the people of the Galilee similarly have concentric, overlapping, and disparate zones of belonging that map out a terrain of power—personal as well as economic, familial, and po-litical histories. I make this assertion to acknowledge the sometimes overwhelming complexity of family planning in the Galilee, and the con-sistencies that I hope to elucidate. In some nexuses of power, hybridity and complexity are not "an infinite interplay of possibilities and flavors of the month" but rather are experienced as reified essence (Lavie and Swedenburg 1996: 3).

The Galilee is indeed a very composite place. My close friend Nadia, who visits from Germany every summer—the daughter of Othman Saadi, a friend and former neighbor of my father's from ʿArrabi, and An-gelica Saadi, a German woman and close friend of many members of my family—Nadia too is part of my Galilee. Othman Saadi is a descendant of religious scholars who came many decades ago from Morocco. Just as my aunt Najiyyi, who has never left the Galilee and rarely leaves the village because she is subject to motion sickness, is also part of my Gali-lee. Yet this aunt's mother, known to me as *mart ʿammi ʿAli*, was not originally from ʿArrabi at all—she grew up in the city of Haifa and as a young woman moved to ʿArrabi, where she married my father's uncle. My memories of her, too, are part of my Galilee. The women born in ʿArrabi who married their first cousins next door as well as the many "foreign" brides—women who came from all parts of the world, from the former Czechoslovakia to Sweden to Morocco, from Italy to South Dakota—all are part of my Galilee.

My "Aunt" Miriam, a German Jewish holocaust survivor, and her adopted Yemenite children, whom we visited almost every Sunday of my childhood in the Jewish beach town of Nahariyya, were also part of my Galilee. Fathers Jacob and Thomas, who founded a monastery near my village to emulate the lifestyle of the early Christians in these mountains, were also part of my Galilee. So were the settlers behind the barbed wire on the hilltop overlooking my house who run a yoga medi-tation center, and who collided not only with my fellow villagers but also with Fathers Jacob and Thomas's monastery, whose land they bor-der. And so was Eli "Yasin," an Israeli Jew who bought an old stone house (from the Yasin family—hence his nickname) on the outskirts of my village, and who allegedly reports to Israeli intelligence on activities in the village through the grapevine of young men whom he supplies with hashish. Nadia, Aunt Najiyyi, and Eli Yasin are all part of the Galilee—but not in the same way. Each relates to the Galilee and experiences it and affects it in his or her own ways. But to describe a place as composite is certainly not to celebrate fragmentation.

Multiplicity and complexity contain institutional frameworks. We were all part of the Galilee, Eli Yasin, *mart ʿammi ʿAli*, and I, but we had differential access to systems of power—economic, political, familial, gendered.

My mother was one of those foreign brides, yet her hybrid Chinese-Hawaiian-American background was most often referred to simply as American. Her Chineseness was overwhelmed by her Americanness in the context of American economic and political dominance in Israel. My own multi-ethnic background was perceived largely as Arab, since my father's identity was considered more determinative of my identity than my mother's. While I was considered Arab, I was also considered special when I could skip classes in English as a second language at school or when I wore the T-shirts with big Hawaiian prints my grandmother sent me. My mother was never required to convert from Christianity to Islam, partly because my father is an atheist, partly because of the open-mindedness and open-heartedness of my relatives, but also because we children were assumed to belong to our father's faith (even though he called himself an atheist, socially he was still considered Muslim). Yet in my home we celebrated Christmas, and my relatives came to wish us happy holidays. We celebrated the Muslim Eids with our extended family, and my mother participated fully. I rarely experienced disjuncture between the two religions. Yet the ease with which people accepted my mother and the apparent seamlessness of my identity owed much to the assumptions of a father's dominance and American global privilege.

The assumption of my father's and my Muslimness in the Galilee should not suggest that Islam is all-powerful there. In my predominantly Muslim third grade in public school, I memorized verses of the Qurʾan and listened to the beautiful stories our religion teacher told about the spider and dove that saved the Prophet's life, while the few Christian students were assigned to a Christian teacher.[1] But in my private Baptist

---

1. Palestinians in the Galilee are approximately 68% Muslim, 16% Christian, 16% Druze. The percentages among the total Palestinian population inside Israel differ slightly: 76% Muslim, 15% Christian, 9% Druze. "Christian" includes Greek Orthodox, Greek Catholic, Roman Catholic, Maronite, Protestant, Anglican, Baptist, and Copt communities.

high school, we—Muslims, Christians, and Druze—sang "The Gospel in One Word Is Joy" with Bob the minister from Tennessee. There is hybridity here, but there are also systematic configurations of power. That most private schools for Palestinians are (missionary) Christian is one aspect of this power. That all Palestinian students—even in the private Christian schools—are required to study Jewish religious texts as part of a mandatory unit in Hebrew is another.

That I experienced multiplicity does not necessarily mean that there were no patterns in it. My joy in the seventh grade at seeing the film *al-Qadisiyya* about Muslim conquests of Persia, was tempered by the remark of my cousin Salwa (who went to a Quaker school in the West Bank) that the Muslims forced people to convert to Islam with their swords. I realized and she realized (in a seventh-grade way) that we had received different versions of history. Many of us in the Galilee are aware that there are many senses of "us," even when we are sometimes able to ignore them.

This hybridity in a context of power is demonstrated in this brief history of my village written by my uncle in his doctoral dissertation:

> Like most Middle Eastern towns, . . . ['Arrabi] is built on the ruins of several previous settlements. Occupation of the site, however, has not been interrupted for the last two thousand years. Several wars brought destruction, but it was always immediately rebuilt.
>
> . . . The first historical source . . . to mention a town in the location . . . is the book *Milhamot Ha-Hashmoneam* (i.e., the Hasmonean Wars), connecting it with Jonathan, a leader of a Jewish army rebelling against the Seleucids. During the rule of Herod it became the third largest town in the whole Galilee and was surrounded with a wall. In the year 67 AD it was destroyed by the Roman forces under the ruling governor and all its population were killed.
>
> During the Byzantine rule, the town was inhabited by Christians and recently (1969) the ruins of a church from that period were uncovered near the present existing church. It is believed that the town was an important administrative seat during this period.
>
> Since the coming of the Arabs to the area, it has been mainly an Arab Moslem town. It existed during the Crusaders' period and is mentioned in maps from that period under its present name.
>
> During the Mamluk period ['Arrabi] again assumed importance and became the seat of a large district.
>
> The period in the history of ['Arrabi] of which its people are most conscious and most proud is that of Zahir al-Umar, the Bedouin who dominated the political life of Northern Palestine for nearly 40 years, from 1737–1775. Zahir al-Umar was a member of the Zeydani Bedouin tribe that lived for a while close to ['Arrabi], raiding the neighboring Druze village of Salama in

revenge against a Druze chief who married a Moslem girl from 'Arrabi by force. . . .

In 1710, Zahir al-Umar was authorized by the Ottoman authorities to collect the taxes from 'Arrabi and the neighboring villages. Soon he turned the area into his own feudal domain, recruited an army from these villages and conquered additional areas. The building he constructed, from which he ruled, is still standing in ['Arrabi] and carries his name. Later he shifted his capital to Tiberias and later to Acre, from which he ruled the whole northern part of the country.

After Zahir al-Umar left 'Arrabi, it slipped back into insignificance, from which it started to re-emerge only after the beginning of the twentieth century.

According to the UN decision of 1947, to divide Palestine into an Arab and a Jewish state, 'Arrabi was supposed to belong to the Arab section. It was, however, occupied without war by Israel in 1948. (Kanaana 1976: 55–56)

Yet from the vantage point of the present day, this complex history is sometimes evoked as mythically Islamic or as mythically brotherly and religiously tolerant. For Palestinians in the Galilee now, the events of 1948 are not just another in a long series of events; from this vantage point 1948 seems like a watershed year, after which everything changed. My grandmother revered one of the small shrines in the center of the village as the shrine of a holy man. Today, having been "reclaimed" by religious Jews and surrounded by a locked fence to protect it from the people who a few years earlier had revered it, it is considered Jewish. I was never taught that Salama used to be a Druze village—Wadi Sallama today is a Bedouin village. While the information is somewhere in the history books, it is not on the minds of most people in my village. The Israeli school system never taught me about the Islamic era in Palestine, which lasted about 1,300 years; it tried to keep that out of my mind. And my Communist cousins taught me about the feudalism of that era as they knew of it, especially after the eighteenth century, reinserting it into history and making me look at it in a new way.

I present this autobiographical information to introduce myself to you as your guide through this book, but also as an illustration of how diverse and plural the Galilee is, and yet how certain patterns can run through it. The Galilee contains Muslims, Christians, Druze, and Jews, small villages, large cities, and Bedouin settlements, people that belong to different lineages and possess different amounts of wealth—all categories that people identify with at different moments. What *are* those moments and what are the structures that allow some categories to gain valence over others? In the Israeli state, one influence over the ways in

which people identify with these categories and places has been the decision to limit or not to limit the size of one's family. That decision has
become an important marker of identity, a crucial site for the negotiations and contestations of political, economic, and social boundaries. As
Palestinians have become increasingly proletarianized, incorporated
into a consumerist economy (usually at the bottom), and depicted by the
state as an overfertile "problem population," the number of babies one
has becomes one of the main ways to trace power.

Chapter 3, "Fertile Differences," demonstrates how classic modernization theory, which constructs the "Third World" as uncontrollably
and irrationally overreproductive and thus poor, has infiltrated Palestinians' thinking about self and other. The language of Third World
population studies gets taken up by people in that world, so that many
Palestinians accuse their supposedly more fecund neighbors of being
"just like the Third World," making no effort to control their reproduction. Other Palestinians reverse the argument and call the modernists
selfish and materialistic. In either case, the differences in family size and
contraceptive use have come to define one's status.

WORKING THE FIELD

Much of this book is based on one year of fieldwork during which I lived
with my parents in the Galilee in the room that I grew up in. Much of it
is also informed by a longer experience of being from the Galilee. I do
not say this to evoke the supposedly unquestionable legitimacy of a na-
tive anthropologist, but rather to say that I sometimes cannot point to
the specific "data" or "sources" on which some of my claims are based.
Some of my arguments are products of a combination of memory, nostalgia, intuition, personal attachments, and missing my husband in New
York. I encourage you to read this personal history in my text.

As anthropologists have for so long claimed, the boundaries between formal research and the everyday are fuzzy. During my fieldwork
months I engaged in formal research activities such as setting up formal
interviews, visiting maternal and child health clinics, hiring a male research assistant, responding to an invitation to lecture to a women's
leadership group in a Druze village, discussing research methods with
other women researchers in the area, attending a conference on women
and violence in Haifa, and e-mailing back and forth with a sociologist
in Belgium. But I also went to the mall with my cousins, attended

friends' engagement parties and children's birthday parties, helped my aunt with her gardening, watched music videos with my friends, went to congratulate a neighbor on the success of her in vitro fertilization. A visit to a Palestinian girlfriend who was studying at the university in Jerusalem and rented an apartment for a short period in a Jewish settlement or to my uncle who is a professor of anthropology at Birzeit University in the West Bank were not planned as part of my research agenda, but I went home with a writing pad full of notes. This blurred boundary between work and nonwork makes for a more holistic approach to my topic, but also for a feeling that I am overanalyzing everything—overzealous to see family planning everywhere I look. This too you may want to read in my text.

One of my best friends, 'Arin, invited me to have lunch after her youngest brother's first communion. The family joked about her brother's altercations with the nuns and how he almost got kicked out of the preparatory class. 'Arin said her parents don't care about religion much, but they want her brother to be like his peers and not to feel left out. I was very interested in this conversation and asked so many questions that it was obvious that I was considering it as part of my research. The family didn't seem to think this event was such a big deal, especially the boy himself. His family hadn't invited anyone else to the lunch. 'Arin said jokingly, "Rhoda is more interested in the communion than we are."

While I did live in my parents' home, I traveled beyond it in mind and body. Although I had originally conceived of my study as centered on one bounded location, as my work unfolded I found myself drawn beyond those boundaries. People in one location urged me to contact their friends and relatives in other areas. When I visited my cousin's wife's sister in 'Arrabi to interview her, a sister-in-law who stopped by for coffee told me, "You should really interview women in my parents' hometown, B'ayni. They have the highest birth rate in the world. My younger sister can take you around."

People made babies in contexts not always confined to their immediate places of residence, and I was carried with the flow of these expanding and contracting contexts. When I did go to B'ayni, this village with the supposedly highest birth rate in the world, I dropped in on an old friend of mine, Salam.[2] Her mother-in-law came to borrow some yogurt culture when I was there, and she told me her husband had lived in the

---

2. I have changed most names and a few personal details to protect the privacy of individuals.

city of Haifa for a long time and was so influenced by foreigners that he wanted her to have fewer children. This comment led me to call an old friend I knew from Communist Party summer camp, a Bedouin woman who went to Haifa University and had stayed on in Haifa as a journalist. She knew some of Salam's father-in-law's old neighbors in the city. But she also invited me to lunch at her parents' house in her village, where I met her brother who had married a Russian woman. Reproductive politics in B'ayni and Haifa were embedded in a larger context, in conceptions of urban and rural differences and notions of modernity and tradition. As I journeyed between places, I recognized them as important locales for the circulation of meaning and power, but also as places that were intricately linked to others.

While not "imprisoning the natives" (Appadurai 1988) in my arbitrary and narrow construction of place—a single neighborhood, village, or city—I have chosen to focus on the Galilee, a larger but nonetheless circumscribed region. Its boundaries are certainly porous, are often pushed and pulled in various directions, and overlap and are engulfed by other boundaries, but the Galilee is a dimension of space that is powerfully present in the minds and social interactions of people. It is a practice of location that I deploy along with many other Palestinians. The Galilee is an important locale for the circulation of meaning and power, for the formation and re-creation of identities.

Part of the "placing" of the Galilee, like so much else in Israel, thus has to do with boundaries, numbers, and religion. Palestinians who live inside the 1948 borders of Israel, unlike those living in the Occupied Territories, in new autonomous areas, or in the diaspora, are citizens of the state of Israel. Numbering around 23 percent of all Palestinians, they are largely descendants of the relatively few Palestinians who were not expelled from the emerging state of Israel during the 1948 war. Nearing one million people, these Palestinians today find themselves an ethnic minority of about 20 percent of Israel's population. Half live in the northern region of the Galilee. Estimates of their concentration there range from 50 to 75 percent, depending on how the region's boundaries are defined (Falah 1989: 232; Yiftachel 1995: 222). According to the government's definitions, "non-Jews" were 51.4 percent of the 943,000 residents of the area in 1995 (Central Bureau of Statistics 1998). At stake in these numbers and borders is the character of the Galilee— pictured by Palestinians as their enclave and by the state and many Israeli Jews as a wild frontier to be settled and Judaized.

Palestinian Arabs in the Galilee largely refer to themselves as either Palestinians or Arabs.[3] The choice of terms and their meaning have a history. The state of Israel has historically chosen not to use the term "Palestinian" because its use would imply recognition of Palestinians as a national group that has rights. Its preference is for "Arab," which identifies these people with Arabs in other countries, whom they are welcome to go and join. Most Israelis also routinely speak of "Arabs" while conveniently overlooking "the fact that the term 'Arabs' silences the link which Palestinians have to the disputed homeland" (Rabinowitz 1997: 13). As Rebecca Stein notes, to translate "Palestinian" as "Arab" is to sanitize and rewrite a threatening history (1996: 103). Moreover, the Israeli preference for the term "Arab" to refer to Palestinian Arabs also conveniently erases the existence of other Arabs in the country— Arab Jews. These identity politics lie under the surface of such terms in the Galilee and should be kept in mind.

According to Israeli government data, Palestinians in the Galilee live in 73 localities—4 Arab cities, 69 Arab villages, and 3 "mixed" localities (Central Bureau of Statistics 1998). These localities are "approved by government planning institutions"; some 50 Arab villages with nearly 7,000 residents in all are unrecognized. Jews in the Galilee, with roughly the same population, live in 295 Jewish localities, a fact that reflects the patterns of both numerous small Jewish settlements, planned and placed strategically by the state to balance out and Judaize the Galilee, and the destruction and emptying of more than 100 Palestinian villages and towns in the 1940s.[4]

I thus wove through these patterns in the Galilee and outside it, following the contexts in which people narrated their making of babies and culture. One of the important places to which people travel—in more ways than one—is "the West." What is clear is that we are no longer dealing with an isolated location (and as the brief synopsis of 'Arrabi's history suggests, perhaps we never were), as the insertions of world development theory's reproductive measure into the Galilee illustrates. People indeed describe themselves as trying to "follow in the path of

3. When Nadim Rouhana asked a sample of Palestinian university students in Israel in 1989, "How would you define yourself?" 43.5% chose Palestinian in Israel, 25.7% Palestinian Arab, 10.6% Israeli Palestinian, 5.5% Palestinian Arab in Israel, 4.5% Palestinian, 4.1% Arab, 2.7% Israeli, 2.1% other, 1.4% Israeli Arab (Rouhana 1997: 122).
4. More on this history of land, population, and Judaization policy may be found in Chapter 1.

the First World," or as taking a better route to get there. By having fewer children, many people hope to be able to provide them with recently conceived "necessities": computers, Coca-Cola, Adidas, Swatches. Chapter 2, "Luxurious Necessities," explores emerging conceptions of "household economy" in a context of changing patterns of employment and the penetration of commodification. New requirements, needs, and desires have been created rapidly. Family planning thus becomes part of a consumerist strategy to provide more of these new "necessities" to a smaller number of children. This strategy is clearly linked to the increasing association of large families with poverty and "backwardness." Thus in some ways, people make babies, families, and culture in a kind of global economic context writ local.

My riding of the ebb and flow of places of identification in the Galilee was both facilitated and circumscribed by my connections. I have more than fifty first cousins on my father's side, most of whom are married and have children. Even my close family transcends the boundaries of my village—one of my uncles and one aunt live in Nazareth; another uncle lives in Ramallah, in the West Bank. Many of my female cousins have also married outside our village and have extensive networks of relatives and friends in the various places they have settled. I went to five schools (including two regional magnet schools) in three locales between kindergarten and twelfth grade and have stayed in touch with friends from each of them. My father is a well-known doctor and has numerous professional contacts. My mother has been a high school teacher in two villages for twenty years and knows students of several generations. All of these networks played important roles in my study. Everyone I interviewed had one or two degrees of separation from me via these networks. While these connections lubricated my interactions, usually allowing for some degree of familiarity and trust, I make no claims to having a representative sample. While I tried to choose people from a variety of backgrounds, I most often wound up meeting people whom folks already in my networks chose as suitable subjects for me. One of my cousins, Samiyyi, asked me many questions about my research. When she heard about the number of women I had interviewed, she told me I should really be talking to more men because "this subject [family planning] is their decision, women only carry out the orders." As far as I can tell, Samiyyi herself chose to continue having children until, after four boys, her fifth child was a girl, without any pressure from her husband. Yet she insisted on setting up an interview for me with a man she thought I would find "interesting" for my research.

Note that I do nonetheless have a considerable number of people from the Galilee whom I talked to and talk about, some of whom I was (or became) closer to than others. As will become clear, I chose not to follow the trend of taking a single person's story, or three persons' interactions with the participant-observer, as the basis for my analysis. There are many disadvantages and limitations in my choice. The individuality and life context of some of the men and women I introduce are diluted.[5] My relatively brief introduction of a larger number of people of many backgrounds can more insidiously mask the fact that you are meeting them all through me.

Yet the alternate strategy of focusing on one person's more comprehensively represented experiences creates parallel problems. The small number of subjects, though their individuality and specificity can come to life more vividly than those of a larger number, may in the end come to be seen as representative of an entire culture.[6] Moreover, providing a life context for people's opinions or decisions can serve as the basis for simplistic or reductionist "explanations" for them. When presented alone, the life context can emerge in relative isolation rather than in relation to other life contexts. Additionally, such in-depth accounts can potentially create a sense of intimacy and exhaustive knowledge that lends itself to easy closure, just as brief introductions and superficial descriptions of income level or religion can do.

My decision to cast the net more widely was a choice between alternatives that were both problematic. What eventually tipped my research and writing in the direction that it has taken here has to do with the constant encouragement, even prodding, that I received from people in the Galilee to interview and consider a large number of subjects. These demands were frequently embedded in basic positivist assumptions about research, problems, and solutions. While I certainly questioned these assumptions, my work is "tainted" by my methodological decisions.

To my advantage, my strategy allows for a great variety of opinions to emerge, and thus for a sense of openness that a few life histories might foreclose. At the same time, it permits me to highlight what I believe to be telling patterns within the variety and multiplicity—patterns that might not emerge from a single account. At its best, this polyvocal style

5. While rereading the revisions to this book, I occasionally lost sight of the people whose names I had changed. This experience made me realize my shortcomings in capturing the people I know.

6. Asad 1994 discusses the unacknowledged parallel between such anthropological narratives and case studies that are presented as typical.

traces important rhythms and systematicities of power within the plurality, hybridity, and complexity of experiences.

Sometime in the middle of my year of fieldwork I realized that while I had many intimate relationships with women, which I felt gave me deep insight into my topic of research, I had few such relationships with men. When I talked to anyone except my close male cousins and friends, the conversations on family planning were awkward: either I was embarrassed or they were. I certainly did not have the same sense of ease and fluidity I felt with many women and girls. I was interviewing an acquaintance's husband one day, and when I got to the question "Have you ever used contraceptives?" he looked away, called his sister to get us some coffee, and launched into a half-hour lecture on the many advances Arab women have made in the workplace. So I decided to hire a male research assistant, Manhal, an outspoken and sociable sociology student whose brother was engaged to a friend of mine. I am not sure how far this strategy was able to push the limitations of my being a woman, since all the men Manhal interviewed knew I would listen to the tapes or read the notes, but I did try to push them. Many of the quotes from men are doubly filtered—first through Manhal, then through me.

Obviously people's perceptions of me and my research are an essential part of this project, not only because such perceptions influenced the things they told me, but also because they constantly tossed my questions back to me. Inasmuch as I had been married for three years and did not yet have any children, my going around asking people why and when they had babies was just begging for the questions to be turned back on me. Ethnographic attention was often focused on me.[7] Although I had not planned to engage in this kind of reflexive dialogue so extensively and with so many people, I found myself doing so at their insistence. The fact that I had married an American (of Jewish and Christian background) fascinated many people, and the fact that I was still childless surprised many others. That detail, combined with the fact that I was living in my parents' home for lengthy periods of time without my husband, led to suspicions of infertility and impending divorce. Many people I met immediately looked at my left hand to see whether I was still wearing my wedding ring. Once when I opened my wallet and our wedding photo fell out, an acquaintance remarked, "Oh, you're still

---

7. I will spare you the litany of instances in which I was interrogated during my research. I have incorporated the more interesting and (for me) telling instances in the body of the narrative.

carrying his photo around. I told them you weren't divorced." People pointedly asked after my husband's health. They frequently said, "You're so *lucky* that he lets you go away for so long," simultaneously conveying admiration for my husband's broad-mindedness and tactfully accepting my cover-up story about research rather than confronting me about our alleged divorce. In response, I found myself pathetically invoking the power of computers and corporations—the flows of things and power that I examine here: "He's very busy, he can't take more than two weeks of vacation a year. He works for NBC's multimedia department." While the mystery of what computer multimedia might be was satisfying to many of my listeners and familiar to some, my invocation of the big American media company was not. "You mean MBC," people would say, referring to the Saudi-owned satellite network out of London, which probably would have seemed more impressive.

Yet the overall acceptance of my somewhat deviant behavior and of my research, despite occasional criticisms and disapprovals, again has to do with my father's support of me, my elite education, my relative wealth (my nuclear family is probably upper middle class in the Galilee), and my connections with the United States.[8] Again, these are venues for the exercise and circulation of power. My connections with the Chinese-American community, the support of my mother, and my feminism were probably not what legitimated me.

The fact that I was (or had been, according to some) married was also an advantage, to the extent that it made me privy to talk about sex and babies. Had I attempted this research a few years earlier, my supposedly virgin ears would probably have been protected from the many lewd jokes, explicit information, and tips on contraception that I heard.

Most of my fieldwork was conducted in colloquial Arabic with a variety of regional dialects, with some classical Arabic, Hebrew, and English words interjected, often to signal the speaker's modernity or rejection of it.[9] My translations of Arabic are another level of filtration you should read into my text. When I have felt unable to translate words ac-

8. Although the United States is often condemned in the Galilee as an imperialist power that has supported Israel consistently, it is also envied as a seat of cultural, economic, and technological power. Chapter 1 explores this matter further.

9. Colloquial dialects vary even within the Gaililee. My transliterations follow local pronunciations, with a bias toward 'Arrabi's *fallāḥi* style. I also used colloquial versions of village and city names, thus eschewing both Israeli official names and classical ones. The system used for Arabic is based on the IJMES one, modified for local pronunciations. For Hebrew transliteration, the Library of Congress system was used.

curately, I have transliterated them. Bear in mind that some of my transcriptions and translations are inadequate to portray the eloquence, wittiness, and playfulness of people's words. My renditions occasionally lose some of the speakers' original humor, persuasiveness, and significance. Moreover, the interpretive work and the academic vocabulary I use for my own analysis and theorizing may imply a simplistic and false contrast between the anthropologist who analyzes and theorizes and my subjects, "who merely relate experiences without having thought about them" (Rand 1995: 21). I attempt to quote many people as they analyze and theorize on the subject at hand, academically and otherwise, to dispel this false contrast.

But not only are these my translations of other people's words, and not only are they words said in front of me (or my research assistant), they are momentary and contextual articulations and expressions. People may say other things at other moments, or do things contrary to what they say. (I certainly do.)

Although some people may appear passive vis-à-vis my role as writer, many of them are certainly not so in person. Late one evening when several relatives were visiting at my family's house, someone mentioned that one of my cousins might be moving back from Jerusalem to the village with his wife and children. They commented that the wife, who is from Jerusalem, said she would have another child if they moved to the village because she would be an outsider and would want another son to empower her. My father looked over at me and said, "Isn't that interesting, Rhoda?" One of my older female relatives got excited about this topic and wanted to tell us more. My dad asked me if I wanted to go and get my tape recorder, but I was tired and I said I could write it down later. My aunt said, "Pardon me, my dear, but do you think you can remember everything we say now tomorrow morning? I think it's better if you go get your tape recorder."

Even in the structured and hierarchical context of a lecture, the audience often talks back. I attended a lecture sponsored by the Communist Party's women's democratic movement in Sakhnin and given by my cousin's husband, an American-trained doctor of clinical psychology. The lecture was attended by about fifty or so women of various ages, educational backgrounds, and degrees of religiosity (several women were wearing Islamicist dress). There were also about twenty men, mostly middle-aged party regulars. The lecture was on the role of fathers in forming children's personalities. During the question-and-answer period, one man in the audience who said he had two wives and nine children launched into his own extended lecture on the difficulty of any involvement of fathers in child raising because they are the main bread-winners. After ten minutes the women in the room started whispering, laughing, and finally talking loudly to drown him out. One woman shouted across the room, "You're wrong, sit down!" When he finally did so, many women had questions for the lecturer. One woman para-phrased him liberally: "Yes, I agree that women sacrifice everything for their kids, not like men." Another woman said his lecture was not very useful to those in the audience with older children, since "the general lines of a personality are formed in the first five years of life and then the circle is closed." She then argued with the lecturer about Freudian the-ory. Indeed, academics and researchers, like nonprofessionals, are ques-tioned and challenged in the Galilee, as I suspect this book will be.

That I was one of only two children in my family—a family whose decisions on the issue of family planning were visible and noticed—very likely encouraged some people to express agreement with my family's choice. It had the opposite effect on my old campmate Suha; she pitied me: "I want more than just a boy and a girl. Rhoda, you have only one brother, so you know how it feels. Isn't it horrible? My children need more sisters and brothers." It did not prevent a friend's grandmother from telling me, "This young generation of women are all whores. They just want to sit on their asses and eat grilled meat—they don't want to bother with raising children."

The point of this discussion is not to say flippantly that everything is contested. That the college-educated woman could engage the psychol-ogy lecturer in theoretical debate only emphasizes the power of these in-stitutions and forms of knowledge. That the women in the audience de-manded that their husbands assume some responsibility for child raising by glorifying their roles as sacrificing mothers emphasizes that resist-ance often partakes of the power of the dominant. That Suha felt sorry for me because I had only one male sibling emphasizes a gendered struc-ture of power, and that my friend's grandmother criticized young wom-en's reproductive decisions by questioning their sexual morality and commitment to the family highlights the power of those elements in so-ciety. Indeed, contestation and resistance often draw on other forms of domination. It has become a truism that resistance mimics power. And indeed, Palestinian resistance to Israeli population policy, which encour-ages Jews to have more children and Palestinians to have fewer, contin-ues to locate the site of political contest in women's wombs. Thus Pales-tinians have advocated either having larger families (to outbreed Jews, just as the Israelis fear) or smaller families (in order to afford to modernize them and thus to challenge Israeli domination with the quality of their children rather than the quantity). But in both resistance strategies and in Israeli population policy, reproduction and nationalism continue to be tightly paired.

However, to say that power meets resistance but that resistance mimics power is not to throw one's hands in the air in the face of hegemony—the specific consequences must be analyzed and evaluated as particular and contingent. Resistance reconfigures power along a variegated scale. In the case of population politics in the Galilee, one of the consequences has been the alienation of Palestinian women from the main source of family planning services available to them, government-sponsored clinics. This consequence can be evaluated in terms of the negative impact on these women's health. Thus "resistance-mimics-power" analyses can remain politically engaged.

My subjects were accustomed to researchers conducting studies in their communities. A large number of Palestinian academics have circulated there before me. In my immediate family, my uncle and one cousin are professors of anthropology, so I am entering well-charted waters. I draw on and owe much to their work. Yet the open-ended and unstructured style of anthropology is not held in wide esteem in the Galilee. "Where is your survey questionnaire?" I was constantly asked. "We'd love to see your data results when they're complete." "Scientific" research methods have gained ascendancy in the Galilee.

Part and parcel of this ascendancy of science is the increasing medicalization of bodies, in addition to their commodification. Significantly, these modernization processes are perceived as having altered the very state of gender and the body. In fact, these changes are often constructed as the primary features of modernization, resulting in new conceptualizations of reproduction and sexuality. Chapter 4 examines some of these bodily interventions in the Galilee, from the sale of cosmetics to IUDs to in vitro fertilization, as rich grounds for the exploration of the class, nationalist, and gender components of childbearing. Walk with me through malls, private clinics, newspaper editorials, sex education classes, and advertisements for plastic surgery as I explore these innovations and their involvement in the power plays of identity and reproduction. The modernization of the body in the Galilee has involved a new training of sexuality through particular forms of consumption, sex education, and the medical control of reproduction. I examine the various forms of contraception and new reproductive technologies, including assisted conception, that have been introduced and the resulting power dynamics.

As I conducted this research, I sometimes felt I was imposing on people by demanding their time and energy, but many people seemed to really enjoy talking about these topics. Among the most enthusiastic were Iftikar and Buthaina. Iftikar was my classmate from the fifth to eighth grades, and I had fallen out of touch with her until I ran into her on the street one day. She was excited to see me because she was getting engaged to a man whose sister was a relative of mine by marriage. Iftikar invited me to her birthday party, which was attended by her current and former coworkers at an egg-sorting factory; Buthaina was her best friend from the factory. Their boss was a Palestinian subcontractor for the kibbutz that owned the business. During the next couple of visits back and forth, Iftikar and Buthaina asked me about my work, and eventually I interviewed them. As my questions built from "What would be your ideal family size?" to "Why do so many women prefer having boys?" to "Would you ever consider accepting donated sperm if you were infertile?" they became increasingly animated. They talked to me for hours. When I met with them again a couple of weeks later, one of their sisters and a friend were present, and Iftikar and Buthaina urged me to interview them. I didn't have my notebook with me, so I forgot some of the questions I had asked Iftikar and Buthaina earlier, but no matter—they reminded me of the things I forgot to ask. They sometimes paraphrased my questions in much more elegant terms than I had used. I borrowed a piece of paper to write notes, and Buthaina asked me, "Are you really going to use this paper? I hope you don't lose it or throw it away. These are important things." Another friend of mine insisted that I interview her sister because she thought it would help me at the same time that it would help her sister "to get to talk about some of these things, to get it off her chest." Obviously not everyone was as excited as these women were, but my continued interest in these topics is sustained by the enthusiasm with which my research was met. Issues of family planning are of deep interest to me but also to many Palestinians in the Galilee.

Some people I interviewed expected something back from me. Abu Riad, who helped women conceive boys with a "scientific" formula, wanted me to take his picture and show him "his section" of the book once it was done. My friend Salam, who helped me make many contacts in her village, wanted to talk to my father, who is a physician, to find out whether he had heard of a scientific formula to conceive male chil-

dren. My father said that as far as he knew, no such thing existed. When
Salam called a few days later, she mentioned that she had finally found
a doctor who did know. In fact, when I asked people if they had heard
of such methods for conceiving boys, many of them asked me if I knew
of a way. Khaldiyyi said: "I don't know how they do it, but yes, I have
heard of it. Do you know, Rhoda, how they do it, so we can tell my
daughter about it?" Khaldiyyi's daughter, who had three daughters,
joined the conversation: "Yes, I hear all the teachers talking about this
at work. They even say there are hormones that you can buy at the phar-
macy." Khaldiyyi added: "They used to tell me when you sleep with
your husband, sleep on the right side and you'll conceive a boy, but it's
not true. Tell us, is there a new way to do it?" My answer—that as far
as I knew, there was no proven way to determine the sex of a baby short
of medically assisted conception—was not what they wanted to hear.

Some of the information people expected from me I could provide. A
social worker who was thinking of getting her master's degree, for instance, wanted to know how to go about getting a scholarship to study
abroad. Other implicit expectations were well beyond my limited abili-
ties. A former schoolmate confided during an interview that even though
she had been married for six years and had two children, she still felt incredible pain every time she and her husband had intercourse. My lack
of expertise in such matters was a source of frustration to me as well as
to her. I told my friend to ask her gynecologist; she had already done so.
I asked her whether her husband rushed her too much and whether he
was gentle; she said, "It's not him at all—he's great. It's me." I bought
her lubricant jelly, but she said, "Rhoda, I can use this for now, but I
can't use it all my life. It's been six years." She told me that I was the only
soul she had ever told this to except her husband and the doctor, and
there I was, unable to help. Safa' Tamish, a sex educator, expressed the
same frustration when she was unable to help people with their problems. She gives sex education workshops and at the end many people approach her and confide in her about their own or their friends' problems—but unlike me, she is planning to go back to school to train as a
sex therapist. Her plans are part of the process of modernizing the body,
which people perceive as both beneficial and warping.

Finally, part of the connections between the local and the global is the
position of the Galilee as my text about it circulates beyond its boundaries. When my husband read a draft of this introduction, he warned me
that exotic-sounding details such as Salam's mother-in-law stopping
by to borrow yogurt culture might lend themselves to Orientalism. I

contemplated cutting these references, and especially deleting paragraphs on clan politics and wife beatings, which could be seen to confirm stereotypes of Palestinian culture. Generally I resisted this urge to censor, because silence would constitute a type of recapitulation. Moreover, I was not the only one to consider the possibility of playing into Orientalist biases. It has influenced many performances of culture and identity in the Galilee, including the ones performed for the sake of my research.

People were aware that my narrative about them would eventually travel in global circuits—circuits that have not been too kind to them. People's accounts were already products of their own interpretations, not raw data waiting to be interpreted by me, and these interpretations often took into account the ramifications of this global travel. It seems hardly necessary to point to the fact that subjects themselves act as editors, cultural critics, theorists, and text makers, often self-consciously so, who calculate the dangers of Orientalism (Rand 1995: 17). I mentioned to a close family friend, Abu Mursi, some of the practices women told me they use (in addition to biomedical ones) to heal and protect their children, such as guarding them from the evil eye. He was only half joking when he replied, "I hope you're not going to take these silly things with you and tell the Americans about them. That's not what you're doing, is it?" But Abu Mursi's characterization of these things as silly, as well as the Western conceptualization of such practices as superstitions, is precisely what I am trying to address. These biases are built into the way such practices are deployed.

Many parents in the Galilee prefer to have more sons than daughters, but their constructions of their preference are clearly informed by the negative impression it may make at home and abroad. That is why it is often constructed in specifically "modern" and global terms. "All cultures like boys because they are patrilineal—it is only logical to want male heirs," one woman told me. Locating this desire within modern nationalism, a narrative that is widely accepted globally (although Palestinian nationalism is often not), is another option. The emergence of "scientific" methods for conceiving boys has made for the possibility of rationally planning a small family (with boys); that is certainly a modern desire. Logic, nationalism, and science are used today to construct a preference for sons.

While this work focuses on the Galilee, it certainly has some relevance to family planning in other areas in which Palestinians live, as well as to the dynamics of reproduction in other societies. Indeed, I suggest

that my analyses may offer an approach useful in the study of other societies and may provide an important angle from which to view life beyond the Galilee.

I hope to illuminate some of the cohesive forms of political, economic, and social structures in which family planning has emerged as
a central category of distinction, domination, and contestation in the
Galilee. Modernization has inserted itself in profound ways. Nationalism, economic transformations, medical regulation, new forms of social
stratification, and changing gender relations have strikingly been articulated through discourses and practices of reproduction. This process
encompasses many nuances, individual variations, internal inconsistencies, and exceptions. But a distinct pattern of "modern" over "backward" emerges, the (negative and positive) consequences of which are
strongly felt in the Galilee. Reproduction has been politicized and maternity nationalized. Women's bodies are deeply inscribed as reproducers of the nation, whether by bearing few or many children. Family planning has become an essential new household economic strategy. The
economization of family planning has emerged as both a set of practices
of material acquisitiveness and a salient belief system. Development theory, with its binaries of modern and primitive, controlled and uncontrolled reproduction, has come to resonate strongly in the Galilee. Social categorizations of urban/rural/Bedouin and of clan and religion
gain new valence through new conceptions of reproductive difference.
The ideal production of small, spaced, controlled, nuclearized, consuming, gender-balanced families has become an important means of
contesting and negotiating shifting categories of personhood and community. Medicalization and scientific innovations have not only transformed reproductive behavior but also influenced social values. Finally,
shifting gender relations are manifest in changing expressions and practices of family planning. Preferences for giving birth to boys rather than
girls are being constructed as compatible with modernity.

It is striking how powerfully modernization has transformed the lives
of Palestinians in the Galilee. Arguments for and against modernization
define, shape, and limit the debates on gender, nation, class, and religion. These transformations have not affected all Palestinians equally or
in the same way, but no Palestinian can ignore them. Planning a family
(whether small or large) is today a point at which Palestinians can engage, emulate, contest, and challenge ethnic politics, economic transformations, medical interventions, and social organization—all changes
that they cannot afford to ignore.

ONE

Babies and Boundaries

What is the significance of population and reproduction in thinking, creating, and sustaining the Israeli nation-state? To answer that question I first explore the connections between demography and modern nationalism and present population policies as technologies of power intrinsic to recent conceptions of the nation-state, ones with powerful race, class, and gender implications. Using this theoretical framework, I reflect on the history of political arithmetic in the development of the state of Israel specifically, as well as in the growth of Palestinian nationalism without a state apparatus. With the Galilee in mind, I demonstrate how imaginings of the nation attempt to inscribe the bodies of women and men in new ways, with certain effects on reproductive discourses and practices among Palestinians in the Galilee.

REPRODUCTION AND NATIONALISM

In *Technologies of the Self,* Michel Foucault observes that in late eighteenth-century Europe, "the care for individual life [becomes] . . . a duty for the state." He notes that an obscure book of 1779 by J. P. Frank is "the first great systematic program of public health for the modern state. It indicates with a lot of detail what an administration has to do to insure the wholesome food, good housing, health care, and medical institutions which the population needs to remain healthy; in short, to foster the life of individuals." Oddly, this new care for the individual and

fostering of life coexists with increasingly larger "destructive mechanisms," such as those used in war. This puzzling antinomy may be understood through the "reason of the state" developed during this period,
whereby the state becomes "a kind of natural object" (Foucault 1988:
147, 151).[1]

The art of governing becomes intimately bound up with the development of what was called at that moment "political arithmetic": "statistics . . . related . . . to the knowledge of the state." Individuals become
an object of concern to the extent that they are relevant to the state's
strength: "From the state's point of view, the individual exists insofar as
what he does is able to introduce even a minimal change in the strength
of the state. . . . And sometimes what he has to do for the state is to live,
to work, to produce, to consume; and sometimes what he has to do is to
die" (ibid.: 151, 152). And I would add to Foucault's list that sometimes
what the individual has to do—particularly the female individual—is to
reproduce or stop reproducing.

During the eighteenth century, the Ottoman Empire, which included
the areas that today are Palestine and Israel, did not use such technologies. State power was not measured by political arithmetic, as it was
beginning to be measured in European states. According to Abraham
Marcus, state power in the Ottoman Empire was measured instead by
the success of government institutions in defending the realm against
external attack and in extracting taxes. The authorities "maintained no
systematic medical or education records; no registration of births, deaths,
marriages, and divorces; no data on incomes or employment; and no
cadastral surveys or construction records. Such information was not
deemed essential to the tasks of governance" (1989: 76, 77).[2] It was not
until the late nineteenth century that Ottoman modernization efforts
created a more comprehensive population registry (McCarthy 1990: 2)
that transformed counting "from an instrument of taxes to an instrument of knowledge" (Richard Smith quoted in Appadurai 1993).[3] With

    1. The state, however, has been considered a natural object at different times in his-
tory. It is important to note that critics have questioned Foucault's rather evolutionary and
Eurocentric argument and his interpretation of political arithmetic as a modern Western
invention (e.g., Stoler 1997, Comaroff and Comaroff 1991, Mitchell 1988). Hence, one
must cautiously proceed with the understanding that this specific conception of the political arithmetic of the state becomes increasingly consolidated, rather than newly and exclusively invented, in Europe after the late 1700s.
    2. While marriages, divorces, deaths, and property transactions were registered in the
local courts, the Ottoman authorities did not aggregate them to produce statistics.
    3. These conceptions of state power closely parallel the power of the sovereign body
on the one hand and the new technology of the prison on the other, discussed in Foucault's

this new conception of the state, power is more diffuse, encoded on the bodies of citizens.

According to Beshara Doumani:

> People counting, essentially, was an exercise in hegemony that involved the (re)definition of the individual's place in the Ottoman polity and the use of knowledge to facilitate greater control. In this sense, population counts, perhaps more than any other single administrative action of the Ottoman authorities during the Tanzimat period, had a dramatic effect in that they literally touched the majority of the local population in one brief, but comprehensive sweep. (1994: 13)

Moreover, this new formulation of state power in Europe was accompanied by the rise of new sciences and political technologies created "to observe people in quantitative contexts." The dictionary meaning of the word "population" shifted away from the verb (to people) and became an object that denotes "a natural entity, an issue about which neutral statements can be made, an object open to human control and management" (Duden 1992: 148, 146; see also Hartmann 1995: 24). A new language thus emerged to "marginalistically integrate individuals in the state's utility" (Foucault 1988: 153). William Petty, the seventeenth-century ancestor of statistics, "conceived the idea of quantifying society"; he wrote that "instead of using only comparative and superlative words, and intellectual arguments, I . . . express myself in terms of Number, Weight and Measure" (quoted in Duden 1992: 147).

Interestingly, these new technologies were often created on the colonial frontiers rather than in Europe, in order to manage and supervise subjugated populations (Comaroff and Comaroff 1991; Mitchell 1988: 40; Stoler 1997). For example, one of the early acts of the British colonial administration after the military occupation of Egypt in 1882 was to set up a central office to organize the official registration of births in every Egyptian village. While the immediate purpose of this counting was to organize recruitment into the army, it had a wider value:

> The new methods of power sought to police, supervise and instruct the population individually. It was a power that wanted to work with 'known individuals' and 'noted characters,' who were to be registered, counted, inspected and reported upon. . . . The new medico-statistical practices adopted from the armed forces provided a language of the body—its number, its con-

---

Discipline and Punish (1979). Emergent political arithmetic, like the new technologies of the prison, is a more diffuse form of power that uses the bodies of citizens.

dition, its improvement, its protection—in terms of which political power might operate. (Mitchell 1988: 98)

Benedict Anderson similarly describes the census as an essential institution of power that arose in the mid–nineteenth century and "profoundly shaped the way in which the colonial state imagined its dominion." Nineteenth-century census takers constructed ethnic racial classifications and systematically quantified them.[4] Anderson argues that these racialized identity categories betray "the census-makers' passion for completeness and unambiguity. Hence their intolerance of multiple, politically 'transvestite,' blurred or changing identifications. . . . The fiction of the census is that everyone is in it, and that everyone has one—and only one—extremely clear place" (1991: 164, 166). Moreover, the invented categories of the census began to shape societies and in a sense become "real":

> Guided by its imagined map, [the colonial state] organized the new education, juridical, public-health, police, and immigration bureaucracies it was building on the principle of ethno-racial hierarchies. . . . The flow of subject populations through the mesh of differential schools, courts, clinics, police stations and immigration offices created 'traffic-habits' which in time *gave real social life to the state's earlier fantasies*. (Ibid.: 169; emphasis added)

Census taking was and continues to be "one of the basic rituals of state formation" (Patriarca 1994: 361). As Ian Hacking notes, "counting is no mere report of developments. It elaborately . . . creates new ways for people to be" (1986: 223). By transforming humans into counted "populations," statistical sciences made it possible "to uncover general truths about mass phenomena even though the cause of each particular action was unknown and remained inaccessible." These sciences reduce people to manageable entities that can allegedly be controlled for the "common good" (Duden 1992: 146, 148). In addition to racial categories, population experts, theoreticians, and planners create

---

4. Similarly, Partha Chatterjee argues that a fundamental change occurred with enumeration:

> The impoverishment of the earlier "fuzzy" sense of the community and an insistence upon the identification of community in the "enumerable" sense. Earlier, communities were fuzzy, in the sense that, first, a community did not claim to represent or exhaust all layers of selfhood of its members, and second, the community . . . did not require its members to ask how many of them there were in the world. The colonial regime . . . sought to fashion the conceptual instruments of its control over an alien population precisely by enumerating the diverse communities that, in the colonial imagination, constituted the society over which it had been destined by History to rule. (1993: 223).

labels such as "underdeveloped," "malnourished," and "illiterate" (Escobar 1984: 387). These "counting conventions" (Cussins 1998: 2) then structure the encounter between the state or organization and its "citizens" in such a way that the latter's local realities are "transcended and elaborated upon by the former." The techniques that population studies use for organizing and labeling people and their problems make them manageable for the discipline. These people are then obliged "to maneuver within the limits posed by the institutions" (Escobar 1988: 435).

Most notably, with the rise of population *control* lobbies in the 1970s, sexual behavior has become a matter of public policy whereby governments and institutions attempt to change the most intimate sexual behavior of millions of people. Population growth came to be considered an essential factor in "developing" the Third World, but soon "not the hope of development but the fear of global disaster gave a new motivation to the attempts at population control" (Duden 1992: 153). Citizens and their bodies, particularly female, nonwhite, and poor bodies, are thus seen as vessels of population growth that must be controlled. Even if one were to agree that continual global population growth is undesirable, the dominant articulation of this belief remains racist, classist, and sexist: it holds poor nonwhite women responsible for impending global catastrophe and claims that the world's very survival depends on containing their reproduction (rather than on, say, limiting levels of consumption or industrial expansion in developed countries, or raising the standard of living for people in the Third World). Political arithmetic is often a highly racialized, classed, and gendered form of knowledge/power.

Still, the coherence and totalizing power of such projects can be overestimated. Population policies are frequently unsuccessful, at least by their stated goals: more often than not the fetishized statistics of population fail to demonstrate the desired changes, as population experts frequently and nervously observe. The desired production of "manageable" subjects often seems to remain elusive. Derek Sayer reminds us that a project such as the state "is a *claim* that in its very name attempts to give unity, coherence, structure, [purposiveness, and rationality] to what are in practice frequently disunited, fragmented attempts at domination." He asks us to pose four crucial questions: "First, how cohesive historically *are* hegemonic projects? Second, even if they are cohesive at some level—of intellectuality—how cohesive are they when actually translated into *practice*? Third, even if these projects are successful at both levels, how *confining* are they, anyway? And fourth, who is the *audience* for this performance? Or are we just dealing with stories the elites tell themselves?" (1994: 371).

These questions are paramount in examining how population projects have played out in Israel: How cohesive have population projects in Israel been, intellectually and in practice? What conflicts within and between elites go on behind the mask of the state? Do these disciplines achieve their stated goal and, if not, do they succeed in other unintended ways? Do they empower, oppress, or both? Who is the audience and is anyone listening? How do different people within the Palestinian community deal with these official discourses and practices? Do people challenge one hegemonic project through another?

POPULATION AND THE ISRAELI STATE

While Zionist ideology was neither monolithic nor static, for the most part it became increasingly popular, especially among Eastern European Jews, around the turn of the twentieth century and revolved around the idea of creating a homeland for the Jews in Palestine. By virtue of such a goal, this movement was concerned largely with maximizing the number of Jews in Palestine in relation to non-Jews through immigration, displacement of Palestinians, and selective pronatalism.

The very definition of the Zionist state, as of most other nationalisms, is based on demography and numbers, but the settler colonial history of the creation of the state of Israel heightens this obsession, as well as its consequences. These include the expulsion and dispersion of the majority of the Palestinian people, referred to by Zionists as "de-Arabization" or the "demographic purge," as well as "Judaization" through "the most active immigration policy in modern history" (Friedlander and Goldscheider 1979: xviii), which settled Jews in Palestine against the explicit opposition of the indigenous community. These processes became foundational for Zionist philosophy and "were necessary requirements for the success of the Zionist enterprise" (Kanaana 1992: 47). The calculation of the ratio of Jews to "Arabs" and the often violent separation, rigidification, and essentializing of these identities is a cornerstone of the imagined community of Israel.

To achieve such a nation, Zionists needed to go to great lengths. Zachary Lockman observes that "Zionism was—had to be—not simply a conventional nationalist movement but a colonizing and settlement movement as well" (1996: 27). Although it is sometimes argued that most Zionists were unaware of the existence of the Arab population at the time they were making plans for the region, recently declassified archives and diaries make it clear that Zionist leaders in fact quickly became highly preoccupied with what was referred to as the "Arab problem" (Said 1988: 239). The image of Palestine as an empty, neglected wasteland, exemplified by the slogan "Land without people for a people without land," was constructed through the colonialist cultural tools that were at the disposal of European Zionists. Although there were dissenting voices, their ultimate marginality demonstrates that Zionism's attitude toward Palestinians "had less to do with ignorance than with a particular way of knowing and a particular kind of knowledge" prevalent in Europe at the time—that of colonialism (Lockman 1996: 36). Hence, "because the Zionist movement was committed to the transformation of Palestine into a 'mono-religious' Jewish state, its success required it to be as intent on the destruction of the indigenous Arab society as it was on the construction of a Jewish life in Palestine" (Said 1988: 238). The marginalization of other people is frequently built into nationalist ideologies rather than accidental or coincidental.

In 1880 about 25,000 Jews lived in the area of Palestine (Friedlander and Goldscheider 1979: 15). Since then, starting in the late Ottoman period, the Zionist movement and the Israeli state have carried out an active immigration policy and today nearly 4 million Jews live in the area. The common Zionist belief that Israel "should be demographically homogeneous" (Flapan 1987: 7) also required de-Arabization of the region. Even before World War I, when Jews accounted for about 8 percent of the area's population, some Zionist leaders suggested that Palestinians be transferred to adjacent Arab countries (Wiemer 1983: 30). At the 1937 Zionist Congress in Zurich, "the idea of transfer was accepted by most of the high-ranking Zionist leaders and became a formal policy" (Shahak 1989: 23). Imbued by a culture that saw non-European peoples as inferior, Zionists were able to construct the inhabitants of Palestine as marginal, as a motley collection of people (rather than as an ethnos or nation), and therefore as *movable* (Lockman 1996: 35). While a minority dissented, according to Simha Flapan (a Zionist historian), this view reflected the "long standing attitude of the majority of Israel's political and intellectual elite and the great majority of the masses of Jews in Israel" (1987: 12–13). Even moderate Zionists who are appalled by the idea of transfer continue to conceive of the conflict as a "demographic" or "population" problem. In 1937 David Ben-Gurion declared that the "idea of transfer—which immediately outraged the

Arabs—was morally and ethically justified, nothing more than the continuation of the natural process taking place, as Jews displaced Arabs" (quoted in ibid.: 16). And I believe Ben-Gurion was insightful in seeing the connection between transfer and nationalism. Given the importance of political arithmetic for sustaining the nation-state, transfer is an extreme yet logical and expedient solution, one that has been implemented elsewhere in the world (e.g., Greece, Turkey, India, Pakistan).

Population transfer plans continued to be drawn up and supported by major figures throughout the history of Israel (Masalha 1997).[5] And while transfer was never officially carried through as such in Palestine, the goals of transfer were achieved largely by other means. In October 1948 the transfer committee appointed by Ben-Gurion recommended that Arabs should number no more than 15 percent of Israel's total population (Flapan 1987: 16).[6] This figure is, in fact, not far from the current percentage of Palestinians living inside Israel "proper" today.

The displacement of Palestinians began through land acquisition. Since the end of the nineteenth century, Zionist organizations have focused heavily on buying land in Palestine. Earlier in that century, in 1858, the Ottoman Land Code had introduced private land ownership.[7] This legal change "set the stage for the rise of large estates, especially in the hands of rich absentee landlords, and for the emergence of tenant farmers on such estates, which, in turn, created the legal condition for the eviction of tenant farmers years later" (Kanaana 1992: 52). Furthermore, the authorities of the British mandate (1917–48) sought to abolish the joint land tenure system to enforce the partition of undivided lands into permanently fixed and privately owned parcels, which also facilitated sale transactions (Atran 1989: 725).[8] Before 1948, residents of

5. The examples are abundant. See Masalha 1992 and 1997 for details. In 1951, Ben-Gurion (then prime minister) supported a plan to transfer Christian Arabs to South America (Masalha 1996). In 1964, Ariel Sharon, then an army colonel, prepared a plan to expel Arabs from the Galilee to Syria if a war were to erupt (*Manchester Guardian Weekly*, Feb. 21, 1988). To this day, right-wing Israeli members of the Knesset (parliament) routinely draw up plans for transferring Arabs as a solution to the ongoing conflict.

6. More recently Prime Minister Yitzhak Rabin placed the upper limit on the proportion of Arabs at 20 percent.

7. These reforms were part of the second phase of Ottoman *tanzimat*. They began to take effect in Palestine around 1870.

8. According to Scott Atran, the British authorities had "a century and a half of accumulated colonial wisdom in matters of land settlement—with accompanying surveys, censuses, sanitary measures, economic and 'education' programs," which they applied in Palestine *en bloc*. In relation to the census, as elsewhere in the empire, they "aimed principally to enumeratively fix the nature of goods and people in order to create the commercial and social categories by which the colony could be arranged: lives were thereby

about seventy Palestinian Arab villages were evicted when absentee land-lords sold their holdings to Jewish organizations (Kanaana 1992: 54).

Thus large-scale land acquisition was one of the first steps taken in the Zionist enterprise. It was soon accompanied by large waves of Jew-ish immigration to Palestine, especially but not exclusively around the time of the Jewish holocaust. Demographically, Jewish immigration "in-creased the ratio of alien settlers from one in ten in 1918 to one in two in 1947" (Said 1988: 242). Land acquisition and immigration were complementary policies whereby the newly acquired lands were cleared of Palestinians and settled by Jews. Resale of land to non-Jews was pro-hibited. As Ben-Gurion said, "We have conquered territories, but with-out settlement they have no value" (quoted in Kanaana 1992: 42). Such tactics, again, are not unique to Israel in the pursuit of nationalist homogenization.

During the war of 1948, 725,000 Palestinians fled their homes and became refugees.[9] According to the Israeli researcher Simha Flapan, the so-called Palestinian exodus was due largely to Jewish attacks on Arab centers, the terrorist acts of the Irgun Zvai Leumi and LEHI (Stern Gang), whispering campaigns, psychological warfare, and evacuations ordered by the Israeli Defense Force. "Records available from archives and diaries . . . show that a design was being implemented . . . to reduce the number of Arabs in the Jewish state to a minimum and to make use of most of their lands, properties, habitats to absorb the masses of Jew-ish immigrants" (1987: 7). The expulsion of the majority of the Pales-tinians during 1948, according to Reinhard Wiemer, "was not acciden-tal, but an option which always had a considerable influence on all the major Zionist groups at different times" (1983: 34). Thus the force of arms accomplished in just over a year what decades of migration had failed to do, namely, "to effect a complete demographic transformation in the lion's share of Palestine" (Abu-Lughod 1971: 154).

The existence of such a deliberate plan of expulsion is controversial among Israelis; many Israeli and Zionist researchers have written about it (e.g., Flapan 1987; Morris 1986a, 1986b, 1988; Pappe 1988, 1994). Mainstream Zionist historians claim that Palestinians fled of their own

---

indexed for scrutiny and control by strangers, and fixed into categories that would limit people's adaptive flexibility" (1989: 724).

9. Of these 725,000 refugees, some 250,000 fled to the West Bank, 190,000 to Gaza, and 255,000 to neighboring countries; approximately 30,000 were internally displaced within the borders of the emerging state of Israel.

will, or that Arab leaders called on them to leave. But while this history of expulsion is controversial, the subsequent systematic prevention of Palestinian refugees from returning is not. Ben-Gurion wrote: "I don't accept the formulation that we should not encourage their return: Their return must be prevented . . . at all costs" (quoted in Flapan 1987: 17). The few Arabs who remained within the borders of the new state and who were present in their homes at the time the first population registration in Israel was conducted were allowed to stay. All others were forbidden to remain within or to reenter the newly drawn borders.

The war of 1948 rather successfully achieved the demographic purge necessary for the creation of the Zionist state. But the process by no means ended there.[10] The war of 1948 was a significant part of the demographic purge of Palestine, but was "only a station along a very long process which started toward the end of the last century and is still going on today" (Kanaana 1992: 100). The process of de-Arabization and Judaization continued with the expulsion of more than 300,000 Palestinians from the West Bank and tens of thousands from Gaza during the 1967 occupation (Abu-Lughod 1971: 163), as well as the immigration of large numbers of Russian Jews since 1991. These various strategies of nationalist homogenization are not unique to Israel, and have been used in the creation of many a nation-state, from the United States with its colonial settler roots to Pakistan and India at their partition.

Another feature of the imaginings of Zionism (although not exclusive to it) heightens its obsession with political arithmetic: the state of Israel was never meant to be "a political expression of its civil society, of the people who reside in its territory or even of its citizens. It was meant to be the State of the Jews wherever they are" (Yuval-Davis 1987: 63). For example, Israel's declaration of independence is not officially identified as such; it is called the Declaration of Establishment of the State of Israel by the People's Council. One of the most interesting debates in the history of Zionism took place a few hours before the adoption of this Declaration of Establishment. Meir Wilner, a leading member of the

10. According to Flapan, Ben-Gurion gave orders "for the destruction of Arab islands in Jewish population areas. The most significant elimination of these 'Arab islands' took place two months after the Declaration of Independence . . . as many as fifty thousand Arabs were driven out of their homes in Lydda and Ramlah on 12–13 July 1948" (1987: 13). Twenty more villages were emptied and destroyed after the end of the 1948 war. While forceful expulsion was a less viable option after Israel signed the armistice treaties with the Arab states, "the Military Administration possessed enough means to 'persuade' numerous Arab inhabitants that they would prefer immigration over humiliation and harassment" (18).

Communist Party, proposed to add the words "independent" and "sovereign," but his proposal was not accepted. The debate around Wilner's proposal, Uri Davis and Walter Lehn point out, "highlights the fact that those who formulated the draft consciously avoided words that would have specified the sovereignty and independence of the proposed state, emphasizing only its Jewishness" (1983: 146). The state of Israel is a state by, for, and of the "Jewish people," whereas the sovereign independent state of Israel would be a state by, for, and of its Jewish citizens (147). This conceptualization of the state heightens its concern for Jewish versus non-Jewish demography.

The central Israeli political arithmetic of Arab versus Jew has also been advanced through a variety of laws that effectively structure life in Israel according to nationalist biopolitics. One of the first legislative acts passed by the newly formed Israeli Knesset (parliament) was the Law of Return. According to this law, "all Jews, wherever they come from, are entitled automatically to Israeli citizenship, [to immigrate to and settle in Israel with the aid and assistance of the state], while according to the Israeli Nationality Law, non-Jews, even if born in Israel, unless born to Israeli citizens . . . are not" (Yuval-Davis 1987: 64). The conception of Israeli nationhood is thus based largely on Jewish ancestry, rather than on citizenship or birthplace. Clearly, a formal distinction is made between Jews and non-Jews, a distinction whereby the former are given automatic demographic (and other) privileges over the latter. According to David Kretzmer, "this aspect of the Law of Return is generally regarded as a fundamental principle of the State of Israel, possibly even its very raison d'être as a Jewish state" (1990: 36). The Law of Return is a symbolic, legal, and administrative expression of the imagined community and perhaps one of the most significant institutions through which subject populations flow, producing a hierarchical reality out of imagined categories.

In May 1994, after it was revealed that thousands of non-Jews had immigrated to Israel with forged documents, Avraham Ravitz, a Knesset member from the United Torah Judaism Party, went so far as to call for the abolition of the Law of Return:

> The subject was debated at a meeting of the Knesset's Aliya [Immigration of Jews] Committee where Population Registry head David Efrati said that 300 immigrant families had been sent back to the CIS [Commonwealth of Independent States, the remains of the former Soviet Union] in the past year, after it was discovered they had entered Israel under false identities. Efrati said authorities in the CIS were cooperating with Israel in establishing the

true identities of persons wishing to come here. Efrati also revealed that during this period, 29% of the immigrants had not been registered as Jews because they were unable to prove their Jewishness. (*Jerusalem Post,* May 26, 1994; emphasis added)

Although he was certainly not against the spirit of the Law of Return, Ravitz preferred to rely on investigations made by the Interior Ministry, so that the law would not be circumvented by "false Jews" (Courbage 1999: 37). And although he did not succeed in abolishing this foundational law, his protests clearly demonstrate its purpose.

It is within the context of Israel, as a state not of its citizens but open to all Jews—a state that can potentially integrate individuals who are not yet citizens for its utility[11]—that the Knesset passed in 1952 the World Zionist Organization–Jewish Agency (Status) Law. According to this law, the WZO, the Jewish Agency, and their specialized branches were recognized as equals of the state of Israel. Davis and Lehn note that in this way the state became a partner in the restrictive policies and practices of, for example, the Jewish National Fund (JNF, controlled by the WZO), which specifically serves "persons of Jewish religion, race, or origin." The constitution of the Jewish Agency states:

> Land is to be acquired as Jewish property, and . . . the title to the lands acquired is to be taken in the name of the JNF, to the end that the same shall be held as the inalienable property of the Jewish people. The Agency shall promote agricultural colonization based on Jewish labour, and in all works or undertakings carried out or furthered by the Agency, it shall be deemed to be a matter of principle that Jewish labour shall be employed. (1983: 147)

Since 1948, despite repeated confirmation of the legal and effective equivalence of the Israeli government and the WZO, "the JNF remained unwilling to transfer to the state title to its lands." The explanation was that the "JNF will redeem the lands and will turn them over to the Jewish people—to the people and not the state, which in the current composition of population cannot be an adequate guarantor of Jewish ownership" (ibid.: 156). Land thus becomes extraterritorial: "It ceases to be land from which the Arab can gain any advantage either now or at any time in the future" (Kanaana 1992: 55). In this way, land, population, and ethnic arithmetic come together in the structuring of the state of Israel.

---

11. Note that the *Statistical Abstract of Israel* includes data on the "Jewish Population in the World."

In 1965 Israel also introduced the Population Registration Law, whereby all residents of the state must be registered, with "nation" and "religion" specified. These reified categories are fundamental to imagining the nation of Israel. According to David Kretzmer, the registration of "nation"

> appears to derive from the fundamental philosophy of the State of Israel, that actively discourages an assimilationist approach towards the Arab minority. The philosophy reflects the idea that Israel, as the nation-state of Jewish people, has a definite function: preserving the discrete national identity of the Jewish people. Registration of 'nation' in the Population Registry is one of the mechanisms of maintaining the distinction between citizens of the state who belong to the Jewish people and those who do not. Registration of 'nation' . . . strengthens the dichotomy between the state as the political framework of all its citizens, and the state as the particularistic nation-state of the Jewish people. (1990: 44)

Thus registration places and divides people according to rigid categories of religion and nation.

Comparative ethnic political arithmetic has been a feature of many nationalisms around the world, although they have been particularly central to the history of Israel. While earlier Zionists depended on large waves of immigration and high rates of Jewish natural increase to achieve their calculus, in the late 1930s there was already much concern that this high natural increase was "temporary and artificial, since there was an exceptionally high proportion of young females in the reproductive ages, resulting from immigration" (Friedlander and Goldscheider 1979: 23). Thus the state tried to encourage the Jewish birth rate. A pronatalist award introduced in 1949 for "heroine mothers" who bore a tenth child was discontinued ten years later when it became clear that the majority of the claimants were Arab women (Wiemer 1983: 47; Masalha 1997: 144). Ben-Gurion stated that "any future pronatal incentive must be administered by the Jewish Agency and not the state since the aim is to increase the number of Jews and not the population of the state" (Wiemer 1983: 46; Friedlander and Goldscheider 1979: 126). Just as the Jewish National Fund refused to turn its lands over to the state, which in its "current composition of population cannot be an adequate guarantor of Jewish ownership," Ben-Gurion wanted pronatal incentives to be administered by the Jewish Agency, not the state, to guarantee the exclusion of Arabs (Davis and Lehn 1983: 156). Indeed, contraceptives were officially illegal in Israel until the late 1950s. Long before the national population control commissions were set up in the

West, Israel had created its own commission, which recommended the establishment of a demographic center in the prime minister's office. The proposal was "implemented years before a similar recommendation was made in the World Population Plan of Action in 1974" (Friedlander and Goldscheider 1979: xviii). This demographic center was established in 1967 with the explicit goal of increasing the reproduction of Jewish women exclusively (Yuval-Davis 1987: 61).[12] A Fund for Encouraging Birth was established in 1968 to offer child allowances to Jewish families with three or more children (Kahn 2000: 4).[13] In addition, child allowances in general and welfare benefits have been about 300 percent higher for Jews than those granted to Arabs in Israel.[14] A Law on Families Blessed with Children, introduced in 1983, gives a range of benefits to Jewish families with more than three children.

Abortion, although widely practiced and not commonly prosecuted, was illegal in Israel until 1976, when a law was passed permitting an abortion upon the formal agreement of a three-member committee.[15] Abortion is the focus of major public political debate among Jews in Is-

---

12. The center is still in existence today; by its own account it "promotes the formulation of comprehensive government demographic policy meant to maintain a suitable level of Jewish population growth, and acts systematically to implement this policy. Most center activities take place under the auspices of the Ministries of Construction and Housing, Education and Culture, and Health. Policy is formulated through field surveys and research, demographic conferences, experimental projects and information activities" (http://www.israel-mfa.gov.il/mfa/go.asp?MFAH00hy0). At the inauguration ceremony for this demographic center, "Prime Minister Levi Ashkol emphasized the importance of a high birth rate for the Jewish people, with a reminder of the six million Jews lost in the Holocaust" (Avgar et al. 1991: 7).

13. In 1998 a rumor of a secret plan to reduce the Arab birth rate surfaced:

A former senior official who asked to remain anonymous told Ha'aretz . . . that in addition to the government's public decision to encourage the birth rate in the 1960s, there was a secret decision to ask Kupat Holim [Sick Fund] health maintenance organizations to work to reduce the Arab birth rate, primarily by encouraging Arab women to use contraceptives. He said he did not know what the practical outcome of this decision was. (Ha'aretz, Mar. 18, 1998)

14. Child allowances paid to Jews and Arabs in Israel were equalized in 1995 as a result of a deal between then Prime Minister Rabin and Arab Knesset members. Nonetheless, the state welfare support mechanisms that year pulled 56% of poor Jewish families out of poverty vs. 39% of poor Arab families. This "differential impact is the result of differences in the levels of support provided and the depth of poverty of the recipients" (Swirski et al. 1998: 3).

15. Estimates of both legal and illegal abortions among Jewish women in Israel have been high, since "Israeli women were less enthusiastic than policymakers about keeping birthrates high" (Avgar et al. 1991: 7).

The committee can recommend an abortion on the grounds of (1) physical condition of the mother, (2) possibility that the fetus will be physically or mentally disabled, (3) pregnancy resulting from rape or incest, (4) the pregnant woman's age, and (5) the social condition of the woman (the last provision was deleted, then reinstated) (Portugese 1998).

rael, as it is in some other countries, but in Israel the emphasis is explicitly nationalistic (Yuval-Davis 1987: 85; Yisai 1978: 274).

And unlike many other developed nations in the world, until recently Israel had no systematic program for family planning services because of the powerful demographic and political interests of political arithmetic (Avgar et al. 1991: 6). Israel has thus maintained a relatively conservative approach in this regard (Friedlander and Goldscheider 1979: 129), and even today contraceptives are not an integral part of the public health care system (Swirski et al. 1998: 1; Salzberger et al. 1991: 9). Until the 1980s, contraceptives were available primarily through private physicians and were not covered by insurance (Friedlander and Goldscheider 1979: 128). In the 1980s the Ministry of Health partially initiated a family planning project that disproportionately focused on the "Arab sector."[16] Despite the ministry's reluctance to start family planning programs in Jewish communities, it was eager to do so among Arabs. It was widely known among ministry employees that approval for a general clinic in an Arab area was difficult to get, but approval was all but guaranteed if the proposed clinic included a family planning unit. My father, who worked for the Ministry of Health at that time, said that enthusiasm for family planning for Palestinians coincided with the attitude that family planning for Jews "was not an appropriate topic of discussion in polite company." While the Arab population is generally underserved in the area of health, family health clinics are opened in many areas where no other primary health care facilities are available (Swirski et al. 1998: 21).[17]

The National Health Insurance Law of 1995 includes neither contraceptives nor contraceptive counseling in the benefits package, although "methods of increasing rather than controlling fertility are well covered—including unlimited in vitro fertilization treatments up to the live birth of two children" (Swirski et al. 1998: 13). Indeed, Israel has the largest number of fertility clinics per capita in the world—three times the number per capita in the United States (Kahn 2000: 2; Swirski et al. 1998: 14).

16. The term "Arab sector" is a political designation created within "the ideological parameters of state discourse." It "inhabits the rhetorical/political norms of government policy" and functions "to obfuscate the state history of violent Palestinian deterritorialization" (Stein 1996: 119, 98).

17. This is not to say that the Arab population of Israel is adequately or equally served by the family health clinics. Indeed, it is not (Hussein 1994; Kawar 1987). However, the family planning aspects of these clinics is more developed in Arab areas than other services provided by the clinics (Kawar 1987).

Examples of pronatalism are easily found.[18] To cite just one instance, in May 1986, "following a discussion of worrying demographic trends among the Jewish population—including a slowing birthrate, declining immigration, growing emigration and the problems of assimilation and mixed marriages in the Diaspora—the unity government headed by Shimon Peres once again said it would try 'to ensure an appropriate level of growth in the Jewish population'" (*Ha'artez*, Mar. 18, 1998).

A 1998 journalistic description of the current state of the demographic center is titled "Battle in Bed Still Favors Arabs":

> A tiny division of the Ministry of Labor consisting of a director and a part-time secretary has been left on its own to battle social trends, Western culture, and cold, hard math in its effort to encourage Jewish births and stave off a demographic threat posed by a more rapid Arab birth rate. This reduced staff, with its tiny NIS 360,000 budget, is all that remains of the Israel Center for Demography, whose establishment 30 years ago represented the realization of a key government goal. (Ibid.)

Thus most of the state's selective pronatalist attempts were largely symbolic, although other aspects of its population policy (immigration, ethnic land control, etc.) are highly concrete and tangible. Besides, pronatalism has had "less consensus and less public interest in Israel" than immigration issues, although that interest rose at moments when immigration was low (Friedlander and Goldscheider 1979: 119–120). Ambivalence toward pronatalism can be traced to the difficulty of encouraging the Jewish birth rate without encouraging the Arabs to multiply too. It also reflects the influence of a liberal health-based contraception movement among Israeli state planners.

The ambivalence can be seen in the coexistence of the government's demographic center, with its strong pronatalism, and school textbooks produced by the Ministry of Education that teach basic demographics with a strong Malthusian slant. Fifth- and sixth-graders are taught to view the human, animal, and plant populations through the same lens; all populations can multiply beyond the carrying capacity of the environment. Populations of mice and Africans in particular are studied to demonstrate the danger for poor and undeveloped countries. Students are directed to a "world game" computer program that simulates population explosions in various parts of the world. The text offers the following discussion questions: "Can humans cover the face of the earth

18. See Portugese 1998 for a comprehensive review.

too? How will the globe become and appear if world population growth continues at this rate? What are the expected dangers to the human species?" (Sabir and Mintz 1992: 53).

Thus most of the state's selective pronatalist attempts (although not other aspects of its population policy, such as immigration, welfare, housing, and land zoning) have been largely symbolic: the state has clearly characterized Palestinians, and particularly those living inside its borders, as a "problem population." [19] In any case, mainstream Israeli public debate, as well as the media and the Knesset, has left little room for doubt in anyone's mind as to who should have children and who shouldn't. Golda Meir confided in the early 1970s, while she was prime minister of Israel, that she was afraid of having to wake up every morning wondering how many Arab babies had been born during the night (Yuval-Davis 1987: 61).[20]

COUNTING

Israel keeps close track of how many Arab (and Jewish) babies have been born during the night.[21] The Population Registration Ordinance of 1965 requires that "the person in charge of the institution where [a] birth

19. Much as Europeans stereotyped and condemned Jews for their large families (Khazoom 1999: 14).

20. Moreover, it is not just official policy that is concerned about Judaization and fertility rates; individuals are troubled as well. A reader of the *Jerusalem Post* wrote from London:

> The demographic picture within the pre-1967 borders is that when the State of Israel was established in 1948, the Arabic-speaking Moslem/Christian minorities formed less than 4 percent of the then much smaller population. They now form 19 percent of the current larger one. On average, their growth has been at the rate of some 3 percent per annum, from natural increases only. . . . When extrapolated this shows a Moslem/Christian Arabic-speaking majority in pre-1967 Israel by the year 2056 and achieved without recourse to a $10 billion loan guarantee. . . . As the Arabic-speaking minority expand absolutely, the time required to overcome such Jewish influx [immigration] is reduced to a mere few months. Soviet mass immigration is only a temporary bleep in what is an irreversible advance to an Arabic-speaking state—namely Palestine. The Jews will then become the minority, but not for long—the Arabs will see to that. Mr. Hurwitz, the Arabs will not swamp the Jews, they will obliterate them. (*Jerusalem Post*, July 12, 1992)

21. The Central Bureau of Statistics frequently does not count Arabs as such, but as non-Jews. It often uses categories of religion (Jews and non-Jews; or Jews, Muslims, Christians, Druze), only occasionally Jews, Arabs, and others. Palestinian is not one of the recognized categories. It is important for Israel to "know" its Jews and its non-Jews and to keep them separate, but it's also important not to empower non-Jews by recognizing them as Palestinian. See Lustick 1980.

takes place, the parents of the child born or the doctor or midwife if the birth occurred elsewhere notify the Ministry of Interior within 10 days of the date of birth. Notification of death must be made within 48 hours after the death" (Central Bureau of Statistics 1996: 21). The religion and nationality of the newborn or decedent must be registered. The ordinance was found to be necessary because Palestinians initially resisted registration efforts carried out by the military administration (Reiss 1991: 79). The authorities felt that underreporting of deaths or overreporting of births could facilitate the smuggling of "illegal infiltrators" back into the country—the return of Palestinian refugees—and thus were strict about registration. Measures taken to increase the accuracy of this registration of births include the disbursement of maternity payments—a sum of money is paid to every woman who gives birth in Israel—only if the birth took place at a hospital, or if the baby was taken to a hospital immediately after birth and was thus registered.[22] Although the amount of money is not large, in earlier years it was enough to encourage Palestinians to register infants through hospitals.

The debates surrounding the 1995 census in Israel shed light on the political nature of counting. The Israeli census traditionally includes a question about religion, and the statistics produced by the Israeli Central Bureau of Statistics are broken down into "Jews" and "non-Jews" or "Muslims," "Christians," and "Druze."[23] These categories of identity are central to imagining and sustaining the Israeli nation. Muhammad Qaraqra, the first Palestinian to be appointed as a regional census director, told me that because of their high birth rate, "generally the Arabs in Israel never considered the census a means for their political repression, on the contrary—the Jewish right-wingers feel it represses them." Because the census of 1995 fell in an election year, he said, "some people wanted to send a political message through the questionnaires. Settlers are saying, 'Don't return the census forms until Rabin's government is replaced.' Yossi Sarid [a Knesset member] believes the real reason they are calling for this boycott of the census is because they are afraid of being found out to be just a few settlers." Census results thus have strong political implications.

22. This regulation was also meant to encourage hospital control of births.

23. The last census did not ask about religion because of objections by many rabbis, who believe that counting Jews will bring disaster upon them. Nonetheless, the data are still presented according to religion.

"Professional populations" of settlers in the West Bank allegedly maintain more than one address in order to be counted twice in surveys, thus adding to the demographic strength of Jews in the Occupied Territories. By changing the census results, they hope to gain political power. Similarly, in 1995 the largely Arab "peace bloc" urged that the Israeli census omit the Jewish settlements in the West Bank and Gaza and restrict the count

> "to the area of the state of Israel only ... because conducting a census on the Jews living there while ignoring the Palestinians living next to them is a clearly racist move." The announcement added that the census bureau belonging to the Palestinian authority is responsible for conducting a census in the areas belonging to Palestinians, exactly as Jews living in New York are counted by the American census bureau. (*'Ittihad,* Oct. 19, 1995)

Clearly, Palestinians and Israelis are aware of the political significance of the census and political arithmetic.

Another issue arising in relation to the 1995 census was whether to include East Jerusalem. Ahmed Ghnaym, a Palestinian Fateh official, argued that East Jerusalem should not be included in the Israeli census because "it is a Palestinian city—and not an Israeli one—that has been occupied since 1967, and its inclusion in the census is illegal" (*Sinnara,* Oct. 20, 1995). He added that the Palestinian National Authority[24] would conduct its own census in the Palestinian areas that include Jerusalem, in preparation for the elections. The Israeli Jerusalem Municipality tried to calm fears such as Ghnaym's by announcing (through its Arab assistant general director of the Arab Affairs department, 'Ali Khamis) that "this is only a survey conducted by the State of Israel that aims to collect information on the number of the population. ... It has nothing to do with the Palestinian presence in Jerusalem and the rights of the residents of the city" (*Jerusalem Times,* Oct. 13, 1995). But despite official Israeli statements to the contrary, the inclusion of East Jerusalem is clearly an issue of political control, borders, and identity. The same Jerusalem municipal office that denied any political relevance to the census had itself earlier announced (through its deputy mayor, Abraham Kahela) that

> for the first time since the reunification of the city in 1967, Jews constitute a majority in East Jerusalem ... 160,000 Jews now live in East Jerusalem, while

---

24. The new governing body of the regions of the West Bank and Gaza handed over to Palestinian control, headed by Yasir Arafat.

the Arab population is 155,000. Kahela believes intense efforts by Jews to settle in a number of predominantly Arab neighborhoods accounts for the demographic change. *Any discussion on the future status of East Jerusalem must take the new population balance into account,* Kahela said. (*Washington Report,* Sept./Oct. 1993; emphasis added)

Moreover, a form of demographic purge was taking place in Jerusalem at the time: Palestinian Jerusalem women who were married to West Bankers had their Israeli identity cards taken away. Thus they and their families were denied residence in Jerusalem and were removed from statistics of the state (*'Ittihad,* July 6, 1995).[25] Jerusalem is an intensified microcosm of Israeli biopolitics, where people designated Jews and Arabs are closely monitored and manipulated.

As Elia Zureik notes, counting Palestinians is a

political act laden with controversy. Depending on who does the counting and the categories used, there is dispute over how many Palestinians there are, their geographical distribution, the type of citizenship they can claim, whether they can be classified as refugees or non-refugees, whether their claim to land ownership in Palestine is legal or not, whether they have the right to return to their homes versus homeland, and so on. (1999: 13)

There are political ramifications to counting by Israelis as well as by Palestinians. After the 1993 Oslo agreement and the establishment of the Palestinian National Authority (PNA), one of the first agencies to be created by the PNA was the Palestinian Central Bureau of Statistics (Zureik 1999: 11). When it conducted its first census in 1997, it was considered an important exercise in nation-building. According to the head of the bureau, this census was "as important as the intifada. It is a civil intifada." Israeli police forces prevented Palestinian census takers from surveying East Jerusalem, and the Knesset outlawed the Palestinian census in the area. Prime Minister Benjamin Netanyahu considered such a survey a challenge to Israel's sovereignty (*New York Times,* Dec. 11, 1997).

Since census taking continues to be "one of the basic rituals of state formation" (Patriarca 1994: 361) that "create new ways for people to

25. In addition, Palestinian residents of Jerusalem unable to prove that they currently live there and have continuously lived there in the past lost their right to live in the city of their birth (B'Tselem 1997). According to *Ha'aretz,* "Far from decreasing the size of the Arab population in East Jerusalem, the attempt by the Ministry of Interior to reduce the number of Arabs living in the city by confiscating identity cards has led to a population explosion." The plan to "stop the demographic increase of the Arab population in the city" backfired because Palestinians who held Jerusalem identity papers but lived outside the city started returning to the city to avoid the confiscation of their IDs (Feb. 11, 1998).

be" (Hacking 1986: 223), census data are the subjects of much attention and controversy in Israel and Palestine, as are counts of Palestinians in other Arab countries. In Jordan, for example, it was decided that population counts broken down by Jordanian and Palestinian in 1996 would not be released lest the figures show that Palestinians outnumbered Jordanians. In Lebanon, where no census has been carried out since the 1930s, "successive Lebanese governments made a habit of inflating the size of the Palestinian refugee population [who are majority Sunni Muslim] so as to discourage their stay in the country, and justify their possible expulsion for fear that their resettlement would upset the Lebanese confessional balance" (Zureik 1999: 8; see also Fargues 1993).

Such politicization of numbers is not unique to Israel or the Palestinians. Indeed, the controversy over the 2000 census in the United States suggests the globally sensitive nature of population data. The U.S. Census Bureau was prevented by the Republican-dominated House of Representatives and then by the Supreme Court from using statistical sampling methods to avoid the undercounting of minority populations (Brennan Center 1999). According to a *Chicago Tribune* editorial, "The census debate is deeply political. The results of the census decide how . . . political districts are apportioned and how the political pie is sliced" (Sept. 3, 1998). Ethnic political arithmetic is not unique, but it is certainly pronounced in Israel.

ARAB VS. JEW?

Israeli pronatalism is selective not only against Palestinians but also against some Jews—those of African or Asian origin. These Mizrahi Jews largely make up the Jewish "lower class," whose population has grown at a faster rate than that of European Jews, and who today account for more than half the population of Israel.[26] The complex historical past of the Jews, "with separate histories in different parts of the world, has presented contradictory and cross pressures on the Zionist movement when it attempts to construct the national boundaries of its collectivity without at the same time breaking radically with its ideology

26. Although Arab Jews make up the majority of Israel's population, Israel does "not disseminate the exact official numbers for security reasons" and attempts to obscure this fact by counting Israeli Jews in terms of those born in Africa, Asia, Europe, the United States, and Israel (Giladi 1990: 6).

of religious/ethnic construction" (Yuval-Davis 1987: 68). "Arab" and "Jew" are constructed in Israeli nationalism as two bounded and separate categories; Arab Jews confuse this neat division. Before the establishment of Israel, the majority of immigrants were "European in origin and in social, economic, cultural and demographic characteristics" (Friedlander and Goldscheider 1979: 26). After statehood, large numbers of Jews from African and Asian countries were brought to Israel, sometimes against their will (Shohat 1988: 35). The Orientalness of these Jews was and is considered a problem by the politically and culturally dominant (although no longer majority) European Jews. While Israeli governments have encouraged the more affluent European Jews to be fruitful and multiply, their policies sought to reduce the Easternness of non-European Jews through, among other things, family planning (Courbage 1999). Golda Meir not only lived in fear of Arab babies being born, but also "cried in relief when Russian Jews began arriving in Israel in the early 1970s: 'At last real Jews are coming to Israel again'" (Yuval-Davis 1987: 70).

The essentialized categories of Arab and Jew violently slice through the blurred connections across these imaginary yet real borders of identity. The Arab Jew from Iraq or Yemen or Egypt is rarely called that—one is counted as either Jew or Arab, never both. Thus Zionism undermines "the hyphenated, syncretic culture of actually existing Jews" through unidimensional categorizations (Shohat 1999: 6). This passion for keeping the categories clear and singular is also evident in a disproportionate anxiety about intermarriage—or as some (for example, Bachi 1976: 51) call it, "outmarriage"—between Palestinians and Jews. Intermarriage is illegal in Israel,[27] and despite its rare occurrence, politicians frequently attack "peace" or "dialogue" programs for promoting miscegenation. Intermarriage is perceived as undermining the state. Similarly, interreligious adoption is illegal: "adoption in Israel is predicated upon the adopters and adoptees belonging to the same religion. Therefore a Jewish [heterosexual legally married] couple can adopt only a Jewish child and an Arab couple can only adopt an Arab child" (Permanent Mission 1997: 33).[28] Similarly, surrogate mothers must be

27. Marriage in Israel is under the jurisdiction of the religious courts, which enforce the prohibition against intermarriage; marriages performed outside of the country are recognized.
28. In accordance with the Adoption Law of 1971.

of the same religion as the contracting couple (Kahn 2000: 190).[29] The state finds it essential to maintain strict boundaries between separate categories of religion, boundaries that form the basis of its imagined community.

Furthermore, intermarriage between Jews and mostly non-Arab non-Jews in the West is often referred to as a "demographic holocaust," since the mixed offspring of these intermarriages are assumed to be non-Jews (Yuval-Davis 1987: 76; *Jerusalem Report,* June 15, 1995). In a 1997 cover article in *New York* magazine titled "Are American Jews Disappearing?" Jewish leaders point to "enemies from within" the Jewish community: "a low birthrate, rampant intermarriage, assimilation, rejection of organized religion, and widespread indifference" (32). Intermarriage is described as the trend most troubling to Jewish leaders, "an act of criminal, historic vandalism," "the destruction of the Jewish people in a microcosmic way" (36, 108). Intermarriage and assimilation in the diaspora is often cited as one of the worrying demographic trends that necessitate pronatalist measures among the Jewish population of Israel (e.g., *Ha'artez,* Mar. 18, 1998). Indeed, the Israeli government together with major Jewish donors in North America announced in 1998 a program called "Birthright Israel," which would send every Jewish boy and girl in the diaspora on an all-expense-paid trip to Israel for their thirteenth birthday, with the explicit goal of discouraging Jewish assimilation abroad and encouraging marriage to Jews (*New York Times,* Nov. 16, 1998).

The characterization of intermarriage as a demographic holocaust points to the problematic ways in which the Nazi holocaust has been incorporated into Israeli pronatalism. Zionist ideology sees its goal as enlarging the Jewish people all over the world and making sure that Jewish mothers "produce enough children to 'compensate' for the children lost in the Nazi Holocaust and . . . the 'Demographic Holocaust.'" The Zionist political response to the horrifying destruction the Nazi holocaust wrought has been only "one response, and for a long time a minority one, of the Jews in the 'modern' world to this history, and to their displacement and persecution" (Yuval-Davis 1987: 64–65, 76). The prominent Israeli demographer Roberto Bachi, who headed the govern-

29. In accordance with the 1996 Surrogacy Law or, more accurately, the Embryo Carrying Agreements Law, which permits surrogacy contracts only between couples and surrogates of the same religion.

ment's Natality Committee in the 1960s, bemoans the fact that the "up-surge of Jewish nuptuality and fertility" after the Nazi holocaust was only transitory and that "there was no realization that a higher birth-rate could compensate for at least part of the losses sustained" in the holocaust (1976: 51).

The chief rabbi of Palestine, I. H. Herzog, called on Jewish families in 1943 to increase the number of their offspring in response to the terrible news of the fate of European Jewry, which he suggested might have been a consequence "of the Will of God," since the modern style of living had spread throughout the nation (quoted in Friedlander and Goldscheider 1979: 123). The sins of this modern lifestyle are gendered: women are rebuked for their selfish unwillingness to bear more children. Ben-Gurion often chastised the majority of the Jewish population of Palestine (pre-1948) for "not fulfilling their reproductive commitments to the nation," particularly in view of the state of "demographic and moral decay" of Jews all over the world (ibid.: 122; Wiemer 1983: 46). These sacrifices were constructed "specifically according to gender and age and to a certain extent class and ethnic origin"—young middle-class Ashkenazi women are encouraged to reproduce. The adviser to the minister of health, Haim Sadan, proposed in the 1970s "to force every [Is-raeli Jewish] woman considering abortion to watch a slide show which would include . . . pictures of dead children in Nazi concentration camps" (Yuval-Davis 1987: 84, 87).[30] The measure was only narrowly defeated. Again, the sacrifices and duties for the nation are clearly gendered and linked to reproduction.

Nira Yuval-Davis comments, "A 'demographic race' between the Jews and Arabs in Israel is seen as crucial, then, for the survival of Is-rael" (1987: 61). Some imaginers pit all Arabs in the Middle East and all Jews in the world against each other. Bernard Berelson, among others, seems to bemoan the fact that "no realistic population policy can raise Israel's proportionate population vis-à-vis the Arabs of the region: under the most extreme assumptions it will remain no more than a slight fraction of the territory, with whatever that may imply for political position and military security" (Friedlander and Goldscheider 1979: xviii).

---

30. Another proposal in 1998 would have had the state keep tabs on women who received abortions, and then "send emissaries . . . to the homes of women who have had one abortion in order to dissuade the family from doing so again." As the minister of labor put it, "the Jews should be worried because their number has not increased since the Holocaust" (Ha'aretz, July 9, 1998; see also July 8, 1998).

One must remember that there has been variation within the Zionist movement since its inception. Because different Zionists have had different answers to the question "Who is a Jew?" and thus different conceptions of "the Jewish problem," their solutions have also varied. Many of the differences, however, were of strategy and priority rather than ultimate goals and objectives. Early Zionists, for example, disagreed on key demographic issues such as "(1) the pace of immigration . . . ; (2) population composition—should population growth be accomplished through immigration of a cross-section of the population, the immigration of workers, or of a cultural, intellectual elite; (3) eventual population size" (Friedlander and Goldscheider 1979: 9–10). However, both leftists and rightists share a concern with demography. Zionist "hawks" and Zionist "doves" alike are anxious about a strong Jewish majority in Israel. Hawks who call for the annexation of the West Bank and Gaza Strip (where Arabs are a large majority) propose to transfer the Arabs living there to other Arab countries to preserve a Jewish majority in Israel; doves call for the establishment of a separate Palestinian state alongside Israel in those areas, thus not incidentally preserving the separate and purer Jewish character of Israel (Yuval-Davis 1987: 75). As Shimon Peres put it, "To remain Jewish, both demographically and morally, Israel needs for there to be a Palestinian state" (Courbage 1999: 24).

Thus statistical data collection, marriage and adoption laws, welfare and immigration, regulations of land and identification cards are all made in the name of preserving the nation—a certain type of nation.

NATIONAL HEALTH CARE

Like other state services, health care in Israel has long been organized along the putative racial lines of Arab and Jew. This policy started prior to the establishment of the state, when Jewish voluntary organizations developed health institutions primarily for the benefit of their own community (Reiss 1991: 9).[31] Although there were individual Jewish doctors who wanted to make their services available to all patients, public funding and support were not ecumenically structured.

From the moment modern medicine was introduced into Palestine a mixture of public voluntary and private practice thus emerged which, even when ac-

31. Part of the aim was to protect Jews from the proselytizing efforts of Christian mission hospitals (Shepherd 1987: 228–257).

tual practitioners and manner of treatment were the same, articulated distinctions between Jews and Arabs, between rich and poor, and between sectors of the Jewish public, through differences in communal responsibility for
provision of services, and through differences in patients' responsibility for
payment. These factors affected the immediacy, frequency and continuity of
care, and therefore both the availability and effectiveness of treatment. (Reiss
1991: 13)

Today's national health insurance system in Israel is descended from
early Zionist sick funds with clear nationalist goals. Around 1912, Jewish laborers founded mutual aid sick funds to provide services for "the
nascent Zionist labor movement as a whole in the context of its national
aims." Such benefits were not available to Arabs who worked in these
communities. The various labor unions united in 1920 to form the General Federation of Hebrew Workers (the Histadrut) and developed co-
operative institutions, among them a common Histadrut Sick Fund.
This fund grew into a central health institution for Jews in Palestine, and
later became "a quasi-state agency with a near monopoly in health insurance and the provisions of primary care" (ibid.: 8, 26, 63). The Histadrut was envisioned by its labor-Zionist founders "not as a trade
union federation on the European model, but rather as an instrument
whose primary purpose was to foster the settlement of Palestine by Jewish workers and build a Jewish commonwealth" (Lockman 1996: 65).
According to Reiss, "Notwithstanding a marginal faction within it
which called for binational cooperation, the Histadrut did not cease to
be a declaredly Jewish institution which originated in competition with
Arab labor and thrived on it." It was not until 1959 that the Histadrut
decided to allow Arabs to become full members, and not until 1976 that
it changed its name to accommodate them (from the General Federation
of Hebrew Workers to the General Federation of Workers). Yet even after Arabs were admitted, the Histadrut Sick Fund invested in their communities "at a relative rate which considered second class citizenship for
Arabs to be legitimate within a Jewish national consensus" (1991: 28,
69). Although more citizens of Israel than of the United States have been
insured, most of the uninsured in Israel were Arabs (before the universal insurance law of 1995).[32] And although many Palestinians have in
fact become Histadrut members with allegedly equal rights to social

32. Before 1995, Israel had a voluntary health insurance system that covered about
96% of the Jewish population and only 88% of the Arab population (Swirski et al.
1998: 2).

benefits, those rights do not extend to the equal political representation that would secure them services comparable to those enjoyed by Jews. The Mapai Party (and its successor, the Labor Party), which controlled the Histadrut Sick Fund, used the opening of its clinics as a reward for Arab electoral support, and thus many communities remained without clinics (ibid.: 105).[33]

Another significant health institution developed prior to 1948 was the Hadassah Medical Organization (a branch of the Hadassah Voluntary Organization, the women's Zionist organization of the United States), which focused especially on children and established centers for maternal and infant care, including a milk dispensary. By 1949 it had built a network of ninety such centers, most of which were later transferred to the state of Israel. Originally the Hadassah Medical Organization made "gestures of goodwill" to non-Jews, but as it became increasingly allied with the General Zionists, its binational commitment was replaced by "the prevailing nationalist perspective" (ibid.: 32).

Reiss argues that it was "sectarian sponsorship that established modern medical care in Palestine" and that that was the framework for the development of the Israeli health system. After the creation of the state of Israel, a Health Ministry was formed. While the Palestinians were transformed from a majority to a minority in the new Jewish state, the Health Ministry, like other organs of the state, continued to see them as a security risk, as "socially alien," and as an "anomalous population." The ministry proceeded to set up a special service for Palestinians, the Medical Service for Minorities, which implemented the government's policy of marginalization and neglect (ibid.: 15, 44, 77).

The Arab community is subject to governmental medical neglect or a double standard and has often been allowed to fall through the bureaucratic cracks of Israel's health system. The Health Ministry, like the Histadrut Sick Fund, used the opening of clinics in Arab communities as signs of party patronage. In 1954 the ministry operated about 200 maternal and child health clinics in Jewish communities and only 6 in Arab communities (ibid.: 83). While this ratio has improved over the years, a difference in the health services and conditions between Arabs and Jews is still very much in evidence. Despite the 1995 law of "universal" health

33. According to Reiss (1991: 105), "While in the Jewish settlements the instrumental aspect of the politics of HSF care was no less potent, it generally focused on improvements in the quality of service rather than on its very presence." This withholding and rewarding policy has lasted many years longer for Arabs.

coverage, gaps between "the sectors" continue to exist. According to Danny Peleg of Tel Aviv University, the new law did not include provisions for "corrective measures"; that is, investment in formerly underdeveloped populations. Moreover, "universal coverage" is severely threatened by a strong privatization drive. Peleg predicts that for-profit sick funds will eventually replace the current nonprofit ones, and such a market-driven system will create even more severe imbalances (1997; see also Swirski et al. 1998: 17).

Thus health care, like other state-linked services in Israel, is deeply rooted in a nationalist visions that favors Jewish citizens over others. The logos of three of the four Israeli sick funds are modifications of the star of David, suggesting the Jewish vision of the sick funds' missions (see Figure 1).

JUDAIZING THE GALILEE

In the Galilee, which falls within the 1948 borders of Israel, Israeli political arithmetic is quite elaborate. Palestinians who live here, unlike those in the Occupied Territories, are considered citizens of the state of Israel. They are largely descendants of the small percentage of Palestinians who were not expelled beyond the borders of the emerging state during the 1948 war (although some did flee their original places of residence to neighboring areas and became "internal refugees"). That Palestinians in the Galilee are citizens of the state heightens concern about (as well as potential control of) their demography and numbers. Former Prime Minister Yitzhak Rabin, now remembered by some as a peace-loving hero, placed an upper limit on the percentage of Arab population in Israel: "The red line for Arabs is 20% of the population, that must not be gone over." If the percentage of the Jewish population were less than 80 percent, Israel would then be a binational state, and "we do not want that." He explained: "I want to preserve the Jewish character of the state of Israel not by name only, but also in action, values, language, and culture. This does not mean that no one lives in it except the Jews. But today there are 4.4 million Jews versus 2.8 or 3 million Arabs[34] and this cannot continue" ('Ittihad, Nov. 1, 1995).

The northern region of the Galilee has a large concentration of non-Jewish Palestinians—estimates range from 50 to 75 percent of the

---

34. The 2.8 or 3 million Arabs here include those living in the West Bank and Gaza—demonstrating the complex relationship between Palestinians inside Israel and in other regions.

Figure 1. The logos for the Israeli sick funds. Three of these four logos are modifications of the star of David, suggesting the Jewish vision of the sick funds' missions.

population, depending on how the region is defined (Falah 1989: 232; Yiftachel 1995: 222)— who have been the targets of intensive Judaizing efforts.[35] While touring the Galilee, Ben-Gurion reportedly objected: "Am I travelling in Syria?" and immediately ordered the Jewish settlement of Karmiel to be built in the area (Minns and Hijab 1990: 33).

Settlement and claiming of Palestinian lands have the same priority in the Galilee as in the West Bank and Gaza. In fact, the Settlement Department of the Jewish Agency intentionally does not distinguish between the West Bank and Gaza and Israel "proper"; it categorizes areas only according to the number of Jews living in them (Wiemer 1983: 51–52). With a clear political arithmetic orientation, Israel has expropriated thousands of acres of Palestinian-owned land in the Galilee and transferred ownership to the state (none of the land can be resold to non-Jews); controlled and limited the physical expansion of Arab communities (Falah 1989; Yiftachel 1995: 230–234); and built numerous Jewish settlements, ranging from elevated "lookout" minisettlements *(mitspim)* to large Jewish towns in the heart of the region.

The goal of these measures is "achieving and maintaining a positive demographic balance in favor of the Jewish population." These efforts are particularly intense in the Galilee because of the continued preponderance of Palestinians there, but also because the region was included in the proposed Arab state (rather than the Jewish state) under the 1947 UN Partition Plan. Israel thus fears the rise of a Palestinian separatist movement in the Galilee and tries to control the Arab population by "isolating, severing, and fragmenting the territorial continuity of their settlements."[36] The sites of Jewish settlements in the Galilee are chosen to "break up the territorial continuity of the Arab villages and to act as a barrier to their physical expansion" (Falah 1989: 229, 231, 237, 249).

In 1976 a secret governmental report on "handling the Arabs of Israel" (which was leaked to the Israeli press) frankly addresses the "demographic problem," especially in the Galilee. Submitted by Israel Koenig, then northern district commissioner of the Ministry of Interior, the report sees a virtual Arab time bomb in the high rate of Arab natural increase in relation to the Jewish rate. The basic concern of the report is the state's future ability, given demographic trends, to prevent the

35. According to governmental definitions, "non-Jews" were 51.4% of the 943,000 residents of the area in 1995 (Central Bureau of Statistics 1998).

36. This fear of Arab territorial continuity is clearly articulated in, for example, Sofer 1989.

emergence of organized Palestinian nationalism and demands for equality within the state. In this regard, Koenig recommended that the government "expand and deepen Jewish settlement in areas where the contiguity of the Arab population is prominent," "dilut[e] existing Arab population concentrations," and "limit 'breaking of new ground' by Arab settlements" (Koenig 1976: 2, 3).[37]

The examples of Judaization plans are abundant (see Yiftachel 1991 and 1995 for more details). Information about a new planning map for the Galilee (by the Regional Planning Board) was leaked to the press in 1995. The goal of the new plan was explicitly stated as Judaization: to increase the number of Jews in the Galilee in relation to Arabs and "to distribute them in such a way that they would disrupt any Palestinian geographical continuity." The plan allocates considerably more land to Jews than it does to Arabs as part of an attempt to ghettoize the Arabs (*'Ittihad,* June 9, 1995; Galilee Society, personal communication). According to Yusif Jabbarin, who has studied these plans extensively, Arabs are totally excluded from the plans' "national goals," and are in fact dealt with only as a hindrance to them (Jabbarin 1997; *Fasl ul-Maqal,* Nov. 1, 1996a). Needless to say, no Arabs are among the members of these planning committees.

Similarly, the project Galilee 2000 was designed for the development and expansion of the Jewish settler community in the Galilee at the expense of the Palestinian community, whose human rights and needs are simply considered nonexistent (M. Kanaaneh 1996). Yet another recent example is the David's Shield 2020 plan (by the Housing Ministry), which calls for the doubling of Jewish settlements in Arab-dominated areas, but with a new post-Oslo twist: a central area in the Galilee is reserved to become a romanticized pastoral model for "coexistence" and will attract "coexistence tourists" to support economically the new "more demographically balanced" population (*Yedi'ot Ahronot,* Oct. 31, 1996; *Fasl ul-Maqal,* Nov. 1, 1996a, and Nov. 29, 1996) (see Figure 2).

37. The prime minister at the time, Yitzhak Rabin, would not deny or condemn the report, and Koenig continued to hold high-level government positions for many years (Hadawi 1991: 58; Masalha 1997: 153). A more recent report in the prime minister's office, leaked to the press in 1998, similarly describes Palestinians in Israel as a potential threat, akin to the Germans in Czechoslovakia who demanded annexation to Nazi Germany. To deal with this potential threat, ministers offered several suggestions, including stricter enforcement of the prohibition of polygamy and stopping family reunification processes and the resulting importation of women from the West Bank and Gaza into Israel (*Ma'ariv,* Aug. 16, 1998; *Ha'aretz,* Aug. 17, 1998).

Figure 2.   "David's Shield" plan for Judaizing the Galilee: light gray areas indicate new Jewish urban areas; the star of David indicates six central Jewish
urban locations; the heart indicates model Jewish-Arab coexistence (*Fasl
ul-Maqal,* Nov. 1, 1996a).

The housing shortage in Arab communities that results from these restrictive policies ironically compels some Palestinians to seek residence
in Jewish areas—a move that is met with considerable resistance. The
Palestinian lawyer Tawfiq Jabbarin went through a long legal battle to
force a Jewish settlement to sell him a house, after they had refused to
do so because "they didn't want mosques in the settlement." Another
Palestinian, ʿAdil Qaʿdan, is pursuing a lawsuit against a settlement that
told him that they have a policy of selling only to Jews, since the settlement was created for that purpose (*Kul ul-ʿArab,* June 14, 1995a).[38] Ac-

---

38. These legal battles are premised on the 1992 Basic Rights Law: Human Dignity
and Freedom and its 1994 amendment. Before the enactment of this law, no legal challenge to segregation was possible.

cording to the president of the Supreme Court, who is presiding over this case, ruling on this challenge to the state's right to lease lands to the (discriminatory) Jewish Agency "is one of the most difficult and complex judicial decisions that I have ever come across. . . . We are not ready for this sort of judicial decision, which has unforeseen consequences" (*New York Times*, Mar. 1, 1998). He has urged the parties to settle out of court.

In spite of the considerable effort made by the government, "the demographic impact of the strategy has been small" (Yiftachel 1991: 336). Although the number of Jews settled in the Galilee has increased, especially after the last waves of immigration from the former Soviet Union, the percentage of Palestinians in the area still exceeds that of Jews. Indeed, "Zionism continues to hold itself susceptible to counter-measures by the weakened Palestinians" (Rabinowitz 1997: 77). By the government's own standards, Judaization of the Galilee has not achieved its goals. It has, however, heightened Palestinian alienation from the state. The policies have been strongly protested by Palestinians (and some Israeli Jews). During the Land Day Strike of 1976 against planned massive land expropriations, six Palestinians were killed in my hometown of 'Arrabi as well as in several other villages in the region.

My hometown is still protesting Judaization policies. 'Arrabi and its neighboring villages are now surrounded by thirty-one small Jewish settlements that collectively make up the Misgav Regional Council, with a population of about 8,000. As the anthropologist Moslih Kanaaneh explains:

> In early 1995 the Israeli Government decided to give Misgav Regional Council a contour area of 183,000 donams of land. Nearly 40% . . . of this land area is private property of Palestinian-Arab inhabitants in the neighboring villages . . . whereas the remaining 60% of these 183,000 donams are state lands which were confiscated from their Arab owners in earlier periods. The issue here is that while 8,000 Jews were given 183,000 donams, the 48,000 Arabs in the three nearest villages to Misgav were left with 25,000 donams only. (1996: 10)

These Judaization plans depend on a series of laws that empower the state to take such actions, including a 1953 law ironically called the Law for Confiscating Land for *Public* Interests. As the former mayor of 'Arrabi, Fadil Jarad, points out, "The reference here is to the public interests of the Jewish people, not those of the Arab people" (M. Kanaaneh 1997). Citizens in Israel are treated according to the "common good" as defined by the ethnically specific Zionist project

(Shafir and Peled 1998: 257). The boundaries of the Misgav Regional Council, Jarad explains,

> were set to be exactly overlapping with and confining the boundaries of the lands of 20 Arab villages in the Galilee, such that it constricted these villages and made it impossible to expand their legislation areas in the future. . . . This comes in the series of continuous attempts for taking possession of the land and changing the demographic situation in the Galilee from an Arab majority to a Jewish majority, and this in itself is a racial approach. . . . If our villages get suffocated and the doors in front of our future development get locked, we will be compelled to fight with all the power we have for getting rid of such unnatural situation, which does not fit the natural population growth and natural expansion of our Arab villages. (M. Kanaaneh 1997)

RESISTING JUDAIZATION

Israel's selective population policy has largely been a failure in terms of one of its stated goals and by its own measures: more than fifty years after the establishment of the state, the Arab natural growth rate inside it is still more than twice as high as the Jewish rate (growth rates of Palestinians in the West Bank and Gaza Strip are even higher)[39] (see Table 1).

After being counted and shuffled and recounted and told to control their Third World–like fertility, Palestinians continue on average to have more children than Jews do.

Pro- and antinatalism are more complicated to implement than immigration and land distribution policies. Israeli attempts at using the depoliticized language of population, demography, and family planning are certainly not perceived by most Palestinians as apolitical. The Israeli authorities more or less admit that "none of the active population control policies which are used in other Third World countries have any chance of meeting cooperation among either the 'traditional' or the 'modern' elements in the Arab sector" (Yuval-Davis 1987: 80) (not that these policies have had no problems with "cooperation" in other Third World countries). Palestinians' experiences make it difficult for them to see neutrality in Israel's language of numbers.

However, Israel's policy has been effective in an unintended way. The structuring of Israel's institutions, policies, and discourses on the basis of the distinction between Jew and Arab eventually comes to be mirrored by a reverse calculus among Palestinians, if not equal in power.

39. Moreover, the area (including the West Bank and Gaza) includes considerably more Arabs today than it did in 1948.

TABLE I
TOTAL FERTILITY RATES IN ISRAEL,
BY RELIGION

	1955	1970	1990	1995
Jews	3.41	2.69	2.56	3.64
European/American born	2.84	2.31	2.2	2.63
Asian/African born	4.07	3.09	3.25	5.86
Muslim	8.95	4.70	4.69	7.96
Christian	3.62	2.57	2.44*	4.85
Druze	7.46	4.05	3.51	6.58

SOURCES: 1955, 1970, and 1990 figures from Central Bureau of Statistics as quoted in Goldschei-der 1992: 21; 1995 figures from Central Bureau of Statistics 1999: Table 3.13.

NOTE: According to the *Statistical Abstract*, "Total fertility represents the average number of chil-dren a woman may bear during her lifetime. For computing the rate, it is assumed that a woman tends to give birth to the same number of children as was calculated for all women of her age in the surveyed year" (Central Bureau of Statistics 1996: 22).

* This statistic includes non-Palestinian Christians, especially those from the former Soviet Union.

Before I discuss the role of population politics among Palestinians, a note on Palestinian nationalism is in order. The distinction between in-stitutionalized Israeli state nationalism and the Palestinian nationalism of a liberation/anticolonial movement is "both theoretically necessary and politically important" (Sharoni 1995: 37). There is a powerful asymmetry between the two. Palestinian nationalism has never achieved any form of sovereign independence in its own homeland, despite a highly developed national consciousness and defined sense of national identity. Palestinians have not had full control over state mechanisms usually considered essential for "imposing uniform 'national' criteria of identity," such as "education, museums, archaeology, postage stamps and coins, and the media, especially radio and television" (Khalidi 1997: 10). Print media exist but have been muted and censored by the Israeli state (and it is often in these recognizable silences that Palestinian nationalism emerges). Thus Palestinian nationalism is often produced in the margins and in opposition to, rather than because of, state mecha-nisms. This is especially the case in the Galilee region.

Since 1948, people who consider themselves to belong to the same nation have in fact been subject to a variety of regimes and thus histo-ries in different regions: Israeli military administration, the Jordanian state, the Egyptian state, military occupation, the Israeli state, the Lebanese state, Israeli invasion, the Palestinian National Authority's limited rule, and so on. Thus Palestinian nationalism in the Galilee has a complex relationship to Palestinian nationalism in other regions. There are many commonalities and shared beliefs. At the literal level, some Galileans have even been part of underground organizations that encompass members living in all of these areas. Moreover, most Galileans have supported the supposedly overarching institution of the PLO. They do have a strong sense of belonging to a nation that does not correspond to the formal borders of any state. However, they also have demands that are clearly informed by the realities of existing borders and states—local agendas specific to their region. When Palestinians in the Galilee demonstrate and protest in favor of an independent Palestinian state in the West Bank and Gaza, they do not demand that the Galilee be a part of that state *and* they have an additional agenda and demands as citizens of Israel. This separation between Palestinians inside Israel and those outside has been reinforced by "peace negotiations" that have excluded Palestinians inside Israel as a collective entity (from either side). These are instances of the contracting and expanding zones of identification to which I alluded earlier. In zeroing in on Palestinian discourse in the Galilee, I follow the ebb and flow of these identifications, which are not confined to the physical boundaries of the region, and my evidence is not strictly confined to one geographic zone.

To note this ebb and flow of Palestinian nationalist identifications is clearly not meant to undermine or delegitimate them as exceptionally fragmented or not "real," as many Israeli social scientists have tried to do (Sa'di 1992). Indeed, to explore the contestation and negotiation of shifting categories of personhood and community in the Galilee is not to present Palestinian identity as being in a special state of crisis, chaos, or decline. Contestation and negotiation are in fact standard processes in the construction of identity and the workings of power and are not unique to Palestinians or to the Galilee.

The focus of Zionism on the ratio of Jew to Arab has been mirrored to some extent by a reverse Palestinian calculus and organizations. Palestine does not mirror Israel in that it does not have the same power to enforce its national imaginings. It does not mirror Israel in that its roots are anticolonial while Zionism was a colonial movement. Palestine also does not mirror Israel in that it is not imagined as a monoreligious nation by the majority of Palestinians (as Israel is considered a Jewish nation). However, it does mirror Israel to the extent that ethnic-based political arithmetic has come to play an important role. Palestinian leaders and intellectuals reject Israeli population politics by deploying a counter-arithmetic that numbers all Palestinians dispersed around the world, as in the following statement by Edward Said: "Palestinians now number over 4.5 million persons, . . . The fact that it has been impossible to make [an accurate] count of Palestinians is symptomatic of their plight, for in few places where Palestinians live are they enumerated as Palestinians in national censuses" (1988: 261). Although Said recognizes the census's potential as a tool of state domination, he believes "it would comprise an act of historical and political self-realization" (1995: 18).

This desire to enumerate Palestinians wherever they live suggests some essentializing of their identity, since some descendents of Palestinian refugees now bear the nationality of their host countries and many others intermarry. As Christina Zacharia notes, a unifying census of a physically fragmented people, dangling in precarious positions in exile, requires "the explicit recognition that there is something real that congeals Palestinians wherever they are actually located" (1996: 38). Such a desired recognition of "something real" that then needs to be counted lies squarely within the parameters of ethnic-based political arithmetic. This point is clearly meant not to deny the validity of Palestinian demands but to note their obvious implication in nationalism and its demographic counting games.

The first Palestinian census was deemed so important that the Palestinian Central Bureau of Statistics even considered imposing a curfew on Palestinians while its census was being conducted in order to ensure accuracy. Palestinian resistance to Israeli state power has included a demand for a census of Palestinians in the Occupied Territories and New Autonomous Regions, as well as all over the world. The power of Palestinian numbers must be known (Zacharia 1996). The resistance partly adopts nationalist biopolitics that set the terms of competition— numbers. As Leila Ahmed has noted, narratives of resistance tend to "appropriate, in order to negate them, the symbolic terms of the originating narrative. Standing in relation of antithesis to thesis, the resistance narrative thus reverse[s]—but thereby also accept[s]—the terms set in the first place by the colonizers" (1992: 163–164).

While Palestinian nationalism is not merely a reaction to Zionism, its relative disempowerment has made proactivity difficult. Moreover, numbers are the basic premise of modern democratic politics globally. As Zureik notes, the fact that the Palestinian and Israeli projects are "asymmetrical . . . in terms of power relations does not alter the nature of the process. By being the weaker side in this encounter, the Palestinian effort has aimed at adopting practices in population count which are aimed at countering Israeli designs" (1999: 19).

Before the 1900s, the struggle of Palestinian villagers, tenant farmers, and intellectuals against the sale of land to Jewish immigrants and the Jewish Agency was not yet articulated in entirely nationalistic terms. Mandate Palestine, in fact, was a relatively recent geopolitical/administrative unit (Kanaana 1992: 3), and neither Palestinian nor Arab nationalism had yet become clearly formed or widespread in the area. In the early twentieth century, however, Palestinian nationalism began to take shape. It was influenced by major currents in the Middle East such as Ottomanism, "Islamic trends, the growth of nation-state nationalisms in Arab states," and such parochial factors as "strong religious attachments to Palestine among Muslims and Christians, the impact over time of . . . administrative boundaries and enduring regional and local loyalties" (Khalidi 1997: 21). It was also strongly influenced by Zionism.

One of the early public Arab protests against Jewish immigration was formulated soon after the Balfour Declaration (1917) when the Third Palestine Arab Congress officially complained to the British authorities. In the late 1920s a series of Arab riots, strikes, and boycotts took place and yet another British commission, the Shaw Commission of 1929, found that "the Arabs have come to see in the Jewish immigrant not only a menace to their livelihood, but a possible overlord of the future." Most important for my argument, the Shaw report goes on to present graphs showing the time when the Jewish and Arab populations would be equal in size (Friedlander and Goldscheider 1979: 68).[40] Such "phantom population statistics" (Anagnost 1995: 32) appear over and over again in the subsequent history of the region and become the fetishized maps of warring demographically imagined nations that cadres of demographics "experts" produced on both sides (though more on the Jewish side than on the Palestinian).[41]

The response of many Palestinians to Israeli political arithmetic at the formal political level has been largely to advocate either large families or small ones. On the one hand, some Palestinians claim they should di-

40. During this mandate period, Zionist planners set up commissions to anticipate demographic trends among Arabs (Friedlander and Goldscheider 1979: xvi).

41. A population projection published in *Journal of Palestine Studies* predicts that a Palestinian numerical advantage (in all of Palestine) will reappear sometime around 2010 (Courbage 1999: 27).

rectly defy the Israeli population control plan by having as many children as possible to fuel the revolution and to outbreed Jews, just as the Zionist planners fear—the Zionist demographic struggle in reverse (Tamari and Scott 1991: 159).[42] While Israelis such as Israel Koenig have warned against an Arab time bomb and called for "obstructing any natural increase in the Arab population," diluting existing Arab population concentrations, and Judaizing these areas (Hadawi 1991: 157–158), some Palestinians have embraced the Arab time bomb as a form of resistance and have called for encouraging the natural increase in the Arab population and Arabizing areas where Jews are now in the majority (Ayoosh 1994). Shortly after the release of the Koenig report, Tawfiq Ziyad, former Knesset member, dramatically emblematized the Palestinian response by sending a black death-announcement card to Koenig informing him of the birth of Ziyad's daughter. My father told me that several of his women patients decided to stop using contraceptives at this time, in direct response, they told him, to the release of the Koenig report. While this resistance is not equal or parallel to Israeli nationalism, such reversals often mimic the power structure that they resist.

The PLO and now the Palestinian National Authority in fact seem to support a pronatal policy for Palestinians (Giacaman et al. 1996; Abdo 1994: 2). Diab Ayush, the deputy minister of social welfare, believes that "the demographic factor is one of the main factors in preserving the land [of Palestine], building it up, and determining its identity." He recommends a "consensual" redistribution of the Palestinian population to Arabize the region, alleviate crowding, and allow for Arab population growth (1994: 2, 16–17). The Palestine Red Crescent Society sees "the high fertility of mothers among the Palestinian community . . . as something positive, as a reassurance of the continued existence of the nation" (1993: 2).

Moreover, this Palestinian obsession with numbers is being articulated by drawing on a mythic and hierarchically gendered past, as in Ayush's statement that part of Israel's demographic policy is "limiting Palestinian population growth in several ways and attempting to transform the Arab population into a minority relative to Jews. Most prominent of these policies is . . . prohibiting polygamy among Arabs in Palestine, even though that contradicts the Islamic system of marriage"

42. This position is parodied by Emile Habiby's Pessoptimist, who works for the Israeli secret service and uses birth control to prove his loyalty to the state (1989: 97).

(1994: 7). Many participants at a Palestinian family planning conference in 1992 advocated polygamy as part of the solution of the Palestinian population problem.[43] This is not a unique perception: on an Arabic talk show on Israeli TV, an elderly Palestinian man from al-Naqab
declared he was proud of defying Israel's ban on polygamy by marrying
eight women (not all at once) and having eighty-five grandchildren,
since Israel's policy of outlawing polygamy and of raising the legal age
of marriage was aimed at keeping the Arab birth rate down (*Dardashat,*
aired in Oct. 1995).[44] Like the modern lifestyle denounced by Chief
Rabbi Herzog, the traditional Islamic lifestyle proposed by Ayush and
others positions women's bodies as fields of contest through which nation and community are defined.

The discourse of high fertility is reflected in the Palestinian press,
which frequently celebrates Palestinian numbers. The caption of a photo
on the front page of *al-'Ittihad,* showing Palestinian boys making the
victory sign (see Figure 3), reads: "Every Month, Four Thousand Newborns in Gaza." The fact that all the children are boys suggests that the
reproduction of sons is at the heart of this celebration of fertility. Palestinian discourse is rife with such demographic stories.

The second Palestinian position, which is more popular in leftist
circles, is that in view of the economic difficulties facing Palestinians,
they should have fewer children so as to be able to educate and modernize them. From this perspective, a few highly educated, professional,
middle-class Palestinians are more challenging to Israeli domination
than a lot of uneducated poor ones. Hassan Abu Libdi, director of the
Palestinian Central Bureau of Statistics, argues that high Palestinian
population growth rates are a considerable burden on the economic infrastructure: "If we just sit back and enjoy the fact that one day we may
number more than the Israelis, we'll sink under our own weight." Just
maintaining standards of living and services at their current level, he
warns, will require an immediate injection of billions of dollars (*Jerusalem Report,* Aug. 26, 1999). Hence he is a strong supporter of lowering
fertility rates for the good of the nation. This perspective is also evident
in a poster encouraging later marriage (see Figure 4).

43. Many pronatalists support polygamy, even though statistically polygamy does not
necessarily yield higher birth rates.

44. Abner Cohen similarly notes that "the law prohibiting polygamy is interpreted by
some as an attempt by the Jewish authorities to prevent the natural increase in the Moslem
population" (1965: 135).

في كل شهر، ٤
آلاف مولــود
جديد في غـزة

Figure 3. "Every Month, Four Thousand Newborns in Gaza" (*al-'Ittihad*, May 25, 1994).

Both Palestinian views on the issue respond to Israeli population policies by continuing to associate reproduction with nationalism. The language and terms used by Israel, while being openly and actively resisted, continue to provide the signs and the points for acts of reversal (Comaroff and Comaroff 1990: 246). While advocates of both Palestinian perspectives consider themselves in defiance of the Israeli agenda, they have unwittingly accepted one of its basic premises by closely associating nationalism with reproduction and women. The politicization of reproduction is not unique to Israel and Palestine: "The adage that 'there is power in numbers' underlies the urge of [many] post-colonial nations and dispossessed minorities to assert their legitimacy through counting their populations" (Zureik 1999: 10). The modern techniques of biopower have become instruments of both domination and liberation. Foucault, among others, has identified the state's attempt to transform the sexual conduct of couples into concerted economic and political behavior as a major feature of the modern state. Moreover, by attempting to infiltrate the family and reproduction, the state has made them into possible sites of resistance.

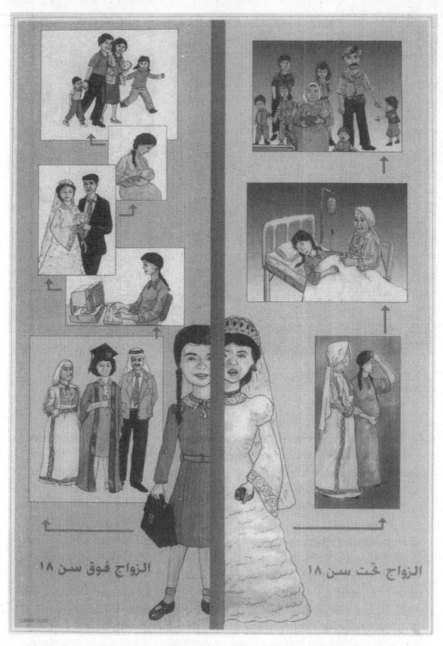

Figure 4. "Marriage under Age 18/Marriage above Age 18": this poster for the Palestinian Family Planning and Protection Association valorizes the scenario of delayed marriage and small family. On the left, the woman is educated, works, is happily married, and has at least one boy and one girl; she wears modern clothes. On the right, the same girl is depicted in traditional clothes, having a difficult pregnancy, unhappily breast-feeding, and surrounded by seven children.

MOTHERS OF THE NATION

All of this has had important implications for the people seen as responsible for producing numbers—women. In fact, underlying the whole discussion of political arithmetic is an attempt to encode women's bodies—both Jewish and Arab—for state power. Women are considered markers of national boundaries, not only symbolically but physically as well: they have the duty to produce the babies that the nation requires (Yuval-Davis 1987). They are recruited for the nationalist project as reproducers (Massad 1995; Peteet 1991: 184; Sharoni 1995: 35), and their bodies and fertility are made the loci of intense contest. Such symbolism of mothers of the nation clearly resonates with many nationalisms around the world. Kin-based metaphors of nationhood that hold women responsible for the demographic strength of the nation in Greece (Paxson 1997), Madonna-like images of mothers of martyrs in Northern Ireland (Aretxaga 1997), and eugenic "mothers of the race" imperatives in early twentieth-century imperial England (Davin 1978) all demonstrate that the politicizing of reproduction by Israelis and Palestinians is certainly not unique, despite their varying contexts and forms.

This inscription of Palestinian women's bodies was clear in the West Bank and Gaza Strip during the intifada, when communiqués of the Unified National Leadership of the Uprising addressed women primarily in their reproductive capacities, as mothers of prisoners and martyrs, or when tear gas caused them to miscarry (Massad 1995: 475). In a refugee camp in Lebanon, one woman described Palestinian women as having *batin 'askari,* a military womb that gives birth to fighters (Peteet 1991: 185) (see Figure 5). The politicization of reproduction is similarly evident in a poster that can be found hanging in many Palestinian homes in the Galilee (see Figure 6). It is also closely echoed by the following lines of poetry, popularized as a song:

> Write down, I am an Arab!
> Fifty thousand is my [ID] number
> Eight children, the ninth will come next summer
> Angry? Write down, I am an Arab! (Lustick 1980: 11)

The fetishization of fertility has made Palestinians, especially women, targets of nationalist rhetoric that deeply politicizes their reproduction. Because Palestinian men *and* women are invested in this nationalization of reproduction, such narratives inform the ways in which they negotiate their reproductive decisions. Women are not passive bystanders of

Figure 5.   The Palestinian widow of a martyred fighter thinks "patience." The
Israeli soldier looks worried by her pregnant belly. Drawing by Naji il-ʿAli, a
Palestinian political cartoonist who lived in Lebanon.

a struggle between Palestinian and Israeli men, but active participants
(in delimited ways) in these constructions of nation and reproduction.[45]
Thus the imagined community of the nation and its multiple configurations shape the ways in which members of that community imagine
themselves, their duties in life, "the right thing to do." Although it is not
the exclusive and perhaps not the primary factor, the nationalist framing of reproduction is certainly a component of the cosmology of family
planning in the Galilee. This component, unlike economic rationality
or access to contraceptives, has not been widely recognized or adequately theorized, despite its resonance in many areas beyond Israel and
Palestine.

This is not to say that the historical configuration of women, reproduction, and nationalism determines in any simple way the number of
children Palestinians in the Galilee have. Making babies or not involves

45. To see women as such passive bystanders would be a narrow view that "assumes
that women's first interests reside in an unquestioned gender identity and ignores . . . the
links between women and their communities" (Aretxaga 1997: 10).

Figure 6. Palestinian artist Sliman Mansour's painting *The Intifada . . . the Mother* depicts the Palestinian masses emerging from between the legs of the Palestinian woman. Prints can be found hanging in many Palestinian homes in the Galilee. (Courtesy of the artist.)

a complex range of beliefs, calculations, emotions, and aspirations, from the widely discussed economic motivations to the intimate and poignant love of children, to the forgetting of a pill. Reproductive decisions play on a shifting combination of socially constructed emotional and material desires. Nationalist framings of reproduction are only one component of this web of longings, albeit one that is not widely recognized. As might be expected, "reproducing the nation," whether through having another child or using contraceptives, is particularly emphasized in political contexts, as during election campaigns, when it is not uncommon to hear men and women declare the need for larger families and swear to have more children who will grow up to vote on their side (although what side that is varies, as do political strategies). But in other contexts, other desires and plans are evoked.

Moreover, given that there is no consensus on the appropriate reproductive strategy for the nation, Palestinians may choose to have either more or fewer children. The dual nationalist discourses—the existence of the small-family *and* the large-family perspectives—have allowed for a multiplicity of reproductive strategies and decisions. The inscription of women's bodies has thus not resulted in strong pressures on women to have either more or fewer children. Indeed, most Palestinians agree with both perspectives to some extent: that it is a national and even human duty to reproduce, *and* that it is important to ensure a good life for one's children. My friend Suha told me, "It's only natural to want to get married and have a family as a service to your people. What else is life for? But you don't want the children to become a burden, either—you want them to be comfortable and happy." Similarly, Hanniyi told me, "If we had more money, I'd have more children for Palestine. I do have these feelings and convictions but I can't afford them—I don't want to throw the children of Palestine out on the streets." Rita Giacaman argues that Palestinian National Authority officials have taken contradictory positions on population, both pro- and antinatal (1997: 23). According to the head of the Palestinian Central Bureau of Statistics, these contradictory opinions have resulted in a policy of no policy (*Jerusalem Report*, Aug. 26, 1999). An article in a popular Arabic magazine with significant circulation in the Galilee presents such a contradictory position:

> It is clear that humans in their nature tend toward procreation, for the size of the [world] population increases without interruption . . . causing conflict between nations, provoking wars, an increase in unemployment, a decline in the standard of living, and the spread of diseases.

Some say that lack of procreation is a factor in spreading peace, tranquillity, enjoyment of a life of plenty, and prevents the manifestation of some hereditary diseases.

Some believe that the process of population control leads to the extinction of nations and the decay of morals. Some scientists say that control leads to depriving the nation of geniuses.

The supporters of increasing progeny say that limiting it is a sign of narcissism, distance from human spirituality and its aspects that compel man to participate in life. The care of a human for himself makes him contribute constructively in the building of his society.

The educated class are the ones who enjoy high salaries and the contented life, who are averse to marriage and resort to methods of contraception. This opens the way for the poor class, who are ignorant of this information, to rain on the nation a storm of progeny, who live at a low economic level, spread diseases, and beget a sick progeny, who detract from the quality of the nation and weaken it. (*Manbar* 1995)

The fact that both positions can be compelling and valid in most people's eyes, combined with the tension between them when money is scarce, allows people to employ different strategies at different points in their lives.

Ideal Palestinian modern femininity is, in fact, commonly scripted in nationalist imaginings as a combination of the two positions: the small *and* the large family. As the women's pages in the daily newspaper illustrate (see Figure 7), the model Palestinian woman of today is a supermom of sorts—educated, employed (in a "feminine" profession preferably), strong enough to face the difficulties of modern life and deal with the complex and racist bureaucracies and barriers she and her children face, yet soft, feminine, fertile, nurturing; she cooks hearty meals, invests herself in her children's education, makes a good name for her husband by having a proud line of children, produces a solid new generation for the nation. An article in a woman's journal published by the Jerusalem Center for Women's Studies, titled "My Homeland in a Woman," is worth quoting here:

The Palestinian woman is the first teacher. . . . She is the carrier of the idea of Palestine in this land. . . . She has the great and rare humane role as "guardian of our generations" in revolutions and intifadas as well as in horizons of peace. . . . The Palestinian woman has constructed institutions . . . building Palestinian society in its lively, social, legal, economic, cultural, and human aspects. . . . We cannot forget woman's role in our land in education, and the shaping of the Palestinian human's memory from the moment he comes into life. . . . Woman is the inspiration of artists in all of the human

Figure 7. The "Woman" page of the Communist 'Ittihad consistently promotes fashion, cooking, and politics—here Ungaro design, coconut sweets, and an officer of the Palestinian women's police force (al-'Ittihad, Aug. 4, 1995).

ages. . . . The Palestinian woman is kneaded from the dough of this homeland's earth, fragrant with its orange and lemon flowers, worked with its
Za'tar and olives. . . . She is a homeland named Palestine, the stem of our first
birth. (*Kul un-Nisa'*, Apr. 1996)

In this cascade of obligations, women are constructed as nurturing
mothers, yet at the same time as political subjects (but mainly through
mothering). Because this litany of requirements can be conflicting and
contradictory, it creates a space for a variety of decisions and desires.
The internal contradictions between the multiple requirements of femininity afford women room for some choice—within the limits of this
ideal.

But even as opinions on family size may vary and shift, it is clear to
almost everyone that these negotiations produce not just babies but
Palestinian babies. Palestinian men and women see themselves as responsible for giving birth to babies who are Palestinian, based on an
imagined biological/genetic foundation—a conflation of birth and genetics with nationality. Children are thus clearly nationally or ethnically
identified by their "Arab blood." This imagined biological identity emphasizes fatherhood (Massad 1995: 472); in a "mixed race" marriage,
paternity is considered more dominant and determinative of identity
than maternity. This emphasis on the Palestinian identity of children as
determined by biological Palestinian paternity allows many people to
consider the marriage of a Palestinian woman to a man of another nationality an act bordering on treason, or at the very least a "loss for the
nation" (her children will not be Palestinian), while the marriage of a
Palestinian man to a woman of another nationality is seen as adding her
to the nation, bringing her into the fold. Certainly my marriage to an
American was often evaluated as a loss for the community. Accepting
an anonymous or non-Arab sperm donor for artificial insemination or
adopting a non-Arab child is often regarded in similar terms. Political
arithmetic has resulted in a reification and rigidification of identity
within the Palestinian community. As with the census, the fiction here is
that "one, unambiguous, stable and complete identity marker" can be
found (Anderson 1991: 166).

The preference for giving birth to boys is also linked to nationalism's
political arithmetic. Recall Foucault's statement concerning the utility of
the state (1988: 153): it is males that make up its power, while females
assist in producing the numbers. Rick Wilford argues that nationalism commonly constructs women as the symbolic form of the nation,
whereas men are invariably represented as its chief agents (1998: 1).

Partha Chatteerjee has argued that at its core postcolonial nationalism in India was "a male discourse" that created a new patriarchy, which "invested women with the dubious honor of representing" certain domains of a "distinctively modern national culture" (1993: 136; 1989: 622). Indeed, a wide variety of national cultures have been modeled on specific gender and sexual norms (Parker et al. 1992: 6). These nationalisms often favor a distinctly homosocial form of male bonding (Anderson 1983: 16) and often legitimize the dominance of men over women (Mosse 1985). Ubiquitous emblems of modern nationalism, such as tombs of unknown soldiers, assign gendered duties, reverence, and rights to men of the nation. Thus it is not surprising that among the complex and changing motivations behind the preference for boys in the Galilee is the belief that giving birth to a boy is an important contribution to the nation. As one article (written by a woman) put it, women's main concern in life should be the making of men, whom they breast-feed "the milk of glory, honor and courage" (*Sawt ul-Haq wal-Hurriyya*, June 16, 1995). Only by producing boys do women truly become "mothers of the nation." The older concept of *'izwi* (strength) of the clan was measured by the number of adult males belonging to it. Boys were necessary for protecting members of the family "in case any trouble breaks out." As the saying went, "boys were born with their stick in their hand" and their first words were "mama, dada, ax, stick" (*'ammā, 'abbā, balṭa, 'aṣā*). Today, however, clannishness is considered unacceptable within the framework of nationalism (even as it is often mobilized in its service) (Swedenburg 1995). Thus the concept of *'izwi*, which once referred to the clan, has been transferred and transformed into the realm of national struggle, to the *'izwi* of the nation. Boys are now important not because they can fight locally (although that is not entirely irrelevant) but because they can stand up to the Israeli state, its police, bureaucracies, and individuals. "Palestinians want boys because they are the backbone of the nation," a teenage girl, Fatin, told me. Women see themselves as giving boys to their families, communities, and the nation.

In these ways, nationalism conjures a gendered world in which women are principally mothers of the nation, reproducers of boys, and makers of national *'izwi*, with limited participation in other realms. Moreover, women are targets as well as active participants in these constructions. Although nationalism can be characterized as male-centered, it is its ability to involve women and give them agency (in delimited ways) that makes these discourses particularly powerful. While gender is depicted in multiple and competing ways in the Galilee, the nationalization of reproduction and its gendered duties can translate into actual, and not only symbolic, limitations on women.

CLINICAL ENCOUNTERS

Perhaps the most limiting effect of Israel's political arithmetic is the way it influences women's encounters with health professionals. The political nature of reproduction and medicine in general is now widely recognized among social scientists (e.g., Ginsburg and Rapp 1991, Hammonds 1987, Harrison 1994, Hubbard 1995, Kapsalis 1997, Martin 1987, Patton 1993). This politicization is particularly evident in the Galilee. The main sites of prenatal, infant, and family planning services available to Palestinians in the Galilee have been government-sponsored maternal and child health centers (MCHs) (later called family health centers). The framing of Palestinian reproduction in terms of a demographic war has added to the roster of separations that usually exist between "client" and "provider." While many women around the world are separated from their providers by class and education (Simmons and Elias 1994), in the Galilee we must add nationalism to the list. Although increasingly many workers at these clinics are Palestinian, some women feel they are working in an institutional framework that does not necessarily have their best interests in mind. As one woman, Iman, told me: "The Jewish doctor wishes he could tie all our tubes. I told him, 'I'm going to have another baby and name him Muhammad and you can't stop me.'" [46]

Given the globally sensitive nature of population issues, their ascendance in close association with state power, their particular centrality in the history of Israel, the ethnically structured health care system in the country, and Palestinian resistance, which continues to recentralize reproduction within nationalism, it does not come as a big surprise that family planning services for Palestinians in Israel are fraught with tension. All of these factors come into play at the site of clinical encounters for Palestinian women in the Galilee.

The fact that state-sponsored medical services are made suspect by political arithmetic is further demonstrated by the success of clinics es-

---

46. Most of the gynecologists accessible through the family health centers are male and Jewish. They routinely give younger women contraceptive pills and older women IUDs, offering little choice or consultation about alternative methods (Badarneh 1994: 24; Hussein 1994: 64; Portugese 1998: 129).

tablished by the Islamic Party. This relatively small network of clinics has been noted for its wide range of low-cost MCH services. Although these clinics were seen by their founders as part of their call to Islam, the gynecologist whom I met (who was not religious herself) told me that "the secret of our success is that we treat women differently. They feel more comfortable with us. They can trust us." These clinics' non-governmental and Arab status has contributed to their popularity.

The government-sponsored clinics are certainly not boycotted or disparaged outright, since they do offer needed services. But many women feel as Iman does. Israeli motives for encouraging family planning are considered sufficiently suspect that many women lie to the doctors and nurses, hide information from them, delay reporting, do not trust them, and sometimes speak badly about them in the community. One nurse, Lubna, told me that her sister-in-law confronted her: "She came up to me the other day and said, 'Why do you treat the women so they don't have more children? This is what Israel wants. No, let them have children.' These women accuse me, as though I'm doing something bad." Two nurses, Salma and Jihan, complained that their clients seemed alienated from the clinic: "They just don't feel this institution is theirs." Moreover, many clients mentioned their reluctance to disclose new pregnancies to the nurses because they expected that the news would upset them. Political arithmetic thus diminishes the quality of communication in the clinic, though there is no formal coercion involved. This diminished communication and lack of trust cannot be in the best interest of women's health.

In the spring of 1995, Arnon Sofer, a prominent political geographer at Haifa University who has been involved in various official plans for Judaizing the Galilee, stated that the most serious threat Israel faces is the wombs of Arab women in Israel (Masalha 1997: 149). Palestinians, men and women, are well aware that their fertility is of grave concern to Zionists and are thus often suspicious of family planning, even when it is provided by non-Israeli institutions. In the West Bank and Gaza, the staff of the Jordanian Family Planning and Protection Association (FPPA) (note the need to emphasize protection along with planning in the very name of the organization) was highly sensitized to the political delicacy of family planning. Staff members I interviewed told me that they did not send their workers into areas where people had recently been killed or wounded: "How can we tell them not to have children when their children are being killed? It's not appropriate." The staff also emphasized that "we never use the word 'limiting' [taḥdīd]. We emphasize spacing and not limiting. People can have as many children as they want." The Palestinian National Authority also very deliberately uses the word "spacing." Dr. Mohammed Afifi, director of health promotion and education at the Ministry of Health in Gaza, stresses: "We don't speak about limiting the number of children" (*Jerusalem Report,* Aug. 26, 1999). Similarly, the United Nations Relief and Works Agency for Palestine Refugees in the Near East (UNRWA) felt compelled to meet with religious, social, and political leaders in the West Bank and Gaza to obtain their approval for their family planning projects before initiating them in 1995.

If the family planning services of UNRWA, the Jordanian FPPA, and the Palestinian National Authority can be suspect to Palestinians, those offered by the Israeli government are more so. Playing on such fears and sensitivities, a disgruntled former employee of the Israeli Ministry of Health (who is Jewish) complained in the 1970s to the Arab League that "the Israeli government was forcing Arab women to be sterilized because their birthrate was far higher than the Jewish one" (Mackay 1995: 31). The International Planned Parenthood Federation investigated and found no evidence of forced sterilization, but the employee's choice of accusation indicates the anxiety surrounding Palestinian reproduction in Israel.

Moreover, the Zionist legacy of the health care system in Israel clearly contributes to making state family planning services suspect to Palestinians. As I have argued, health care in Israel, long sectorally organized along the putative racial lines of Arab and Jew, emerged from institutions whose primary purpose was explicitly Zionist to the exclusion or later marginalization of the majority of Palestinians. Indeed, today's government-sponsored family health centers, the main sites of family planning services available to Palestinians in the Galilee, evolved from the milk kitchens created by the Hadassah Medical Organization, whose nationalist Jewish perspective was clearly articulated.

As a result of this legacy of health policies, the same statistics that the Israeli government collects to imagine its racialized dominion can be used to show racialized differences in health, such as the infant mortality rates in Table 2.

As Silvana Patriarca notes,

Although it cannot be denied that the fortune of statistics is inextricably linked to the fortune of the modern nation-state . . . their mode of operation is far from being smoothly functional. Since categories and classifications used in statistics and reproduced in official discourse by state agencies tend

TABLE 2
INFANT MORTALITY RATES IN ISRAEL PER
1,000 LIVE BIRTHS, 1980–1994

	Jews	Arabs and Others
1980–1984	11.8	22.6
1985–1989	8.8	16.8
1990–1994	6.8	13.5

SOURCE: Central Bureau of Statistics 1996: 134–135.

to acquire . . . a life of their own, the outcome of statistical representations can be highly uncertain. Official statistics create and crystallize units of observation and categories that may produce effects different from those sought by their makers. They can, for example, be used to further the political agenda of oppositional forces, by making more visible phenomena such as poverty and crime. (1994: 361)

The infant mortality rates according to nationality collected by the government of Israel have become significant in attempts to critique the state and its differential treatment of Arabs and Jews.

On the reproductive front, Israel's pronatalist tendency is tempered by a liberal faction that favors contraception and prefers to rely on immigration of Jews and by a general fear that encouraging the Jewish birth rate would encourage the Arab one as well. As mentioned earlier, it was not until the 1980s that the Ministry of Health initiated a family-planning project, and then it targeted the Arab community. My own research was frequently met with enthusiasm among Israeli Jews, especially Health Ministry officials, because of my perceived promotion of family planning for Palestinians. This is the context in which Palestinian women in the Galilee seek family-planning and reproductive health services at the MCH centers, the main sites where they are available.

My discussions with one of the pioneers of family planning in Israel, Dr. Beatta Davidson (a family acquaintance), shed light on the ambivalence regarding family planning in Israel.[47] Dr. Davidson had one of the first clinics to offer family planning services, which were, according to her, "a forbidden topic at the time." Her services were underground and illegal; her feminist and liberal medical convictions were strong enough

47. The discussions were in English.

to compel her to defy the Histadrut Sick Fund policies. Funding from an American source enabled Dr. Davidson to attend a population conference in India in the 1950s. There she was asked why Israel sent a delegate to the conference when Ben-Gurion was awarding a prize to every mother of a tenth child. Dr. Davidson replied, "On this issue, Ben-Gurion and I do not agree." Her attendance at the population conference so enhanced her prestige that the Histadrut Sick Fund finally gave her support for a clinic—not for family planning but for "consultations."

Dr. Davidson told me she saw her target populations for family planning as (1) Moroccan Jews, whose extended family structure Ben-Gurion was trying to break down; (2) Romanians, who had up to fifteen and twenty abortions; and (3) Arabs, who "still" had large families. Dr. Davidson received so many patients that she could hardly keep up. She did not seem fazed by her observation that most of the Arab women she saw during this period were sent to her by their husbands. She believed that Arab men who "lived with the Jews" saw "how much we invested in our children" and wanted the same benefits for their own. According to her, Arab women had not gained this insight. She told me of one client who was crying because her husband would not let her back in the house without an IUD. Many of the women spoke only Arabic, and Dr. Davidson said she developed a limited vocabulary "from here to here," pointing to the area between her chest and upper thighs, even with the help of language classes. Dr. Davidson's colleagues told her that she was crazy: "They told me, 'How dare you?' They were extremely afraid that it would be perceived as a demographic war. But I never felt that. None of my work ever had any repercussions. I never had any complaints or problems." Although Dr. Davidson represents a more liberal Zionist view and had the best intentions in providing her services, her perspective too—not to mention that of the Israeli medical establishment—is shot through with contradictions and ambivalence. The distinction of Arab and Jew strongly comes into play, despite or in addition to humanitarian goals.

Given the Zionist sectarian foundation on which the Israeli health care system has been based, the Zionist emphasis on the political need for a Jewish majority, the state's reluctance to provide family planning to Jews, and the inscription of women's bodies as a locus of nationalist contest, it is not surprising that even with the best of individual intentions, the quality of communication between client and provider at the maternal and child (or family) health centers leaves much to be desired.

With a symbolic vocabulary "from here to here" as the tool for discussion, even "from here to here" may not be all that well served.

CONCLUSION

Note that family planning as encouraged by Israeli state organs holds little legitimacy for Palestinians as an Israeli discourse per se. However, the use of other existing tropes, paradigms, or class positions can lend appeal and efficacy to such otherwise delegitimized projects.

This brings to mind one much discussed instance in which reproduction was a factor in both nation-building and resistance to it, the case of Fascist Italy. In an attempt to reverse Italy's declining fertility rate, Mussolini set a goal of increasing the Italian population from 40 million to 60 million in less than twenty-five years. Coercive measures, such as the banning of contraception, abortion, and paid employment for women, were supplemented by propaganda campaigns and rituals of legitimization such as the annual celebration of prolific couples. Elizabeth Krause writes that by painting the state as a patriarchal family writ large, Mussolini allowed some citizens to experience solidarity with the state through tropes of kinship, gender, and reproduction (1994: 272). Lesley Caldwell suggests that beyond the cataloguing of Mussolini's repressive policies, one must address the modes in which the state attempted to effect and disseminate its vision among particular populations of men and women, including dependence on already existing paradigms embedded in Italian society, such as the Catholic construction of women as biological reproducers and nurturers (1986: 136, 115). Although these strategies had limited success, the productive as well as the repressive elements of state activity must be examined.

Returning to the Galilee, one might ask whether Israeli family planning projects are able to appeal to Palestinians beyond the realm of state politics. And my answer is that to a certain extent they do—by appealing to Palestinian desires for "modernity" and middle-class status. It is no coincidence that family planning pamphlets show a photo of a single male child with a Westernized young mother and father huddling over a book (see Figure 8).

It is striking how much nationalisms have been configured on women's (and men's) bodies. Recent literature has suggested that a wide variety of nationalisms have been modeled on gender and sexual norms (Parker et al. 1992: 6), and that such national uses of genders and sexualities is mobile and multifaceted (Povinelli 1994). In the Galilee, too,

تنظيم الاسرة

حقائق ومعلومات

وزارة الصحة ـ قسم التثقيف والارشاد الصحي ـ اورشليم

משרד הבריאות
המחלקה לחינוך לבריאות

תכנון המשפחה

Figure 8. The cover of a pamphlet on family planning issued by the Israeli Ministry of Health appeals to Palestinians in its invocation of modernity and middle-class status.

there are significant links to be traced among gender, reproduction, sex, health, nationalism, and the state. The heightened emphasis on women as reproducers of the nation in response to Israeli population politics has limited female participation in the nation and has further alienated women from institutions that could improve their health and help them in their reproductive strategies.

Let us remember that a project such as the state is a "*claim* that in its very name attempts to give unity, coherence, structure, [purposiveness, and rationality] to what are in practice frequently disunited, fragmented attempts at domination" (Sayer 1994: 371). The audience for these performances "is not asleep," as a Palestinian editorial assures us ('*Ittihad,* Nov. 15, 1996), and has responded in more ways than one. However, that audience has challenged Zionism with something that resembles it in some ways. In both cases, it is the wombs of mothers that are ultimately considered uniting. An article in the Hebrew daily *Ha'artez* reports that Ihab al-Ashqar, an intifada activist, "would habitually tell his Israel secret service interrogators and his prison guards: 'Do you know what the major problem facing you Israelis is? You think you are different from us, as if we are not born, like you, after nine months in our mothers' wombs'" (*Ha'artez,* Apr. 20, 1997).

TWO

Luxurious Necessities

LADDER OF CIVILIZATION

Jamil, who owns a falafel store, said his seven children are a thorn in Israel's side. But he also told me he bought a leather couch for 11,000 shekels (roughly U.S.$3,000) because he saw Israeli government officials sitting on one like it on television.

Many Palestinians in the Galilee resist Israeli domination but also express awe for Israel's technological superiority (as well as that of Israel's financial backer, the United States). Few dispute this fact or its importance. Some even go so far as to accept Israel's argument that the state has "developed" the Arabs in Israel, and consider themselves the most developed Arabs in the Middle East by virtue of their colonization by Israel—even as they consider Palestinians in the West Bank the least developed Arabs in the Middle East by virtue of *their* colonization by Israel. One of my cousins was talking about a trip with her family to newly opened Jordan, where they visited Petra. She mentioned that there are floods in Petra that "kill tourists every single year. It's so dangerous." Her mother shook her head and said, "They should do something about that." My cousin's husband commented: "If the floods were in Israel or America, they would have done something about it, they would have built a dam or something, but not in Jordan." My cousin added bitterly, "That's why Israel should occupy Jordan first, develop it, and then afterward they should make peace."

Palestinians have been subjugated by Israel's economic policies and indeed see themselves—justifiably so—as victims of ethnic-based "underdevelopment." Yet at the same time, they admire the Jewish population's economic "advances." Moreover, they have also partly accepted Israel's argument that their underdevelopment is exacerbated, if not exclusively caused, by their high fertility rate. Palestinians in the Galilee have largely accepted—perhaps been forced to accept—the claim that a lower fertility rate will lead to greater economic development. In this context, family planning has expanded from a remedy for underdevelopment to become itself a sign of the modern (Anagnost 1995: 22).

The conceptualization of history as linearly progressing, and the corollary that "Arab society" or "Palestinian culture" or "Eastern civilizations" are slowly advancing or trying to advance toward a Western universal model, is widespread in the Galilee. This underlying premise of Israeli discourse (Eyal 1996) has insinuated itself into Palestinian material and ideological identity work. The media (Arabic and otherwise) bombard readers and viewers with constant reference to the modern (*'asry*) as positive. The superiority and inevitable dominance of "the modern" can be found in everything from furniture advertisements, Islamic movement literature, and cake recipes to family planning promotions. A commentary in the Communist daily by a Dr. Fu'ad Khatib reads:

> Writings lost in the labyrinth of Arab reality, a reality that is confused, with broken wings, unable to jump toward the twentieth century. I deliberately do not say the twenty-first. "Climbing the ladder" is done one rung at a time, and we are still flailing at the end of the tenth century economically and the Middle Ages socially and in terms of our thinking. Our fate is like a straw in the flow of a current. (*'Ittihad*, June 6, 1995)

The urgency with which this discourse is deployed seems to derive partly from the fear of falling farther behind and being trampled under the large mechanical foot of modernity. It is significant that for many Palestinians in Israel, this danger is not metaphorical but literal.

A primary signifier of modernity in the Galilee is family planning—having fewer, planned, spaced, modern children in a companionate marriage. A Gaza surgeon who failed in his efforts to set up a family planning awareness campaign explains that "in Gaza, it's not a Third World mentality, it's Tenth World" (*Jerusalem Report*, Aug. 26, 1999). A strong connection is drawn between modernity and reproductive control. While I was telling one of my favorite teachers from elementary school about my research project, the principal overheard us and insisted on interjecting his opinion:

> Quite simply, there is a reverse correlation between family size and
> the level of civilization. This is because the requirements of life in civ-
> ilization are higher: education, a villa, a room for each child, a com-
> puter, a desk, a bed. . . . Before people didn't care about this. The
> early Muslims, for example, said, "We want to increase the number
> of our fighters." They had different requirements than today.

How did the school principal and Dr. Khatib come to conceive of modernity in these ways? This process is closely tethered to an increasingly global capitalist economy that manifests itself in different forms and provokes varied responses across time and space (Mills 1997: 42). The challenge is to discuss these processes of globalization without privileging the global, romanticizing the local, or eliminating the national (Rudy 1998).

"Life isn't what it used to be" has become a cliché repeated daily in the Galilee. The old days were simple; modern life is complex, with many requirements, needs, necessities. Khadiji Haddad, a nurse and health educator at a school in Sakhnin, who is married to the lawyer son of one of the village's sheikhs, noted that "the difference between our parents and us is that life today has a lot more requirements [mutaṭallabat]— things our parents considered luxuries are fundamental for us."

The strikingly rapid pace of these ongoing transformations makes for stark and clear contrasts between the old days and modern life. I have noticed over the years of going home to the Galilee every summer that it has become increasingly difficult to find unique American gifts that friends and family cannot easily find back home, and increasingly easy to buy things that are as trendy in the Galilee as in New York.

With the massive purchase and expropriation of land by the Israeli government, and thus the virtual elimination of agriculture, people for whom farming was the primary source of income have been compelled to work for wages in Jewish enterprises (sometimes on land they themselves used to own) as the cheapest of blue-collar workers (Owen 1982). The Israeli economy, bolstered by massive influxes of U.S. aid and private capital, has long benefited from cheap Palestinian labor (Tamari 1981; Zureik 1976, 1979). The Palestinians have thus served as Israel's army of reserve labor, occupying the lower rungs of the occupational ladder, taking the undesirable jobs that Israeli Jews have not cared to fill, especially in construction, agriculture, and manufacturing (Bornstein

1998: 220). For Israeli businesses, these Palestinian workers are tantamount to "a Third World colony next door" (Moors 1995: 203). Note
that this "economic integration" is accompanied by strong legal, social,
and residential segregation; it is not just market forces that keep Palestinian labor cheap and available (ibid.; Bornstein 1998: 219). The
underclassing of Palestinians has resulted not only from the absence of
a positive policy to integrate them as equal citizens but also from the
state's deliberate efforts to isolate and limit them (Sa'di and Kanaaneh
1990: 8).

Palestinian citizens of Israel are poorer than Jewish citizens (and the
Palestinians in the West Bank and Gaza are poorer still): they have a
consistently higher incidence of poverty, and that poverty is deeper. According to official government statistics, in 1997 about 46.1 percent of
non-Jews in Israel lived below the poverty line (National Insurance Institute 1998). In addition, the supposedly equalizing effect of welfare
benefits lifts fewer non-Jews out of poverty.[1] Not only are Palestinians
overrepresented in low-paid blue-collar jobs, but within any given occupational category they receive low returns in terms of occupational at-
tainments relative to their qualifications.[2] A nationwide survey of the
Jewish population conducted in 1985 revealed that 81 percent of re-
spondents believed it was appropriate for the state to give preference to
Jews over Arabs, 61 percent agreed that Jewish applicants should be fa-
vored for employment in the public sector, and 48 percent said they
were not ready to work with Arabs (Sa'di and Kanaaneh 1990: 8). These
findings suggest the Zionist ideology of prioritizing Jews and marginal-
izing Arabs that underlies many personal interactions, but also government policy: lower child benefits, lower mortgages, substantially smaller
budgets allocated for Arab municipalities than for Jewish settlements of
the same size, and so forth (see Table 3).

But along with these forced and violent changes, Palestinians have
been seduced into seeing the American dream as a hope (perhaps their
only hope) for their children. Many parents hope that if they have fewer
children, they will be able to provide them with recently conceived necessities: computers and Coca-Cola, Adidas and college savings funds.
Although they are at the bottom of the consumerist system, they are

---

1. For example, state welfare support mechanisms in 1995 pulled 56% of poor Jewish families out of poverty vs. 39% of poor Arab families (Swirski et al. 1998: 3).

2. According to the Central Bureau of Statistics, "about 30% of Israeli-born Ashkenazim, compared with 50% of Israeli-born Mizrahim and 80% of Arabs, work in blue-
collar occupations or sales" (quoted in ibid.).

TABLE 3
SOME INDICATORS OF INCOME AND POVERTY
AMONG ARABS AND JEWS IN ISRAEL

	Arab	Jewish
Average monthly income of salaried urban* males (1994)	NIS 2,494	NIS 4,555
Average monthly income of salaried urban* females (1994)	NIS 1,154	NIS 2,235
Poverty rates after payment of transfers and direct taxes (1995)	33%	15%
Employed persons in blue-collar jobs	78%	48%
Persons aged 15 years and above employed	40%	52%

SOURCE: Israel National Insurance Institute 1996; Central Bureau of Statistics 1997.
*Residing in communities of more than 2,000 people.

largely enveloped by it and express their hopes and fears from within it. Aihwa Ong writes that "the disciplining of the labor force is an intricate, long-drawn-out process involving a mixture of repression, habituation, co-optation, and cooperation within the workplace and throughout society" (1991: 286). In any case, very few Palestinians are calling for a return to premechanized farming.

REQUIREMENTS OF MODERN LIFE

An awareness of the changing and increasing "requirements" of life is now considered paramount for entering modernity. Significantly, not everyone supposedly has this awareness or the ability to attain the requirements. Butrus is a 30-year-old father[3] of one son who works as a construction contractor. He told me:

Before they needed labor to work, and all the food was from the land. They didn't have to buy a computer for each of their ten children. My brothers and I are ten, we have twenty cars altogether, each costs about forty thousand dollars. What does that come to? Eight hundred thousand. Do you think people before could even imagine this? Before they used to all live in one room. Now I am renting a house from my own brother, so I can have my freedom in it. People have woken up.

3. Unless I indicate otherwise, the ages given are those at the time of my research. Note that the ages of people born before 1948 are rough estimates, since registration of births was not systematized then.

Butrus's wife, Lamis, added:

> Now each family needs to live alone in a house. Before you'd have
> four families together. The time when a woman was willing to live
> with her in-laws and close the same door on them at night—that time
> is over. The clock's hands don't move backward.

Butrus continued:

> But some men are clueless. [He used the Hebrew term *satum*.] They
> don't look to the future, don't plan. The young men in our village are
> all independent, they're free with their lives. There are no *mukhtars*,[4]
> or masters. Each head of a household is responsible for himself. In
> contrast, in Mghar village, men, no matter how old they get, still give
> their paychecks to their fathers. They are very backward. Indepen-
> dence in the family promotes development and freedom.

Owning one car or more, having your own house, not living with your
extended family, buying your child a computer, and controlling your
household income have become new "necessities," signs that "at least
some of us are waking up from the stupor of the past."

Kamli Sliman, my classmate in high school, held out on getting married until she was 25 and now has a new three-story home and a baby
boy, though her parents still live in a small house and depend on her father's income as a garbage collector. She said she plans to have only two
children because

> there is an impact to economic considerations. It's very simple: spend-
> ing on two isn't like spending on four. . . . The old generation had
> more children. Development and technology are the reason for the
> change. Luxuries *[kamāliyyāt]* didn't exist, high school education
> wasn't mandatory, they didn't have sports clubs one could join, as I've
> done. . . . Before there used to be more good, and children used to get
> full. Today children don't accept just any kind of food, they want
> such a variety. Now people want their children to live at a high stan-
> dard and to educate them. And even when both husband and wife are
> working, they can hardly keep up. [See Figure 9.]

This emphasis on formerly unimaginable technologies and luxuries
as today's fundamentals was repeated to me over and over again. And

---

4. *Mukhtar* is a clan leader institution established in 1861 by Ottoman law to replace
the existing village leadership structure and open the population to external bureaucratic
control.

Figure 9.   Kamli showed me her newborn's room with matching bed canopy, curtains, lampshade, and carpet, saying, "We want the best for our son."

there is a supposedly self-evident logic in this: the need to provide these expensive fundamentals for one's children, to "keep up," requires the modern person to calculate and rationally economize by cutting down on the number of children because "spending on two isn't like spending on four." A new economic rationality was being articulated. Echoing modernization theory's rational, economizing, calculating individual, many people spoke of family planning as common sense to any logical person. The modern conditions supposedly speak for themselves, or, as Haniyyi said, "The circumstances decide, not the husband or wife." Society is seen as consisting of, on the one hand, rational modern people who are aware of the increasing requirements of contemporary life and have logically concluded that they must follow a new family strategy and, on the other hand, those who have not reached this rational conclusion—yet.

THE NEW ECONOMIC RATIONALITY OF THE FAMILY

As I heard repeatedly, the key to being modern in the Galilee is awareness that modernity requires a high degree of daily consumption and a high level of spending. Yasmin, who is originally from Syria and married a cousin in Nazareth twenty-five years ago, has five children. She said,

> There are a lot of expenses in the family. We provide everything for them . . . we even bought them a computer. My daughters spend a lot—we made them used to spending, on clothing, food, and all. The world has developed, having children isn't everything in life. Before, a child would accept anything you gave him, now he doesn't.

Similarly, Yumna, a schoolteacher from Majd il-Krum with four children, told me

> My son Sharif [12 years old] wants pocket money every day, courses, computers, swimming lessons, football team dues, trips . . . when he hears from his friends about a new place, he wants to go to it. He wants to go to a play, wants to buy Crocker jeans and only Crocker, wants specific types of sneakers. And if the child is a girl, it's double the expense: every day there's a new style of hairdo, clothing, shoes, decorated notebooks and book covers. My daughter [11] likes to change her school bag every two months and she refuses to buy anything cheap. . . . Because of the economic situation, people's view of life is different. You not only have to eat and drink, you want to enlarge your house, to go on trips outside the country. . . . Before there was no TV, no radio, no electricity, so life was simple. Today the quality of life has changed.

There is more to life than just having children, and one wants to do more than just survive. Children are choosy, finicky, voracious, and parents want them to have the best. Their consumption habits become a focus of a family's modernity and affluence. Fawziyyi from Tamra, housewife and mother of four, said:

> Life is hard now, it costs a lot, yet we want to give birth and pass on our inheritance. These days a family demands three different meals— breakfast, lunch, and dinner—and each meal must have different dishes in it. Children now won't eat for dinner the same thing they had for lunch. They're very picky. Before, the Arabs' ambitions were in kids [ṭamʿit-ha bil-wlād]; they were insurance in life and a profitable trade. But today everything is too expensive.

It is not that modern families don't care about having heirs and passing on their names, but rather that this enterprise has become costly. A new family economy is necessary. Muna, a high school teacher and mother of four, said that "the young generation think more about economic considerations. They put a lot of effort into the child, and they know that it costs. Today you have to buy milk from a store, and you can't feed a child a dry piece of bread—you have to have those jars of prepared fruit, Pampers, creams . . . And illnesses are increasing—in the winter you need a budget just for medicines." Many parents describe themselves as calculating costs on a limited and sometimes unstable income, and yet investing in each child.

One's attitude toward household economy—whether or not one sees the "self-evident" logic that modernity requires fewer children—is considered of vital importance in the Galilee today. A related question is whether or not one accepts the supposedly traditional and religious belief that a child's livelihood (*rizqa*) is given at birth. While this faith that God will provide is considered religious, it is not clearly Muslim, Christian, or Druze. It is considered part of faith in God—whatever that faith may be. It is not, of course, unique to the Galilee or to Palestinians; Catholics and Protestants in late eighteenth-century Europe sustained "the idea of a providential God who was disposed to supply an abundance of food however many babies might need it" (Schneider and Schneider 1996: 19). Today in the Galilee, this God-sent livelihood often takes the form of the Israeli government's universal welfare—a small stipend, usually referred to as "insurance," of about $30 per month per child.

To depend on the insurance check or to believe that God will somehow provide is to be fatalistic, old-fashioned, and definitely not modern in most people's understanding. My cousin Salah told me: "There are some people who like to have children because of the insurance payments. They have more children so they can increase the payments. They don't think that in the future these won't be enough. People in the × clan think about this a lot. Actually they don't think at all." Taghrid, a Bedouin housewife and mother of four, said that "this belief in *rizqa* is simply wrong. If a human being doesn't work hard, his livelihood's not going to come to him on its own. Although insurance helps a bit, it's not even enough for one child's pocket money." Basmi, a mother of six from Tab'un, felt very strongly that "each child adds on at least a thousand shekels a month—milk, diapers, clothes. It's not true that a child's *rizqa* is sent by God. If I were convinced of that, I wouldn't have had an abortion."

Although several religious people told me that they did believe that God sends a livelihood, they emphasized that this does not mean that one should not plan and make calculations. Wardi (who is Christian)[5] told me that once a child is born, "you can no longer say a word except this, that God will provide. But the livelihood is not going to come to him on its own. It just means that a human being must deal with the situation he's in." Nuhad, from the city of Haifa, who became a born-again Christian three years ago, believed that "that saying about livelihood is silly [habal]—I believe the child is a blessing from God, but that doesn't have anything to do with livelihood."

Suha argues with her mother-in-law about this issue:

> There are so many expenses. I've already opened a savings account for each child. You need to plan for the future, for their university and everything. There's a lot of pressure from my mother-in-law to have more children. [Suha has a boy and a girl.] We had a big fight because I want to wait several years between children. I tell her it's because of the financial situation, and she says, "No, it's sinful to say that. Each child is born and his livelihood is born with him." But I've had two children and no livelihood was born with them. I keep on counting how much I need to spend if I have another kid. My husband makes a lot of money and still we're always in debt. I don't know how other women do it, maybe I waste too much money, I don't know. I know people who make less money than my husband and have more children and they're able to save each month. It amazes me, I don't know how they do it.

From her mother-in-law's perspective, Suha spends too much money on her kids, and unnecessarily opens a savings account for college when the children are only 4 and 6 years old. Not all Palestinians in the Galilee have been enveloped by the modernization orientation. Similarly, Fatmi, who is 28 and has been married less than six months, does

> believe that the child is born and his livelihood is born with him. You shouldn't believe people who tell you they can't have more children because they can't afford them. These aren't reasons, they're more like excuses. The people who say this usually spend on three children what they could spend on five. For example, my aunt Samiyyi spends so much on her three children that if she had more children, the money would be enough for them. Today everyone works and every-

one makes money. There are no economic restrictions to having more children if one wants to. Everybody complains about economics, those who have children and those who don't.

Fatmi's aunt Samiyyi, on the other hand, told me that Fatmi is "young and inexperienced—she doesn't understand yet how important household economy is." Samiyyi doesn't want to spend less money on more children because "it's better to have a small family that lives at a high standard than a big family that lives at a low standard."
One of my relatives worried:

> I hope you're not going to make it out like all the Arab births are because of politics. Because of the economic situation in Israel, we don't look at politics this way. I want a family that's not too big and not too small, that in the future I can educate and who can have suitable conditions and everything. Arabs in Israel don't think about simply increasing their numbers, only in the West Bank maybe. A lot of young men were killed in the intifada there, and with their simple thinking some people want to compensate for that killing by having more children. On the contrary, I believe we should give birth to only a thousand and they would turn out decent [mis'adin]—that would be more helpful.

This view emphasizes the supposed quality of children over quantity in the context of Israeli domination and economic difficulties. Such a perspective manages to blend and balance seemingly conflicting desires: to resist Israeli domination and to imitate it at the same time; to resist its ethnic population policy by adopting its economic strategies for the family.

CREATION OF MODERN STANDARDS

A certain economic rationality has thus become a significant marker of modernity in the Galilee. As I mentioned earlier, this process is related to the incorporation of Palestinians into a global capitalist economy. The most obvious way in which newly imagined and imaginable needs and possibilities have been created in the Galilee is through technologies of mass communication. Print media, television, radio, advertising, and packaging have long been identified as sites for the production of modern, and particularly consumerist, desires. Examples easily come to mind: a teenage girl I knew had tacked above her bed a glossy magazine photo of Cindy Crawford kissing an invisible man without smudging her Revlon ColorStay lipstick; a promotion for Buddy Pudding, a product of Tnuva, the largest dairy company in Israel, promises free toys (see Figure 10).

Schools, clinics, and workplaces—factories, offices, government ministries—are just a few of the other sites for the construction, dissemination, and possible contestation of the symbols and meanings of modernity. It is important not to overlook the role of ruling institutions in this process; "states ration goods and services, they govern credit and retailing practices, they define appropriate standards of consumption with statistics and property laws, they provide the framework of private consumption through social spending on infrastructure, housing, health, education and pension" (de Grazia 1996: 9). At the same time, the state's role is not overdeterminative. The Malthusian sixth-grade schoolbooks, the disapproving glares of a trained nurse, the psychological evaluation techniques a recently graduated therapist brought back with him from France, the Welfare Ministry's definition of family expenditures eligible for reimbursement, and the ways these things get read, reread, ignored, or rejected are part and parcel of how modernity is produced in the Galilee.

These processes of globalization are linked to local dynamics and are caught up in identity politics, as they are in so many places. The politics of seductive targeting and seduced reception at these many sites overlap the politics of difference and race, as any marketing analyst can tell you. The processes through which local modernities are created are linked to who the message makers and performers are, whether they are policy makers, television producers, members of the local subsidiary of AT&T, or civics teachers; how they view their audiences; how audiences view themselves, the message, and the message makers. Thus, how the various Tnuva researchers (who are almost all Jewish) defined the market, how they tried to appeal to Arab consumers, how Arab readers saw Tnuva and the ad's image and text, and why they buy Buddy Pudding (if in fact they do) are all important factors in the production of Palestinian local modernity. These factors are connected with and affect one another in complex ways.

Much of the appeal of modernity is its claim to universality and inevitability, its power to, as a newspaper advertisement for a diet drink proclaims, "unite the rich and the poor . . . man and woman . . . worker, employer, and actor . . . the young and the old . . . the Asian, the American, and the European" (as-Sinnara, Aug. 26, 1994). Yet it appeals in

Figure 10. This ad by Tnuva for Buddy Pudding, which appeared in a Communist Arabic paper, reads: "How many times have you dreamed of going into a toy store and taking every toy you desire? The dream comes true. . . . The Buddy campaign gives you the chance to fulfill this beautiful dream. . . . Collect seven lids from Buddy and collect the toys from HyperToy stores" (*al-ʾIttiḥad*, June 9, 1995).

specific, localized ways; the next line in the advertisement claims that Vitalia is the most popular diet drink in Hollywood. The glamour and power embodied in Hollywood films and television programs shown around the world stand in stark contrast to the daily realities of many Palestinians in the Galilee and are invoked to appeal to them. A kind of "parable of the democracy of goods" (Merchand 1985) that holds out the promise of equality through consumption draws on specific images of whom one will be (and should want to be) equal to by drinking Vitalia. Moreover, who buys the drink and for what purposes is not overdetermined. Consumption is not simply "a particularly insidious form of false consciousness in the face of capitalist hegemony," since "commodities can serve as important vehicles for the construction and contestation of identity" (Mills 1997: 54, 40). Consumers are not simply passive victims of dominant ideology, they can be "creative users" who respond in various ways to the messages encoded in products by manufacturers (Urla and Swedlund 1995: 306). Consumption can thus serve multiple and sometimes contradictory purposes; that is precisely what makes it so powerful.

Many of these products and ideas have a universal appeal, and have a tremendous capacity to penetrate beyond any simple East/West or North/South divide. However, part of the appeal of the Hollywood diet drink, and many other products, is premised precisely on this divide. Its appeal is not that it is produced universally—everywhere or anywhere in the world—but that it is produced in the United States specifically. Part of the appeal of the "most popular diet drink in Hollywood" is the opportunity it presents to the consumer in the Galilee, who is in so many ways at the bottom of the heap, to partake in the powers of Hollywood, in the powers of the First World. By consuming certain products, Galileans can become—even if for a fleeting moment—part of an imagined world or an imagined cosmopolitanism and not just an imagined community (Appadurai 1990: 7; Schein 1997). Products allow consumers to imagine alternative realities— identity, history, and geography are central to consumption (Kemper 1993).

Global exchanges and networks are not in and of themselves new to history (Rolph-Trouillot 1998). Indeed, Palestinians have long exchanged and purchased goods in economic circuits that extend beyond their immediate boundaries (e.g., Doumani 1995), but the speed, quantity, frequency, and social significance of these transactions have changed. Goods and ideas that flow through international networks tend to become "indigenized" and take on specific local significance (as opposed to simplistic claims of world homogenization) in a subtle play of "indigenous trajectories of desire and fear with global flows of people and things"; in other words, local structures of meaning and power (Appadurai 1990: 3, 5). As Roger Lancaster notes, "it would be a most interesting task to try . . . to show how a changing global economy is inserted into local 'traditions' through everyday material practices; to follow people transacting their goods, ideas, and lives very much on a global scale—all without losing sight of just what hurts in the ongoing, violent history of neocolonialism" (1997: 6–7). The ways in which consumerism and family planning emerge tightly paired in the Galilee is one particularly striking example of this indigenization.

Other commodities and consumption habits become markers of modernity and identity in the Galilee and come into play sometimes in unintended ways. I was especially struck by this phenomenon when I visited the apartment of a friend, Ghada, who is a professional puppeteer, actress, and self-described "artist type" living in Haifa. An outspoken Palestinian nationalist, she has adopted many of the Jewish bohemian signifying products as well as the habits of her health-conscious artist colleagues. Her kitchen was stocked with brown sugar, fat-free milk, decaffeinated coffee, and Brita purified water, all products her mother never buys. She has an indoor cat called Ulysses and an aquarium of fish, and she buys expensive pet food for them. Her living room is furnished with the standard "Bedouin-made" striped carpets and rattan shelves of struggling Israeli artists' homes, a hand-crocheted throw on a rocking chair, a lambskin floor piece and floor pillows, and exercise equipment.

Perhaps Ghada's apartment stands out in my mind because it was imitating an esthetic unlike that of most Arab homes I know. But chandeliers, microwave ovens, dark wood kitchen cabinets, and silk curtains (even where there are no windows) are imitations of modernity and middle-classness that have recently become common. Style, and keeping up with it, has become a major marker of modernity and class. Such items are now significant players in the emerging powerful discourse of family planning, tools in the construction of social identity and status.

Thoughts about consumption habits were powerfully provoked again when I went with my cousin Maha to get our hair done before her engagement party. Whenever Maha objected to the hairdresser's stylistic suggestions, Nadya insisted that "a woman has to go with the *ofnah* [Hebrew for style]." She commented on the fashionableness of the color of Maha's dress, a soft beige-pink, not like "those loud Bedouin colors" that used to be popular. Nadya hung on her salon's walls several "after" photos of her clients, and she had to change them frequently because the hairdos kept going out of style. She received complimentary promotional posters, mostly of blond women, from her hair-products supplier. She selected the "most appealing" of the posters to hang, and changed them frequently as well. She told us that just a few months ago she would have puffed up Maha's bangs and sprayed them stiff, but now she had to make them into a softer '70s retro style with curled strands hanging in front of the ears.

Nadya showed us her newest product, which she was using on Maha—a makeup sealer that is guaranteed to hold makeup in place for many hours. Nadya's husband had been my homeroom teacher in seventh and eighth grades, so she had heard that I was doing a doctorate in the United States. She made a point of handing me the new bottle of makeup sealer so I could read the label and see for myself how modern it was. She asked me if I knew of the latest products in the United States, whether they had really come out with a cream that stops body hair from growing back. Nadya has been very religious for the last few years. She covers her hair whenever she goes out—the day I accompanied Maha to the salon she put on a fashionable bonnet with a Gucci symbol when she went next door to buy some Sprite to serve us.

Maha's future sister-in-law, who had accompanied us to the salon, pursued this line of inquiry for me. While we were getting our hair done in the latest styles, we heard a Jeep passing outside, inviting people to a wedding. During the spring and summer, the most popular time for weddings, public loudspeaker invitations become something of a noisy nuisance. Maha's sister-in-law commented:

> I remember the first time anyone did this, Salah il-Kharbush decided to hire a Jeep with a microphone to invite people to his son's wedding instead of sending out invitations. Everybody told him not to do it, that it would be ridiculous, and everybody gossiped and bad-mouthed him afterward. Then a week later someone else did it, and now everybody does it. Now it's shameful and miserly if you *don't* do it. It's so odd how these traditions are invented.

Keeping up with an ever-changing style is an essential process of modernization and class negotiation. Acquiring the status of modern is not a one-time event, nor is it stable. It must constantly be reasserted and re-created, as its requirements are constantly changing. Moreover, certain objects and habits acquire modern meaning and enter into circulation without the benefit of a marketing campaign. What about those little plastic corner pails for garbage that almost every sink in an Arab kitchen in the Galilee has—how did they become an indispensable sign of a clean modern home? I doubt the marketers at Keter, the largest plastics manufacturer in Israel, had such grand ambitions for the small product (not that they are complaining). Similarly, certain children's toys, clothing, household items, or car accessories can become the latest craze in the Galilee—local fads that rapidly and sometimes unpredictably come into fashion, mutate, and disappear.

It has been argued that "the articulation of social ties through commodities is . . . at the heart of how sociality is experienced in consumer capitalism" (Urla and Swedlund 1995: 282). In the Galilee, consumption and its seemingly endless possibilities are seen as having allowed for a considerable increase in social competition and aspirations of class mobility. Many people told me that everyone is looking at everyone else, comparing, imitating, and competing. This basic dynamic is posited as thoroughly modern. In the past, a sharecropper would supposedly never dream of imitating a landowner's lifestyle. Badriyyi, who was 86 and used to be a sharecropper and a tobacco smuggler, insisted that imitation and competition were a central dynamic in "today's life," which made it both more egalitarian and more greedy: "For example, the young girls see each other, and follow each other. They think if the doctor's wife has these things, I want to have them too. Before, children used to run around without underwear, women would have one dress and it would have three patches in it. Today each child has thirty, forty outfits and still it's not enough. They all want what the doctor's wife has." Note that my mother is a doctor's wife and I am a doctor's daughter, and we were relatively privileged participants in this cycle of trend-setting consumption.

Although indispensable, the little plastic pails in the sink are not automatic guarantors of modern status. Their success as markers of modernity is dependent on certain habituations in dishwashing, sink cleaning, and garbage disposal. The outward appearance of consumption is constantly held up to scrutiny—people compare and inquire, to see whether the signs of modernity are real or just facades for a backward, negligent family, especially a backward mother. Are they just blindly imitating the material goods of others, or are they able to imitate their lifestyle and modern habits as well? Are these goods embedded in modern beliefs? Tharwa from Rayni earlier told me:

I look at the kids I teach in the kindergarten, their clothes, the lunches their mothers make them—my brother's children are going to see this at their schools and how are they not going to want the best? There are so many expenses—there is always a birthday—you need cake and pastries.

But sometimes economic background is just for show. I know this child in my class, their house is a palace and every child has a room. But the boy tells me his mother throws down a mattress for them on the floor every night. He says, "We write our homework outside on the balcony because she has to clean the house." She puts their food in a piece of bread rather than on a plate—it's all appearances. These women who are sitting at home send their children to day care when they're six months old and sit around drinking coffee with the neighbors. They just imitate other people. They're not really advanced.

Primitive mothers acquire the beds and desks of modernity but fail to use them properly—the children don't actually sleep in the beds or study at the desks. The lonely unused beds and desks fail as material markers of modernity because they are not accompanied by proper modern habits and beliefs.

The particular commodities and patterns of consumption that become important markers of modernity among Palestinians in the Galilee, the way they are supposed to be used, and the way they signal modernity are all linked to, but not simply determined by, market interests. They are also linked to specific politics of race, gender, and class.

PROPER UPBRINGING

One of the important habits of modernity that one must acquire, in addition to its materials, is proper child raising techniques. Taghrid insisted: "There is an effect to the economic side, but it's not everything, there is upbringing [tarbiyi], and that requires more than money." Khadiji Haddad, the nurse who said that "things our parents considered luxuries are fundamental for us," included among those things proper child raising: "Before, the concept of mental development [she used the Hebrew term hitpathut] didn't even exist." Proper upbringing and family planning require material as well as social investments.

Money isn't everything, but schooling, an essential component of proper upbringing and an important site for the production of modernity, requires money. From kindergarten supplies to university tuition, proper upbringing can be expensive. Taghrid, who had worked for a few months in a day care center, told me: "I realized from that job that children's toys really help in their development, and they're expensive." A computer seems to be the cutting-edge item for proper education, although the children often wind up only playing games on it. Computers, often several models behind the market in the United States, are sold by local dealers for around U.S.$2,000.

In addition to the expenses, according to the principles of modern child raising in the Galilee, parents must give more care and attention to each child. Taghrid holds that "child raising today is harder, before they didn't care or know about it," a belief I heard repeated many times. Modern mothers (more than fathers) are required to raise modern babies. "Even though I didn't go to university," Taghrid said, "I get a lot of books about the principles of education [*uṣūl il-tarbiyi*] and read them." Despite all the amenities and mechanizations of modernity that in some ways have made life easier for many women, Taghrid said, "I didn't want to have more children because they're difficult to raise. Not only economically difficult—and thank God we don't deny them anything—but in terms of effort. I am the one who gets it [*mākilt-ha*]. There's always work, tiredness . . . you don't have time to scratch your head, always for the children." The effort and the modernizing attention Taghrid gives to her children seemed to outweigh the running water, electricity, and appliances her mother didn't have in the past.

Family planning, in its economic, reproductive, and social senses, is so closely linked in modernity that the term easily slips into each of these meanings. Dalya, 28, a trained religious leader and mother of two, gave me a long lecture about important aspects of family planning:

> I want to expand your question about family planning to the planning of the Muslim house, which includes many complementary aspects—cleanliness and purity, lowering of the voice, emphasis on proper education of children. My neighbors look at me and they say, "The Muslim woman is introverted and antisocial," because I don't spend my time drinking coffee with them and gossiping. But in fact I am properly planning my family and home.
>
> There are several levels of family planning [she is taking this out of one of the books she has set out on the table], from cleanliness and purity, to organization and orderliness and nice dress, to lowering of voices and guarding the secrets of the home, science and worship, and to emphasize these to the children and to teach them obedience, to

teach the children economizing in dress and food, to have good relations with people and treat them well, not to discriminate between
sons and daughters. It really means planning your family to make
sure you can do all these things for them—you can't have twenty kids
and take this good care of them, it's only rational.

People think the Muslim woman bores her husband because she's
always dressed the same and doesn't use makeup. But the Muslim
woman at night, when there are no more men to enter the house,
must decorate herself. You can come and see that my closet is full of
the latest fashions, clothes, makeup, perfume. Under my head cover
my haircut is just like yours. As you came in, did you see the worker
laying down our new ceramic tiles? It's the latest style. Our home is
an organized Muslim home.

Planning the modern Muslim family is expressed not only in the number of children but also in the way they are raised: a combination of material and social investments that are closely linked.

CRITIQUES OF CONSUMERISM

Contemporary family life in the Galilee is often characterized as more
advanced, "civilized," free of archaic obligations, and generally more
fun than "traditional" family life in the past. Khaldiyyi, a 53-year-old
mother of nine, told me: "Enjoying life today is more about traveling
abroad, going on car trips on weekends, eating at the seafood restau-
rant. Before no one could imagine this or afford it, and enjoying life was
all about having children, marrying them off, having grandchildren . . .
which involved a great amount of work and effort." The possibilities
and aspirations of people have changed. Khaldiyyi added: "The old generation didn't know about having a barbecue on Lake Tiberias or owning two cars, nor did they know that they should want this. There's a big
difference between the generations. Before they used to show off with
pregnancies. Today people go on trips more, the days are nicer—so
people have fewer children." Competition among women to have children has supposedly been replaced by competition between them in consuming and "enjoying life" the modern way.

Quite often, however, the perceived need to economize rationally and
plan your family emanates not from an embrace of modernity but rather
from a fear of its dangers. As Nuhad, who lived in Haifa, said:

The young generation is more aware that the economic situation is getting harder. The more time progresses, the more the problems. For example, in Haifa people have few children because of the housing crisis. A couple of years ago we were living in an old house, full of dampness and mold. How can we think about having more children? The housing crisis is the biggest problem in Haifa—rents are high and incomes are low. If it's not a person's will to have few children, it's the will of the conditions.

Many mothers told me that the worst thing that could happen to a child was that he or she would lust after something a friend had and the parent could not afford to provide it—an ever-present possibility in a community where more than 60 percent of children live under the poverty line (Sa'id and Kanaaneh 1990). The child would then feel beneath his or her friends, of a lower class, backward, and deprived. The impossibility inherent in one's condition while one is surrounded by all the signs of possibility is not uncommon. The need for economic rationality and family planning frequently arises from the fear of poverty and the constant threat of underprivilege.

Indeed, the materialism that has come to characterize modern life is heavily pursued and desired, but also heavily criticized. Wardi told me:

All the requirements of life changed: from the day of Randa [her oldest daughter, who is 28] to the day of Wishah [her youngest son, who is 22] a lot of change took place. Today you quickly feel like you're coming up short with your child. Life has changed a lot—and not always for the better. The young generation doesn't appreciate these things the way we were able to. In the age of speed, people prefer material things, and I say this is wrong.

Life was much nicer before; when you needed yogurt culture or an egg, you'd just borrow it from a neighbor. There was intimacy [*ulfi*]. Now people are closed to each other. Now you're ashamed to borrow something from the neighbors because that makes you look bad.

Our neighbor Imm 'Adnan similarly expressed disapproval of people's supposed materialism and abandonment of morals and traditions, even as she approved of material advances:

Today the young generation wants to stop having children. My oldest son tells his wife that if she gets pregnant again, he'll send her back to her parents. They feel it's too difficult to have more children. They want to do what Israel does. Before, there used to be hunger and we did all the work by hand and we had no hospitals. Today in Israel everything is plentiful and available. The Arabs in Israel are better off than all the other Arabs, especially the poor ones in Gaza, and yet they dislike children. They say they can't provide for them even though everything is available. They're selfish and immoral and I tell my sons so. The young women of today want to take care of themselves and get dressed up and look good. I tell them, "Have more children and you and the children can get dressed up and look good."

When I accompanied my aunt on a senior citizens' bus trip, one of the men on the bus heard that I was doing research for the university. When he asked, I told him I was studying family planning, and he said, "Oh, yes. Today there is family planning. Not like before, when they needed sons and daughters to work the fields. Still it was better before." When I asked him why, he said there was "less trouble and headaches." This man, Kamal, and his family used to be small landholders, but he told me about a very poor man who used to work other people's land in exchange for a small amount of grain:

Poor man, every time he'd clear a plot of land and cut back the growth, the landlord would take several months to go check on his work, and by that time it would have grown back. The sneaky landlord would refuse to give him his grain until he did the job right. So the poor man would have to do the work all over again. And to this day that working man still insists that people were better off in the old days. There was no headache.

When Kamal saw my look of disbelief, he explained:

You forget that before there was no money for the wife to ask for. No wives to say get me this and get me that, bring us this and bring us that, the children need this and the children need that. If a husband is lucky, his wife won't be too demanding. Before no one ate meat— just cracked wheat. Now if there's no meat, children won't eat. This is not an easy life for a man.

Many of these critiques of materialism are based on a modern nostalgia that is strongly gendered and raced. Like Kamal's complaint about demanding wives, an article that appeared in *al-'Ittihad* dramatically critiques modernity through the medium of a young woman (July 28, 1995). The author ridicules his friend's wife, Kamli, for insisting on using a special newfangled machine to dice onions and garlic, so that her hands won't smell, and contrasts this attitude with the sacrifices of his mother and the older generation, who diced onions by hand. The author notes that Kamli looks down on her mother-in-law as backward because she refuses to use the modern device. The truly primitive of the two, he says, is young Kamli: her head is like "a fancy sparkling box," decorated but empty. According to him, an Israeli friend of Kamli's recommended this device, and Kamli imitates her. As Kamli supposedly boasts end-lessly about her material acquisitions and technological gadgets, the au-thor wishes she would be struck dumb, so that he could see her beauty without having to hear her talk. He then ponders how rare real Arab mothers are today.

Whether disapproving of people's perceived immorality and materi-alism or fearing poverty, many people criticized modernity and its eco-nomic and consumer basis. The joltingly rapid transformations that have occurred have certainly not been kind to most Palestinians. They have been forced and seduced onto the lower rungs of the Israeli and global economy. But they have come to express many of their hopes, de-sires, and fears largely from within it and using its terms. Over the last decades, economic transformations have involved new patterns of em-ployment, but also changing patterns of need and consumption and changing conceptions of household economy and economic rationality that idealize small modern consuming families. Family planning thus be-comes part of a consumerist strategy to provide more of these newfound needs, often under harsh conditions, to a smaller number of children. An amalgam of commodities, consumption patterns, household organiza-tion, and parenting strategies have all become part of this new sensibil-ity, increasingly considered to be a hallmark of the modern.

THREE

Fertile Differences

When I asked my old friend Fadya how some of the girls we had gone to school with were doing, she told me that many of them had married upon graduation and had several children. She called them *primitivim,* a Hebrew word derived from the English "primitive." My elderly aunt who had nine children herself said that people no longer have large families because life has "advanced": "Before we didn't know anything. But now only those who are wild keep on having a lot of children, living by their instincts." Lamis, 23, said her Muslim neighbors "never plan anything. They're like goatherds, like barbarians. They just give birth and throw the children out on the streets without thinking about how they're going to provide for them."

"Primitive," "barbarian," "irrational": these words have entered the vocabulary of Palestinians in the Galilee in profound ways. The language of modernization theory (Greenhalgh 1996) has infiltrated their day-to-day sexual, reproductive, and parenting practices. The discourse of population studies about the Third World has been taken up by people within that so-called Third World. Indeed, Palestinians today accuse other Palestinians of being just like the 'olam shlishi (Hebrew for "Third World")[1]—wild, animalistic, herdlike, driven by instincts, and unable to control their reproduction, unlike their rational, cultured, civ-

---

1. Palestinians' use of Hebrew rather than Arabic terms for "primitive" and "Third World" points to a genealogy of this discourse. They are telling loan words.

ilized selves, who carefully plan their lives and are advancing in the footsteps of the First World. Palestinians distinguish themselves and define each other by looking through a modernist lens at how people make babies.

This newly formed modernist discourse has its flip side: the counterdiscourse of romanticized traditionalism that reverses the terms of the argument.[2] Although such talk is less common, some Palestinians call the modernists selfish, rabid individualists, frivolous, materialistic, sexually loose, unthinking imitators of the West with their tiny families, while they see themselves as self-sacrificing real Arab mothers and fathers, producing children and thus upholding traditional morals, the family, and the nation.

In either case, supposed differences in number of children, spacing of births, and parenting techniques have come to be important markers of status that shape the ways people perceive and rank each other. Palestinians in the Galilee subscribe to one of these views and sometimes oscillate between them. But for all the gradations of opinion, reproduction is a topic of concern to almost everyone. Reproductive measures are key markers used to negotiate and daily re-create essential categories of identity: the modern, the primitive, the urban, the rural, the Bedouin, the clan, the Muslims, the Christians, the Druze, the local, the foreign, the Jews, the Arabs. To borrow Betsy Hartmann's term from a different context, "reproductive rights and wrongs" (Hartmann 1995) are strategically deployed as part of the local negotiations of personal and collective identity and daily engagements of power.

Reproductive practices and discourses have become an important marker of self and other because, first, they are a central framework in *Israeli* definitions of self and Palestinian other. Since Israel is by definition a Jewish state, it characterizes Palestinians, especially those living within its borders, as an undesirable problem population whose fertility and reproduction are highly threatening. Israeli views are dominated by images of Palestinians as breeders, irrational out-of-control reproducers, especially in the Galilee, where Palestinians outnumber Jews. The rhetoric of development and modernization—that "they" need to stop breeding—here is heightened and takes on strong racial overtones (as it does in many other locations around the world [Ginsburg and Rapp 1995]).

2. Although this antimodernist discourse harks back to an authentic past, it is largely a contemporary production shaped by and in response to the modernist version.

It is thus ironic that Palestinians have partly come to mimic this structure by defining themselves in terms of fertility and using reproductive
control as a measure of modernity or, alternatively, Arab authenticity. It
is not surprising, however, that options for empowerment and advancement in the Galilee largely follow lines of power that Palestinians simultaneously are subject to and try to resist. It is not uncommon that dominant structures define the few means through which empowerment is
conceivable (Comaroff and Comaroff 1990). Thus Israeli state policies
and rhetoric are part of the reason that Palestinians use reproduction as
a register of difference, the same register with which they have been evaluated and marginalized.

A second reason for the salience of the reproductive measure, especially its more common modernist version, is the incorporation—as un-
even and hierarchical as it is—of Palestinians into the Israeli economy,
albeit at the bottom, and their exposure to a highly consumerist culture.
As we have seen, many Palestinians have come to aspire to provide their
children with the goods they see in the marketplace and in the media.
Family planning thus becomes part of a consumerist strategy to provide
more of these things to a smaller number of children.

A third factor in the salience of the reproductive measure is medicalization. The past decades have witnessed the rapid penetration of modern medical services into the Galilee. That hospital deliveries there went
from 0 to 100 percent in the space of forty years suggests the extent of
this change. The Palestinian community is relatively underserved; basic
indicators such as infant mortality rates and life expectancy lag considerably behind the better-served Jewish community (Central Bureau of
Statistics 1996; Swirski et al. 1998; Reiss 1991). Yet Western medicine
now shapes the way people view their bodies, conceive of sickness and
health, and seek care. This has also given shape to new conceptualizations of reproduction and sexuality. In *The Woman in the Body,* an important text on the medicalization of reproduction in the United States,
Emily Martin argues that not only does medicalization transform the
physical processes of birthing, but new cultural values become embedded in these processes as well. Martin tries to get at "what else ordinary
people or medical specialists are talking about when they describe hormones, the uterus or menstrual flow. What cultural assumptions are
they making about the nature of women, of men, of the purpose of existence?" (1987: 13). Medical expansion and scientific innovations not
only transform the processes of body care physically but can transform
social concepts and values as well. It is clear that basic assumptions

about the superiority of science and modernity are embedded in talk about reproduction in the Galilee. Moreover, with the introduction of scientific methods of contraception, they have become entangled in the construction of identities.

Ann Stoler (1991) has argued that sexual control in European colonies was far more than a trope or discursive symbol for other meanings, but was indeed "the substance of imperial policy" (54). Stoler writes that "sex in the colonies was about sexual access and reproduction, class distinctions and racial demarcations, nationalism and European identity—in different measure and not all at the same time" (87). I see a similar effect in Israel— modernization, if I may reify it in this way for the moment, similarly attempts to regulate "sexual, conjugal and domestic life" to differentiate between colonizer and colonized, Jew and Palestinian, the modern and the backward.

The negotiations of identity—of self and community—through reproductive discourses and practices are not just abstract debates about identity and modernity, although they involve a great deal of that too. Much is at stake. The potential consequences of (successfully) labeling someone as "reproductively primitive" or "reproductively modern" can be felt in very unabstract ways. These evaluations are germane when one applies for a job, considers an offer of marriage, opens a new business, runs for local office, and organizes a political demonstration.

I was struck by the potential power of reproductive ranking when I visited a preschool class in 'Arrabi. There were two teachers: Silviya, 28, was originally from Nazareth and had recently married into the village; Ahlam, 34, was a Muslim woman born and raised in 'Arrabi. Each woman had one son and one daughter. When I visited their class, I was struck by the certainty with which these two teachers had already decided which of the thirty 4-year-old children was essentially smart and which was stupid. The ways in which these teachers decided intelligence had a great deal to do with their reproductive categorizations. Which of these children belonged to a family that the teachers considered reproductively modern? Which of them spoke, behaved, dressed in ways that signaled their parents' investment in modernity and contemporary parenting? The answers could be found in an accumulation of seemingly insignificant details, such as the food in a child's lunch bag; a bag of Bugle chips was a sign of the modern; a *labani* (yogurt cheese) sandwich signified the primitive. Although a *labani* sandwich requires more time and effort to prepare and is more nutritious, the teachers saw it as less "advanced." This is not only a matter of class—it is possible to be rich

Figure 11.   Only certain children, those considered part of a reproductively modern family, were called on by the teacher to recite songs, answer questions, or dance in the center of the room. Photo taken by the author at a kindergarten-class celebration of Mother's Day in 'Arrabi.

and primitive at the same time, as discussed earlier. It has to do with the perception of a person's relation to the spirit of the times, to modernity. The number of children a couple produce has become a crucial measure for allocating this essence, positive or negative, among Palestinians.

The two teachers' expressed perceptions of reproductive stigma may well have a profound impact on their students' lives. When I visited the class, only certain children—the "modern" children—were called upon to recite, sing, answer questions, or dance in the center of the room. The "stupid" kids from "primitive" families were marginalized and ne-glected (see Figure 11). Already in preschool they were perceived as not doing well in school, a perception that can work itself out in self-fulfilling ways. Obviously, Silviya and Ahlam hold a lot of power over these children. This is not to say that these teachers are mean-spirited or bad, but their view of the world inevitably affects that world.

These negotiations of identity are not to be oversimplified. Like most negotiations of social categorizations, the teachers' stigmatizing alone is not the whole of the children's experiences; they are not necessarily doomed by the teachers' categorizations. Not everyone agrees on the standards of the stigma, and not everyone agrees on the lines along which they are drawn. Silviya and Ahlam, in fact, disagreed on the degree of "brightness" exhibited by a few of the children. The definitions and requirements of modernity in reproduction are shifting. Stereotypes are flexible tools; there is no one-to-one correlation between, for instance, the number of children a woman has and how modern she is perceived to be. Reproductive practices are not the only measures of hierarchy used. Moreover, if Palestinians are constantly ordering and hierarchizing one another according to a modern/traditional reproductive binary, this does not mean that even people who strongly subscribe to this binary are incapable of making alternative, nondualistic representations. They often do. What is clear, however, is that these deployments of reproductive stereotypes "are implicated in a wider set of relations of power" (Stoler 1991: 55). That people are playful, maneuvering, and creative should not be understood as contradicting this.

As a member of a middle-class, two-child home who delayed childbearing for several years after marriage, I was probably perceived by many as being pro–small families. This perception may have encouraged people to express a pro–small family ideology to me, but as you will soon see, not all of them did. The use of the reproductive measure as a central category of difference in the Galilee is more than a product of my positionality.

CITY VS. VILLAGE VS. BEDOUIN

Today the division of Palestinian society into citified *(madani)*, farmer/villager *(fallaḥi)*, and Bedouin sectors is increasingly signified through reproductive discourses and practices. As among other social categories, there are multiple configurations of the borders and relationships among the three groups. The most common ordering places city above village above Bedouin. However, the shifting official status of different places of residence, the conditions of urban poverty, nostalgia for a mythic traditional past, and Palestinian nationalism's idealization of the peasant revolutionary complicate the hierarchy considerably. Still, a great deal of the orderings and borderings of these categories are negotiated through reproductive measures.

As part of modernization's urban bias, rural folk are considered peripheral and slower at "integration" into and "embrace" of modernity. As an American, my mother was constantly asked by city folk how she could stand living in a village—"Why don't you move to Nazareth or Haifa?" Citified Palestinians often dismiss farmers as "coming from under the cows," while farmers in turn frequently assert their sophistication in relation to the even more rural Bedouins. But reproductive practices have increasingly become a measure that Palestinians use to locate different places and their inhabitants in a hierarchy, the city being reproductively most modern, followed by the village with higher fertility, and then the Bedouins. On a recent visit home, one of my girlfriends from Nazareth commented on the rapidity with which I became pregnant after I discontinued contraception: "Wow, that's 'Arrabi for you!"

Nuhad is a 36-year-old secretary and mother of two girls. She is originally from the village of Tur'an, but her father's job required the family to move to Haifa. Nuhad's husband, Ghassan, 28, is from the village of Mghar, but he too moved to Haifa to work as an ironsmith and then settled there with Nuhad when they married.[3] Nuhad assured me that people who lived in villages had more children than anyone else in Palestinian society, much more than urban Palestinians. According to Nuhad, villagers who moved to cities tended to change, but those who stayed in villages "continue to have families that are too large":

> I have a sister-in-law back in the village. She knows her family's economic situation is difficult and still she keeps on having children, one after the other—they have four and live in one room. Sometimes they don't have the price of a bag of milk. The father wants to enlarge the family and the wife made two mistakes [unplanned pregnancies]. This is shameful—it's not fair to the children. They don't go to school, they're just thrown in the streets. This is ignorance. There is also competition between the women in the village . . . they compete to see who has more children. And if they have girls, they keep on giving birth until a boy comes—it's an instinct for Arabs.

Nuhad seemed to feel that people in the cities, even if they are originally from the village, can overcome this reproductive instinct and become what she describes as responsible, civilized reproducers. Thus the city has a civilizing effect, the opposite of the primitivizing village. When I asked her about Bedouins, she said: "Oh, forget about them, they don't

---

3. Such moves are difficult. Israel's regional planning policies, meant to control and contain Palestinian population growth, have resulted in lack of urban–rural migration. See Falah 1989.

even know what contraceptives are. If they saw a condom they'd probably think it's a piece of gum in a wrapper."

Her husband, Ghassan, told me, "It depends on a couple's background, on their level of culture. People who are not cultured and civilized have children by mistake."

Nuhad added: "Certainly it's only human to make mistakes, in certain cases. For example, with the day-counting [rhythm] method, it's
possible to miscalculate a day or two. But I use a thermometer and keep
a record so that everything is scientific and precise—you need a woman
who has awareness, then you won't have mistakes."

While most people (including Nuhad) attributed this putative difference in the reproductive practices of different places to "an old mentality" that controls villagers, others believed it was a product of less developed economic conditions. Lawahiz, who is from 'Arrabi village, said
that "city folk are forced to change their attitudes toward reproduction
because everything there is more expensive, people rent their homes, and
they have more expenses." Salam from B'ayni village similarly said:
"There's a lot of difference in giving birth. City people have fewer children, perhaps because their life, from an economic standpoint, requires
more material things. In the villages, people still eat from planting vegetables around the house and that's enough—you don't have to buy as
much." Salam said this despite the fact that she had no garden or fields.
The perceived different economic environments of city and village supposedly produce opposing attitudes toward childbearing.

The allegedly slower transfer of this citified reproductive mentality
to the villages is considered to be in progress, however, sometimes quite
violently, as in the case of Salam's mother-in-law, Khadra, aged 57:

> My husband used to live in the city, and he read in a book that breast-
> feeding is bad for the health and that the child should drink cow's
> milk, but only from one cow. And he used to bring me jars of for-
> mula for the kids—it was very expensive. But he told me that breast-
> feeding was bad. He wanted to imitate the city folk and the Jews and
> didn't want me to have any more children. He only wanted two boys
> and a girl. He didn't want me to have so many kids. [She had eleven
> children.] Once he tied my hands behind my back and hit me on my
> stomach so the child would come down. Every time I'd give birth to
> another child, he'd tell me, "If you'd given birth to a calf it would
> have been better, at least I could sell him." I used to be afraid to sleep
> next to him when I was pregnant, because he might hit me in the

stomach. He used to work hard to support them. That's why he didn't want too many. My husband was an only son, so I wanted to give him a lot of sons.

Khadra's husband gave an alternative rendering of this history:

I was ashamed that my wife had so many children, though I love them all. Because this makes us seem backward. People at work used to tease me that my wife is always pregnant. You know women, they're old-fashioned and traditional. She couldn't comprehend my desire to give my children the kind of life I saw in the city. I wasn't able to do that because of my wife. After eleven children I finally got her to get a sterilization operation. What are we, goats? She told me that the sin of the operation will be in my neck.[4] I told her, "Put it right here, deep in the bone of my neck [slapping his neck], I don't care."

I didn't ask Khadra's husband about the physical violence, because she didn't want me to bring it up in front of him. Note that Khadra's desire to have more children than her husband wants runs counter to the dominant, population-statistics view, which sees women as enthusiastic about reducing their fertility and men as obstacles who don't care about the consequences of their sexual behavior.

People in the villages surrounding B'ayni constantly referred to the fact that it had the highest birth rate in Israel, and sometimes in the world, "as studies and statistics have proved." According to Ghassan, the reason was that "half the village is Bedouin. They think that honor means having a soccer team for a family. They're oblivious of the modern world."

The boundaries of Bedouinness are in some ways ambiguous. The category often stands for a subculture or subethnicity within Palestinianness, but the line between Bedouins and other Palestinians, such as villagers, is blurred. Many Palestinian villagers and city folk, for example, claim to be descendants of Bedouin peoples in the distant past. My own family consider themselves village farmers *(fallaḥin)* who are descended from Bedouins who came from what is now Jordan many generations ago. Similarly, Bedouins incorporate former peasants who, because of drought or loss of land, adopted the nomadic ethos (Jakubowska 1992: 86). And while today's Bedouins used to be seminomadic, shrinking grazing lands and aggressive state planning have forced them

4. Many Muslims consider elective permanent sterilization a sin.

to become sedentary. Indeed, the constitution of Bedouinness has been influenced by Israeli state policies that have institutionalized their separateness. Like villagers, they have largely had to abandon grazing and agriculture for wage labor, and are generally the poorest segment in society. They have been forced either to settle in existing villages or government-designated "development villages" or to settle illegally on what land they are able to hold on to. These "unrecognized villages" cannot be found on any official map of Israel; their inhabitants are pressured into giving up their land to the government and moving to the designated development villages. These approximately 70,000 Palestinians in 123 villages (not all of which are in the Galilee) have been refused water lines, electricity, roads, permanent housing structures, health services, and other services.

Israel has tried to emphasize divisions between Bedouins and other Palestinians (Jakubowska 1992: 85). As part of its divide-and-rule policy, Bedouins are required to register as such: their ID cards read "Nationality: Bedouin" instead of "Arab." During the period of military administration, "the regime also cultivated the internal fragmentation of the Bedouin" by requiring them to register according to their tribal affiliation (Lustick 1980: 135). They are encouraged to volunteer to serve in the Israeli armed forces, unlike other Palestinians (except for the Druze, as will be discussed). Yet despite this special treatment, Bedouins loom large in Israeli fears of the Arab demographic time bomb. According to the newsletter of the Abraham Fund, a Jewish coexistence group based in New York,

> Israel's Bedouins pose one of the largest and most complicated challenges to successful Arab-Jewish coexistence efforts. With a birthrate higher than any other Israeli Arab group (8.5 per family) and way beyond the Jewish rate of birth (2.1 per family), the Bedouins and their problems are becoming increasingly difficult to ignore. Their total population comprises 10% of Israel's Muslim Arab population and they are the least integrated of Israel's Arab communities . . . the Bedouins' growing numbers and extended family structures, which reach into the West Bank and Gaza, make coexistence efforts aimed at this isolated, indigenous people a looming Israeli priority. (Socolof 1997: 1)[5]

---

5. The fear of Bedouin fertility is clearly articulated in press coverage of a 1998 Sharon Bourg plan to transfer ownership of land in the Negev from Bedouins to Jews. According to a senior Agriculture Ministry official interviewed by a leading Hebrew newspaper, "It's an all-out war. If we weren't here, the Bedouins would be. Unfortunately, most of the Negev isn't in our hands, and it is unthinkable that if we don't bring Jews to live here, within a couple of generations we will lose the Negev" (Ha'aretz, Mar. 4, 1998). The official laments that it is impossible to know exactly how many Bedouins live in the Negev:

Thus the separation of Bedouins from other Palestinians is partly a construction of Israeli state policy that has systematically "underdeveloped" them, even more than it has other Palestinians.

However, this separation is also performed by Palestinians and Bedouins themselves, often along lines similar to those drawn by the Abraham Fund, those of reproduction. Though their political agendas may differ and probably clash, both Butrus and the Abraham Fund writer distinguished Bedouins as overreproducers. In B'ayni, which is actually a merger of the Bedouin settlement Njidat and the village of B'ayni, residents who are not Bedouin (or only claim to have been so 600 years ago) are quick to distinguish themselves from their Bedouin fellow villagers. Salam told me that "Bedouins have a lot of children and they don't even feel like they're raising them because they stay out on the land. They don't notice there are so many of them." This despite the fact that most Bedouins have lost their land and are proletarianized.

'Ilabun is another village where Bedouins were "integrated"—that is, forced by the state to settle in an existing village to which they were annexed. Although the Bedouins in 'Ilabun have officially been part of the village since the 1950s, both villagers and Bedouins see themselves as living "*next* to each other" (rather than, say, together) and imagine a boundary between them despite their official joint status. Furthermore, Bedouins in 'Ilabun often distinguish themselves from Bedouins who do not lived in integrated villages by asserting their reproductive superiority, just as villagers do. Taghrid, 38, said, "We live next to a Christian town and we're influenced by them, we become more aware. We're no longer like other Bedouins because we've developed more. For example, we have smaller, more organized families." Thus Bedouins in mixed villages or cities and Bedouins in all-Bedouin villages, while viewed by non-Bedouins as inferior, also internally order themselves through (among other things, but especially) measures of reproductive modernity.

COMPLICATIONS

This dominant hierarchical narrative, city-village-Bedouin, fewer children–more children–most children, is complicated by the growth of

---

"They marry four or five wives, have twenty or thirty children, and scatter them all over the desert. It's hard to get them out of there." Of the Israeli policy of concentrating Bedouins in towns, he says: "The moment you lock them up in apartments, there's not a chance that they'll want only so many children. Instead of twenty or thirty, they will have to make do with two or three because they won't have the room."

village populations so that their size now qualifies them to be officially recognized as cities. The reproductive status of residents of a village that turns into a city is ambiguous—they are seen as being "in a transitional phase," not yet freed from their rural background. The recent official recognition of Sakhnin as a city was widely parodied by its residents: "How yucky villagers are!" *(Araf yi'rif ahl il-'ura),* said in an exaggerated city dialect. A frequently repeated joke was about a farm girl in Sakhnin who woke up one morning after the village became a city and asked her father about the grapes in front of the house: "Baba, what's that dangling from the vine?" (again in exaggerated city dialect). For many citified people, it is precisely Sakhnin's rapid population growth—in other words, its primitive reproductive behavior— that has made it officially a city, so it cannot qualify as a civilizing space. As Nuhad said: "Do they think a city is in numbers? A city is in its style, in its services and development."

Butrus (the man who owned twenty cars with his brothers) pointed out to me that "there's a lot of difference from village to village. In Mghar they're so conservative that my friend's wife doesn't come in to serve us coffee when I visit, she knocks on the door and her husband goes out and gets it, so we don't see her. She stays stuck back there with a slew ['or] of kids. I can't even imagine that happening in my village." In Butrus's view, cities are reproductively more modern than villages, but some villages are more citified and modern than others.

The imagination of internal homogeneity or patriarchal dominance is often conjured in the deployment of village, city, or Bedouin stereotypes. But marriage between people of different places, especially the movement of women from one place to another, makes for some spatial breaks and disruptions. Fatmi, 28, is a trained Islamic teacher originally from 'Arrabi who recently married in adjacent but smaller Dayr Hanna. She was very critical of her new village and found it backward and inferior in comparison with 'Arrabi. She thought the reason was that

'Arrabi is much larger and so has more educated people and more services and everything is available in it. In Dayr Hanna there are very few educated people and there's strong clan feeling. There are a lot of fights between the Husayn family and the Khatib family and they all hate each other, from the old to the young. The other day there was a fight here and I couldn't believe what I was seeing. It happened for no reason at all. They're really backward in Dayr Hanna. They even marry off their daughters young so if a daughter has a problem getting pregnant, she still has time to get treated and have kids. They marry them so young so they can have a longer period for this treatment. But that's wrong. A girl needs to develop her personality. I was married at twenty-six. Because of early marriage there are a lot more spinsters in Dayr Hanna. If a girl is over twenty, no one wants to marry her anymore. I don't like early marriage. Today life is different; you need education, and the Prophet said, "Education is the obligation of each Muslim man and woman," and this takes more time today. Life requires [bid-ha] so much today. Before, during the time of the Prophet, they used to live in tents. No one lives in tents anymore.

For Fatmi, Dayr Hanna is stigmatized by its clannishness and by the oppression of women caused by its single-minded focus on reproduction. She said, "This obsession with fertility is illogical." Yet Fatmi's hometown, which she sees as developed, might be considered backward and primitive by a more citified woman; with the flexible tools of the reproductive measure, one person's modern town is another person's primitive village.

Sunbul, a chemist from the village of Kufur Yasif who "married into" the city of Shfa ʿAmir, challenged the dominant city-over-village paradigm and told me that some villages are even more civilized and thus more reproductively modern than the city:

I'm from Kufur Yasif and we're not a city, but I don't know why, we were always more developed than the others. We have more educated people and my mother and father were satisfied with only two girls—no one ever interfered with them to have more children. Here in Shfa ʿAmir, it's larger than Kufur Yasif, but the environment is such that everyone likes children. If [Bill] Clinton lived in Shfa ʿAmir, they'd drive him crazy asking him to have more children. I grew up in an environment where they don't like to reproduce a lot. Even young people in Shfa ʿAmir have more children than the old people in Kufur Yasif. Generations have changed, but still the young people are saturated [mitsharbin] with the parents' ideas. Married women in Shfa ʿAmir have a lot of children like before, like the originals [ʾaṣliyyin]. Their minds are a little primitive, even the educated ones. The women who come from outside change the environment a little. In villages they have more children than the city, but villages like Kufur Yasif and ʿIlabun have fewer—it doesn't matter if it's a village or a city, what matters is the level of civilization.

The conditions of city poverty further complicate the master narrative of urban modernity and superiority. To begin with, the majority of the Palestinian urban elite left the area around the time of the 1948 war. Acre, for example, is a city whose Arab population is almost entirely made up of refugees from the surrounding villages. "Mixed cities" like Acre and Haifa, which have a Jewish majority as a result of Zionist policy and individual initiative, have a particularly conflicted position vis-à-vis modern reproductive standards. Most of the Palestinian residents of these cities have been ghettoized in slum neighborhoods, the ubiquitous "side effects" of modernity and progress. All-Arab cities such as Nazareth, the largest Palestinian city in Israel, also have pockets of poverty, as well as a severe housing crisis, because of the state's refusal to allocate additional land to them for population expansion. The housing crisis has led many Palestinians to seek residence in neighboring Jewish towns. The "panoptical" city of Upper Nazareth, as Martina Reiker calls it (1992: 123), or Natzerit Illite—the Jewish city overlooking the Arab city of Nazareth—was created explicitly to Judaize the area's population, which was (and still is) largely Palestinian (Rabinowitz 1997: 73). Because of the housing crisis in the Arab city, many Palestinians have tried to rent or purchase homes developed for Jewish settlement there, but have met with resistance. The widely publicized attempt by an Arab woman to purchase a flat in Upper Nazareth "led to a campaign to keep upper Nazareth free of Palestinian Arabs" (Reiker 1992: 124). Much of this segregationist argument has involved stereotyped portrayals of Palestinians as an "ever multiplying stock" (Rabinowitz 1997: 60), out of control, invading reproducers.[6] This Israeli political discourse at-

---

6. Approximately 10% of the population of Upper Nazareth is now Arab, mainly highly educated young families (Rabinowitz 1997). The situation is similar in the city of Karmiel. Avi Feldman, a candidate for mayor of Karmiel in 1998, warned against turning Karmiel into a binational city: Karmiel

"was planned in the context of making the Galilee Jewish, and [binationalism] can be prevented." Feldman outlined his plan for lowering the number of Arabs who come to Karmiel's parks. "All the parks are full of Arabs. This situation cannot continue and will make the city binational," he said, explaining the problem as he sees it. "I will fence in the parks and impose an entrance fee on anyone who is not a resident of Karmiel. We won't say Arab or Jew. When we impose an entrance fee, and a family of ten shows up and is charged 10 shekels per person, they will stop coming." . . . Feldman said he also plans to cut down on the number of Arabs working in the city. Explaining his opposition to the construction of the Bedouin neighborhood of Ramiya in southwest Karmiel, on lands expropriated from the Bedouin some 20 years ago, Feldman explained: "They keep multiplying. They'll build a mosque and then a school here, and gradually they'll begin to buy apartments next to their apartments and they'll take over entire neighborhoods here." (Ha'aretz, Oct. 22, 1998)

tributes the Palestinians' housing crisis to their inability to control their sexuality, their high fertility—not state policies. All of these "urban problems" lend themselves to a romanticization of the rural, thus complicating the modernist narrative of urban superiority.

UPSIDE DOWN

A less powerful counter-discourse turns the hierarchy upside down to put Bedouins at the top and cities at the bottom. Even as Bedouins are stigmatized, they are idealized as authentically Arab (though not necessarily authentically Palestinian, which is the role played by the farmer/villager).[7] There is thus a Palestinian counter-discourse that asserts the authenticity and pride of Bedouin culture, including its reproductive traditions. While Taghrid said that "I have been forced by my husband and the family to have this many children. I haven't been able to adapt myself to this era," another Bedouin woman, Khabsa, said, "We're proud of our traditions and customs. We're not so quick to forget them. I am Bedouin and my children will be Bedouin and my children's children will be Bedouin. There will be a lot of them, God willing, and they'll be real proud Arabs." This counter-narrative of traditionalism, like the Israeli portrayal of the noble savage, is clearly just as modern as the dominant modernist discourse, and both are configured in terms of reproduction.

Similarly, the idealization of the farmer/villager in Palestinian nationalist discourse disrupts to some extent the dominant discourse of urban superiority (and yet continues to use the register of reproduction). While Zionism has depicted Palestinians as an essentially fragmented, authoritarian, backward society and the peasant in particular as economically unproductive, biologically overproductive, unadapting and perhaps unadaptable to the modern "democratic" state, Palestinian nationalism has reproduced "a modernist teleology that fixes a particular essence

---

7. For the Israelis, Bedouins represent primitiveness in its dual meaning of inferior culture and icon of nostalgia for a lost past. They are seen as an unchanged indigenous culture since biblical times and thus similar to the "original Hebrews" (see, e.g., Shepherd 1987; Stein 1995). Many villagers, Bedouin and non-Bedouin, have tried to cash in on the recent increase in Jewish tourists in search of depoliticized authenticity in the "countryside" by opening up tent restaurants often called *madhafeh* (a Bedouin guesthouse). *A Taste of Galilee*, a brochure put out by the Israeli Ministry of Tourism has a photo of an old man from one of the 123 unrecognized villages in his *madhafeh* on the cover—of course with no mention of his village's lack of recognition, his demand that it be recognized, or his demand to be allowed to build a concrete house and to get running water. Near a photo of wildflowers of the Galilee, this wild man of the Galilee is situated to elicit a modernist nostalgia for a mythologized ancient rural Jewish past.

upon the peasantry" (Reiker 1992: 120). While Reiker, Ted Swedenburg, and others have discussed the subaltern oppositional practice of
reproducing Palestine "through the circulation of select icons of [peas-
ant] material culture and through the remembering, narrating and reconstruction of Palestinian rural topography" (ibid.: 122), my point
here is that this rendering of peasant essence, like that of the city, has
involved the evocation of reproductive practices. This representation of
the peasant icon signified through "traditional reproductive practices"
is present not only in academic writings (e.g., Kanaana et al. 1984), art
(as in Sliman Mansour's work; see Figure 6 in Chapter 1), narrations of
history, and political speeches, but in daily negotiations of reproductive
decisions. As Khadra told me: "People in the cities have mixed with the
Jews too much. They imitate foreigners, and think that's better. They
forget their origins and don't want to have children any more. We in the
villages still hold on to our traditions. If it weren't for us, there wouldn't
be any Arabs left. There are too many problems in the city: drugs, problems with girls, housing crisis, crime. We are more protected here."

This view is sustained as a reaction against modernization's colonial
and exclusionary thrusts, against the internal contradictions and failures of modernization, yet in one way it does not go beyond it: it, too,
justifies its stance by the measure of reproduction.

The growing villages are challenging the simple classifications of
space through their expansion, and some of the characteristics usually
ascribed to the city are increasingly appearing in some of these expanding villages. The ideal village structure has members of each clan living
together in one neighborhood. Shukri 'Arraf, romanticizing the dying
"traditional Palestinian village," describes the neat physical layout of
the village as mirroring the social structure of clans: each geographical
cluster in the village consists of a single clan, "a group of humans belonging to one father" (1985: 11). While most villages probably did not
conform to such a tidy mapping even in the so-called traditional past,
the attempted spatial separation of clans in villages today has certainly
been disrupted. State policy and discrimination coupled with population
growth have pushed young families to purchase land (since inherited
land, which is constantly subdivided and distributed equally among
sons, is often insufficient)[8] and has led to the appearance of new neighborhoods on the outskirts of villages that have a mixture of residents of
different clans.

---

8. Generally, daughters relinquish their inheritance rights (Moors 1995).

Often residents of these relatively new mixed outlying neighborhoods
are viewed as more similar to city folk and more modern. Suha, 26, said
she had a lot of privacy and

> no one interferes in my affairs as they do in my parents' neighbor-
> hood. I have more independence about what I do in my home and my
> affairs with my husband. No one can pressure us, "Come on, have
> another kid." They talk but we're too far away to hear. I can't imag-
> ine what I'd do if my mother-in-law lived next to me. I can't go back
> to that situation, we've changed.

At the same time, these mixed neighborhoods also represent a lost rural past. Suha lamented the fact that while she had more freedom, she
also had less assistance from relatives in caring for her children. And not
having relatives around her made her feel unsafe, "like in the city." For
several months, her husband worked with heavy equipment down south
and was home only three nights a week. She said she was so afraid at
night she took up Islamic praying (but she quit when her husband's job
relocated him closer to home). During this period when her husband
was frequently absent and Suha was seven months into her first pregnancy, her jewelry was stolen from her closet. She thinks the thief was a
woman acquaintance of hers whom she caught snooping in the bedroom. But her mother-in-law accused her of being unfaithful to her husband and bringing men to her house—or how else could she be robbed
in such a neighborhood without realizing it? "You live in this neighborhood, who enters your house without you knowing?" Suha said these
accusations nearly drove her crazy and affected her pregnancy. When
the child was born, the nurses at the hospital "knew how upset I was
without my telling them." They asked her if she had experienced any
stress during pregnancy. "God, did I!" she answered. The modernization of some village neighborhoods thus also complicates reproductive
stereotyping along modern/primitive lines—these neighborhoods are
more reproductively modern than other parts of the village but also reproductively more dangerous.

"The paradigm of nation-building which celebrates the rural as the
fundamental expression of the indigenous and the authentic and which
despises the city as responsible for the loss of both, for detribalization,
corruption and social death" (Holston and Appadurai 1996: 189), is
powerful in the Galilee, yet most subscribers to this paradigm do not actually want to move from the city to the village, nor do they oppose attempts to "develop" villages. Quite the contrary, these romanticizers of

the rural are often simultaneously inventors of the "authentic" rural, thus viewing it in modern ways. Similarly, while Palestinians in the Galilee sometimes express a respect and nostalgia for traditional peasant birthing and family life, few see themselves as replicating it and most aspire to be modern reproducers. Thus the paradigm that celebrates the urban and the modern is still dominant. Rather than contradicting the superiority of the modern, the valorization of the rural past often complements it.

Mahdi, originally from 'Ilabun, is one of the few people I know who took his premodern rural nostalgia this seriously:

> I want to go back to the village, if only I could find a job there. I've been living in Haifa for twelve years now and I know it very well. I like the simplicity of the village. You know, living among Jews makes you forget how to be an Arab. You start denying many things about yourself. I want to be free to do what I want, be as traditional as I want—to speak Arabic as loud as I want, to just eat hot bread and oil with a head of onion, just crunch into the onion. I'd have more children there—they'd have room to play freely, their grandmother would take care of them. Here I'm judged if I have more than one child. There I'm judged if I don't. In Haifa you're not free to live by the authentic standards of Arabs.

Yet Mahdi continues to live in the city. And there are many times when he, too, criticizes other people for their backwardness and their too many children.

It is important, however, not to overstate the case. City/village/Bedouin reproductive stereotypes are dominant but not hegemonic. Some people even believe that there are *no* reproductive differences between city folk, villagers, and Bedouin Palestinians. According to Fardos, 71, "there's no difference between cities and villages. Arabs are Arabs, and everyone is cutting down on their family size now. Women just want suits, every occasion they want a new suit. . . ." For Khaldiyyi, any differences have been erased. While she believes it is true that the cities began modernizing their reproductive behavior first, the villages and the Bedouins have managed to catch up. Thus for her, modernity has an equalizing rather than hierarchizing effect:

> Before, there used to be a difference between the village and the city—in terms of dress, education, reproduction *[khilfi]*. But now it's all the same. Today everyone is on one level, there's no such thing as a city person, a farmer, and a Bedouin—they're all the same. Look at

my daughter Luma, she's married among the Bedouins and has three girls and they don't want any more children for now.

But before, there were a lot of children in the villages and they were full of lice. The nurses used to come to the village to check people's heads for fungus and lice, and they used to shave people's heads and put iodine on them. It was a funny sight. But when the nurse came to my house, she was so surprised about the cleanliness. I had the first bedroom set in the village, and we had fancy heavy sofas.

Moreover, reproductive measures are powerful but they are not the only measure of difference between places of residence. Sexuality, wealth, education, and patriotism are other yardsticks of status. But these, too, are often linked to reproduction. The effects of hierarchizing according to the stereotypes of the reproductively modern and the reproductively primitive are evident. While the criteria sometimes shift and slip into an antimodernization framework, the modernist spirit of both frameworks is clear. This measure has become one of the primary ways in which difference and hierarchy—including that between urbanite, villager, and Bedouin—are imagined, articulated, and daily reasserted.

CLAN

Clan is another significant category of identity in the Galilee that is increasingly constructed by means of the reproductive measure. Not unlike the categories of city, village, and Bedouin, the ordering and bordering of clans has become intertwined with modern reproductive standards.

Israeli anthropological studies as well as Zionist political discourse have long held that the so-called *hamula* (clan) system of Palestinians in Israel is the cause of their relative backwardness, underdevelopment, and lag in adaptation to the Israeli "democratic" system (see Reiker 1992 and Zureik 1979 for detailed discussions). Thus the *hamula* system, which according to this analysis is deeply ingrained in the Arab's Oriental and tribal mind, and not Israeli policy, is the underlying cause of the great disparities in conditions between Arabs and Jews in Israel.

Talal Asad argues that the "*hamula* traditional form of organization" was "the ideological resolution of a Zionist problem—for it constituted a mode of control and an imputed identity for the only political existence

allowed to Arab villagers in Israel" (1975: 274). Rather than seeing the
hamula as a "continuity of tradition," Asad points to its contemporary
creation by the Israeli authorities. Nicholas Dirks (1990) argues that

> in many parts of the former colonial world . . . tradition as we know it today
> was produced through encounters with modernity in the context of colonial-
> ism. Caste, religion, and custom, to mention just some of the most obvious
> categories, were dramatically reconstructed by colonial rule. The British were
> thus implicated in the production of those very components of Indian tradi-
> tion that have in postcolonial times been seen as the principal impediments
> to full-scale "modernity." (25)

In the case of the Galilee, there is nothing post- about the colonial reconstruction of indigenous categories.

During the 1950s (the period with which Asad's article is concerned)
the Israeli military administration distributed employment and job permits through labor committees based on clans. Political parties encouraged "closely supervised '*hamula* lists' to run for local council" (Asad
1975: 271; Lustick 1980: 137).[9] This locking of *hamula* to local council politics empowered clan politics with the privileges of the council,
which "controls all sorts of petty but, in the local context, vitally im-

---

9. This system of manipulation involved, in addition to the *hamula* lists for local council elections, party candidates for the parliamentary elections whose main qualifications
were membership in prominent families and an established willingness to cooperate (Jiryis
1976: 166). The following example of the efforts of a Palestinian parliamentarian illustrates the degree of institutionalization of *hamula* networks in the state of Israel, where
endless permits and bureaucratic barriers require connections:

> Diab Ebeed has described his service to fellow Arabs during the five years (1961–65)
> he was a member [of the Knesset]. He mentions 2,000 letters he addressed to different
> branches of the government. . . . He was able to arrange . . . 1,319 loans to individual
> Arabs. He helped resolve 368 problems between Arabs and the ministry of education
> and smooth 594 individual difficulties with government departments. . . . Comment-
> ing on this list of achievements, a *Ha'aretz* reporter noted:
>   "Knesset member Ebeed . . . makes no mention of any bill he has challenged or pro-
> posed. All his activity and the source of his pride, lies within the narrow scope of
> influencing the appointment of a school teacher, or having him transferred from a dis-
> tant school to one nearer home. . . . In a democratic society, an ordinary citizen may
> expect to attain such things without having to appeal to a member of parliament."
> (168–169)

Although this is certainly not true of all Arab Knesset members, it is the norm for Arab
members of the Zionist parties. Various Zionist parties have tried to exert influence in various ways to gain Palestinians' votes, but the religious parties, for example, are known to
trust "in the persuasiveness of material benefits and offered money" and have been rather
successful in the wholesale buying of votes from *hamula* leaders (ibid.: 180).

portant sources of remuneration, influence, and prestige," such as col-
lecting taxes, deciding where approach roads will be built or electrical
transmission lines connected, countersigning various kinds of permits,
and appointing school administrators (Lustick 1980: 121). Through an
elaborate system of manipulation and patronage, the Israeli government, political parties, and Histadrut (labor union) institutionalized the
clan (Asad 1975: 271–272). The system of vote-recruiting has continued to the present, often involving local Palestinian brokers who are
able to promise certain minor improvements in local conditions in return for votes. As Dan Rabinowitz puts it, "there is very little about this
phenomenon which can be plausibly attributed to 'culture'" (1997:
149). It is systematically constructed.

Ian Lustick argues that "there is a highly effective system of control
which since 1948 has operated over Israeli Arabs," which is based on
policies "specifically designed to preserve and strengthen just those
structural circumstances and institutional arrangements which contributed to the segmentation of the Arab community, both internally and
in its relations with the Jewish sector." Part of this system of control was
"the sustained policy . . . to encourage, maintain and exploit the hamula
fragmentation of Arab villages" (Lustick 1980: 25, 122, 137).[10] Historically, "the Israeli state developed practices . . . that *constituted* the 'Arab
village' as the flawed object of modernization discourse" (Eyal 1996:
393; emphasis added).

However, understanding clan as a modern creation that has often
served as a divide-and-rule tool does not mean that clan can be categor-
ically dismissed as irrelevant. In a ten-page student publication called
"Promising Pens" (Feb. 1995), two tenth-grade girls from my village of
'Arrabi obtained data from the local village council and wrote the following one-page article. After a brief introduction to the geographical

---

10. Talal Asad writes:

The mobilisation of Israeli Arabs periodically according to "hamula" ideology is thus
the expression of a special subjection—as members of an exploited class who are prevented, because of Israel's Zionist structure from developing either a class-based or a
nation-based political organization. Zionist ideology . . . cannot permit the existence
of two politically organized national identities (Palestinian and Jewish) within what is
by definition a Jewish national state. The institutionalization of the hamula in local
government is an attempt to provide an ideological solution to this political contradiction: for through this device it becomes possible to control rural Arabs administra-
tively and also to separate them authoritatively on the basis of an imputed ethnicity.
(1975: 273)

surroundings of the village, the bulk of the article was devoted to a list of clan names with their sizes and percentages, in descending order:

1. Yasin-Nassar: the number of this family's members in 'Arrabi is 2,500 or 19.8%, or the largest two clans in the village.

2. 'Asli: the number of this family's members is 2,100. This is the second family in the village in terms of size.

3. Kanaani [my clan]: the number of this family's members is 1,375 or 10.8%. . . .

7. The medium clans: and they are five—Shalash, Qaraqra, Sa'di, Darawshi, and Sih, and equal in total 2,100 or 16.5%.

8. The small clans: and they are 12, equaling 7.5% or 950 persons.

9. Refugees: and they are the following families: Mi'ary, Namarni . . . (G. Kanaani and Sih 1995: 5)[11]

The fact that these two students represented their village—mostly to fellow villagers—in this way, and the fact that the village council kept records of these data, suggest that clan is an important categorization.

Indeed, Palestinian nationalist culture shares with Israeli nationalism roots in Western Enlightenment models and Marxist developmental stages theory, while at the same time reacting against it.[12] In a move that ironically mimics Zionist thought and practice, Palestinian nationalism has strongly condemned "clannishness" as a backward, primitive, antidemocratic sentiment that must be replaced by nationalism, while at the same time mobilizing "clan politics" in its service (Slyomovics 1998: 138; Peteet 1991: 187). One commentator urges Palestinians in the Galilee to "advance our society" by leaving the "dirty swamp of hamulism and sectarianism" (Fasl ul-Maqal, Nov. 1, 1996b). Another argues that political parties must replace "representation through the family and tribal system" because that phase in history is gone and parties must be "modern, up-to-date, and evolved" (Qatamish 1998). It is true that the

11. A more detailed account, including a pie graph, can be found in the first chapter of 'Arrabat al-Battuf: People and Homeland, published by the 'Arraba al-Mustaqbal Association ('Arraba the Future). The chapter is titled "Short Geographical History" and is written by the principal of the village high school.

12. Again, to point to similarities between Israeli and Palestinian nationalisms is not to suggest that they are somehow symmetrical. As Palestine is not an existing state with apparatuses and mechanisms for the imposition of uniform criteria of identity, it does not have the power to enforce its national imaginings as Israel does. Moreover, the roots of Palestinian nationalism are anticolonial while Zionism was a colonial movement. Palestine also does not mirror Israel in that it is not imagined as a monoreligious nation by the majority of Palestinians (as Israel is considered a Jewish nation). These differences should not be elided.

use of clan politics in the Palestinian nationalist struggle was in large part structurally imposed by the Israelis, but Palestinian nationalism in the Galilee, like many other nationalisms, draws on clan structure both practically and ideologically.[13]

As in many nationalist discourses, it is precisely the tracing of multiple ancient genealogical patrilineages that is frequently held up as the connection between the people and the land, the proof of their indigenousness. Their roots are basically clan lines, and their right to self-determination on this land derives from this, as in the oft-repeated Palestinian insistence that "we are a people of refined origins" *(sha'b 'arīq ul-uṣūl)*.

The phrase "Palestine, land of the fathers and grandfathers" is foundational and ubiquitous in Palestinian nationalist discourse (see Figure 12). The Palestinian National Charter (Al-Mithaq al-Watani al-Filastini), issued by the PLO as a sort of constitution, defines Palestinian identity as "a genuine, inherent, and eternal trait and is transmitted from *fathers to sons*" (as quoted in Massad 1995: 472). Another example of the significance of patrilineal kin continuity in Palestinian nationalism comes from the literature surrounding Land Day in 1976, an important moment in Palestinian history, especially to those still living in Israel, and particularly to those living in the Galilee. The *Black Book* published by the Regional Committee for the Defense of Arab Lands in Israel to document the events of Land Day begins: "The Israeli authorities have not been satisfied to drown Land Day, March 30, 1976, in the blood of the martyrs and wounded among the *sons of our people, living on the land of the fathers and grandfathers . . .*" (Regional Committee 1976: 9; emphasis added).[14] As Israel continues to confiscate lands, Palestinians articulate their protests to this and other injustices in multiple terms: the

13. On the practical side, Palestinians have been forced to compete with *hamula* lists; "Even the Communist Party, whose Arab cadres condemn hamulism . . . has often found it necessary to join coalitions formed by hamulas in order to participate significantly in local affairs" (Lustick 1980: 122; Rabinowitz 1997; Wood 1993; *Fasl ul-Maqal,* Nov. 1, 1996b). Town politicking—the distribution of party favors and appointments—is thus often based on considerations of clan sizes and alliances.

On the ideological side, Rashid Khalidi points out, Palestinian national identity "is and has always been intermingled with a sense of identity on so many other levels, whether Islamic or Christian, Ottoman or Arab, local or universal, or family and tribal." Indeed, among the factors that historically helped consolidate a shared sense of identity have been "regional and local loyalties," including family and clan loyalties (1997: 6, 21).

14. Another example comes from Samih Ghanadry, a Galilee author and Communist Party member, who writes that the Palestinians in Israel "did not choose this homeland . . . but were rather born in it, father from grandfather" (1987: 8).

الأرض – الوطن والبقاء

Figure 12. A political booklet titled *The Land—Motherland and Existence* features this image of a man and his grandson near olive trees (Karkaby 1994).

robbing of a people's livelihood, breaking the laws of property, violating international human rights agreements, attempts at ethnic cleansing, but also inheritance, patriarchal continuity, and clan rights.

It is striking how this focus on patriarchal continuity is deeply dependent on *female* reproductivity, yet in these examples it is not mentioned but simply assumed. Although elsewhere women are constructed as central guardians of Palestinianness through traditional mothering, the preservation of land is imagined as the domain of men.

Thus to some extent, Palestinian nationalist discourse depends on, draws from, and continually constructs clans. Still, in much of its rhetoric, clan and family politicking is condemned as backward, thus unchanging and overdetermined. Yet clan structure and significance have historically strongly mutated. Consider, for example, the Ottoman 1858 Land Code, which to some degree transformed the typical *musha'* (joint tenure) system, in which land was communally owned and managed in accordance with internal family structure, to private ownership, under which land was usually registered in the name of family heads and large landlord, thus institutionalizing their power and intensifying disparities. Or consider the Israeli confiscation of the majority of Arab lands, the marginalization of remaining Arab agriculture, and thus the undermining of the clan-based distribution system.

If clan hierarchies were related to landownership and agricultural distribution during the period immediately preceding 1948, they did not fall neatly along class lines, since different households within each clan had different relations to the *mukhtar*[15] and to (often foreign) sources of economic power and political influence. This disarticulation of clan and class is even stronger today, since much land has been confiscated, water resources are unequally distributed, private agriculture is no longer profitable, and the Palestinian population has largely been proletarianized. As Salim Tamari argues, this dependence on wage labor in the Jewish sector diminishes previous cleavages in wealth (while creating new ones) (1981: 61). This dependence has considerably altered the significance of clan in determining one's economic status. Clan today is a different thing than it was thirty years ago, or a hundred. It is not an unchanging timeless essence, but a product of historical and political-economic engagements.

15. As mentioned earlier, the *mukhtar* is a clan leader institution established in 1861 by Ottoman law to replace existing village leadership structure and open the population to external bureaucratic control.

Clan is not a remnant of the past. It is present as a product of contemporary power relations, state-generated and otherwise, even if it is imagined as an inherited tradition. Several years ago a girl from my clan who was supposed to marry her cousin eloped a few weeks before the wedding with her neighbor, a married man, father of seven children, also from my clan. I found out after they ran off to Tel Aviv together that although they were next-door neighbors, the girl belonged to a different branch of the clan than the man did. This detail became significant. Not only do elderly folks have detailed clan information, but teenage boys in my neighborhood do too: since the elopement they have been getting into occasional fights over this scandal along these clan branch lines. The teenage boys, with the help of their families, reconstructed the clan lineage and determined who among their agemates belonged to each branch of the clan. This reinvented clan structure has fueled their macho competition over who gets to buy one relative's used car or why one relative did not pay another's proper wages. The division in the clan is supposedly rooted in a rivalry between two brothers some hundred years ago, but few people remember the details. The clan structure today is based on recent events and rivalries; the young generation recreated their clan boundaries and became very educated in the details of the structure of their clan, which is now on the verge of becoming two. If this honor–shame scenario and its clan basis are often presented in a language that gives an illusive sense of constancy that confirms stereotypes of the unchanging "fossilized" Arab, I present them as contemporary projects embedded in shifting contemporary power relations.

Clan has never been a stable entity in the Galilee—clans are constantly fracturing into new ones, new families are incorporated or expunged, and boundaries are disputed. Not only is it not a biologically determined clear-cut category, but the importance of clan and its role in shaping individual lives has fluctuated as well. Furthermore, while clan has always been negotiated to varying degrees, today a new measure is used—family planning. Like the urban/rural/Bedouin divide, clan is one of the categories Palestinians use to organize themselves, and current negotiations of rank are often based on perceived reproductive differences.

CLAN AND REPRODUCTIVE DIFFERENCE

An important part of the project of contextualizing clan in the Galilee today is exploring how it is negotiated, reconfigured, and signified by re-

productive measures. Clan boundaries and relationships are today constructed through the modernist regime of family planning. While clannishness as such is looked down upon in certain contexts, it is proudly
evoked in others, especially in the assigning of reproductive stigma. It is
thus possible for Khaldiyyi, mother of nine, to declare the demise of the
clan system and a few minutes later to insist on clan membership as central to family planning differences. Khaldiyyi told me that "before,
people used to want to increase the clan, but today there are no clans.
The best man is the one who has the most money and is famous." Yet in
the same discussion, she commented that "there's a difference between
clans in terms of how many children they have. For example, look at
your relative Kamilya and how she has only three children—her equivalent in the lower neighborhood has a lot more. Or look at my daughter
Luma and compare her with her classmates from the Fulan family.
There's no comparison. Here the women are more learned, they understand more."

Reproductive stigmas often ascribed to certain clans designate their
members as reproductive "others." "Before," "a long time ago," people
supposedly had children to enlarge and thus empower their clan. As discussed in Chapter 1, parents had children to strengthen the 'izwi of their
families. And while this was "natural" in the so-called traditional past,
such motivations are now stigmatized by modern people. "These days"
clan is not important—it is no longer acceptable as a motivation for
having children. Yet clan is acceptable as a basis for assigning this motivation. Clan is thus still important because reproductive stereotypes are
distributed along its lines. It is posited as one of the bases for the presence of a certain "understanding" and "modernity," which prevents
clannish and now irrational reproductive behavior.

Khaldiyyi was ordering not only clan hierarchy by reproductive measures but clan borders as well. Khaldiyyi was bringing together her clan
and my clan in "the upper neighborhood." While there were several
lines of intermarriage between them, these clans were not necessarily allied in any formal way. It is true that geographically most members of
both clans lived in a more elevated part of our hilly village, while the
Fulan family she refers to and others lived in "the lower neighborhood." However, I believe Khaldiyyi also used the terms "upper" and
"lower" to hierarchize the clans. Thus, not only do clans hold ambiguous and contradictory significance; these designations, clan boundaries, alliances, and relative power are shifting and being reconfigured

with the help of the markers of "modern" and "primitive" reproductive practices.

The process of stigmatizing or honoring clans often involves the construction of opposing mentalities. When I asked several men and women who considered themselves as having small families why some couples decide to have large families, a common response was that I should ask these questions in the neighborhood or clan where families are large. Karam, a 32-year-old mother of three from Mazra'a, told me, "I don't know what's going on in their minds to make them do this, you should go to the × clan and ask the people there." Munir, a Druze man from Mghar, also told me that "there are particular clans that like having more children. Probably they're not living like the rest of the people in the village. They have a different mentality. What's important for them is to have children no matter how they live." These statements and others I heard depict parents in certain clans as having a totally different mind-set and lifestyle that are "almost incomprehensible to us."

Clan reproductive stereotypes, like those of city, village, and Bedouin, are not stable or unchanging—quite the contrary, they must be constantly redeclared and re-created in the branding act or speech. As constructs, clan stereotypes stick as long as they are repeated by many people many times. Thus they sometimes don't "work" or last. Their effects are damaging or limiting to different degrees.

COMPLICATIONS

The designations "Khaldiyyi's clan" and "my clan" in a sense refer to Khaldiyyi's *husband*'s clan and my *father*'s clan. The clan as an imagined community depends on imagining patrilineal dominance and unity, which is obviously not always the case. In order for clan to work as an ordering category, to determine the reproductive type of its members, women who marry into the clan must adopt their husbands' reproductive preferences and accept the clan's supposed orientation and traditions regarding family planning. Women take on their patriarchal duties, including the service and promotion of the spouse's clan, to varying degrees, and often manipulate these obligations in new ways. Men can do so as well, as in the case of Sa'id 'Asli, who had a big fight with his brothers some twenty years ago and changed his name to Sa'id Yasin, thus adopting his wife's and his mother's maiden name (his wife was a maternal relative). Intermarriage between allegedly reproductively modern families and traditional ones can, in some instances, disrupt clan and reproductive stereotype homogeneity.

Ironically, clannish reproductive others are also stigmatized as female-dominated. The women in these "certain other clans" are seen as both oppressed, in that they are enslaved to childbearing, and at the same time domineering and overbearing. Perhaps they adopt their patriarchal clan duties to such an extent that they take them over. Iftikar's older sister had just married into one of these "certain clans":

> She got pregnant immediately. What kind of marriage is that? They didn't go for a honeymoon or anything. The mother-in-law and father-in-law interfere in everything, the mother-in-law even tells her son when to sleep with his wife. . . . In the × clan they really love having lots of children. Also their young men stay in their mothers' homes and the mothers pressure them. Men in the × clan love their mothers more than they love their wives.

When I asked Iftikar: "Isn't your sister living in a separate home far from her mother-in-law's?" she replied: "Yes, but my sister has to go there every day and they have all their meals there, and they interfere with everything. In the × clan, the mothers dominate the men."

Children in such stigmatized clans are often referred to as *bazir,* which is derived from the word for "seeds" but is used as a derogatory term, somewhere between "kids" and "urchins"; the term implies their abundance. According to clan reproductive stigma, *bazir*-loving families are usually impoverished, partly as a result of their irrational reproductive behavior. Karam told me: "They keep on having *bazir* even though they can't find food to eat. They don't think, "How am I going to feed another child?'" This familiar attitude is resonant of Malthusian-based development theory, which blames poverty in the Third World on its uncontrolled population growth, or of welfare reformers in the United States who blame the high fertility of "black welfare moms" for their inability to "raise themselves" from poverty.

The discourse that the Galilee attitude echoes most closely, however, is that of Israeli Zionists toward Arab reproductive behavior. This Israeli discourse links the "traditional *hamula* system" to high fertility rates, an important component in the supposed causes of Arab "underdevelopment," thus stigmatizing Palestinian Arabs as self-defeating, irrational reproductive others. Abner Cohen follows this developmental logic and portrays the rapid population growth of the Palestinians as a major cause for the deterioration of the economic conditions of Arab villagers

(1965: 21, 38, 52). The focus is thus shifted away from land confiscation, state policies, discrimination, and the systematic marginalization of Palestinians in Israel. While the Palestinian discourse in the Galilee generally lacks the racial component—although "*bazir*-loving folk" are occasionally depicted as having darker features—it has rather thoroughly incorporated modernization theory's blame-the-victim, reproductive-other attitude.

The *bazer*-loving families, however, are not always associated with poverty. Several people echoed what my cousin Khalid, a social worker, told me: "You see how people in the × clan live? But they're loaded with money. These families spend more than me and you. Only it doesn't show on them. They hide it and let their children run around barefoot like that. Why? Because they don't care." Reminiscent of Koenig's report that Arabs hoard and hide away their money (1976), such statements posit that *bazir* lovers are too greedy or don't care enough about their lifestyle to spend the money necessary to at least appear modern—"like the world." As mentioned earlier, wealth and consumption must be accompanied by modern habits and beliefs in order to mark modernity.

In another variation on the economic theme, Muna, a physics teacher, told me many stories about a certain clan: "They have families of sixteen and eighteen in which not a single person is educated. They serve in the army for the money and now they have a lot of money and they've built houses and they marry the best girls in Sakhnin. They have babies out of ignorance. They now have a style of older women over forty-two getting pregnant. They know their children might come out deformed but they don't care." Thus the stigma is certainly related to poverty but goes beyond it. *Bazir* makers are stigmatized not necessarily for their poverty but for their "backwardness"; not necessarily for their lack of money but for their lack of modernity.

Even when being clannish makes economic sense, it is usually not considered modern, and is still stigmatized. Nisrin, a senior social worker from the city of Shfa 'Amir, commented: "The concept of 'quality over quantity' is central to family planning, but also to many other parts of our lives. But clannism and tribalism are so strong in our society that people want more and more children because they think that will make them strong. Everything here is still clan based—jobs, elections, marriage, etc." There is an admission in this statement that being clannish can be beneficial (if you are in the right clan), but achieving positions or marriage partners in this way is wrong and bad for the community. It's not modern. And it's a cause of "our culture's backwardness."

As mentioned earlier, nepotism and clannishness are institutionalized by Israeli authorities in many aspects of life. Indeed, the three governmental maternal and child health (MCH) clinics in my village are roughly structured along clientele clan lines, although the official rationale is geographic distribution. When I talked to the nurses at these MCH clinics, almost all agreed that the clientele of the clinic in the "lower neighborhood" had a lot more children. Fadwa, one of those nurses, said that "through my work as a nurse I saw differences between clans, especially the × clan, where there is no awareness. At the other clinic, there really is a stronger tendency to plan families. This goes back to one's culture/education [thaqāfi] and awareness. In the × clan they just naturally have children without thinking about it, or about the child's future." Interestingly, Fadwa is originally from the very clan she derides, although she married into another one.

Clan stereotypes—both positive and negative—are not immutable, nor are they unanimously agreed upon. Even people who are widely stigmatized as members of reproductively primitive clans find ways of stigmatizing their own others. My parents' neighbors, the family of Salah Karim, were almost mythologized by many people (including my family) as reproductive others since they had eighteen children, or twenty, depending on whom you asked. In our two-child family, Salah Karim's family was definitely other. But the father of that family regrets not having more children, and my parents certainly came up short in his opinion. Salah Karim's wife (Imm Yusif) was one of my father's patients, and soon after he gave her contraceptive shots after her last pregnancy because she wanted to rest, she began menopause. Her husband was mad at my father for "ruining" his wife—he believed the contraceptives had destroyed her capacity to have children or induced an early menopause. Imm Yusif, the mother of eighteen, had her own reproductive other even as she said she realized she was considered a reproductive embarrassment by her children:

> The secretary at the hospital got to know me because I came back so many times and she'd feel very sorry for me. She'd tell Abu Yusif: "Brother, you have to let your wife rest a little, please, have pity." But Abu Yusif said no way. And I did what Abu Yusif wanted [he is sitting nearby listening in]. My children were embarrassed that I had so many children, they wanted me to rest and they gave me pills secretly. Now they hate large families.

But Abu Yusif used to take very good care of me. Each time I'd have a baby he'd buy meat and save out all the nutritious parts for me. At the hospital, he used to always bring me the lungs to eat. For forty days I'd eat nutritious food, and that's why I was able to tolerate so many pregnancies and why I'd get pregnant again so soon while I was breast-feeding [aghyil]. All of Dar Ihmad [her father's clan, not her husband's; she is appropriating it] take good care of their wives, daughters-in-law, and daughters—they don't let them suffer. Women from the lower families used to give birth in the fields. They used to carry their shoes in their hands and run so they wouldn't wear them out. Once there was a woman from the lower neighborhood who was in the hospital with me and when she saw the lungs that my husband brought me, she put her head under the covers and started to cry because her husband doesn't take care of her. Especially when she has a girl.

Reproductive stereotypes are flexible tools. Imm Yusif, whom many people construed as a reproductive other, stigmatized her own set of backward reproducers.

COUNTER-DISCOURSE

Alongside the modernist discourse of clan-based reproductive difference is a less dominant counter-discourse—equally modernist—that does not consider the stigma of "bazir lovers" a stigma at all. Rather, having a lot of children is a mark of authenticity, tradition, and true Arabness. Kalthum, a 61-year-old woman from a clan that is frequently stigmatized in modern eyes, said: "We're the ones that are right. What's the meaning of life without children? What are those educated people saving their money for? We want to enjoy life, to see our children and grandchildren filling the world. We are Arabs." Thus it is important not to overemphasize the power of the dominant reproductive stigma. While some of its victims may accept their inferiority in relation to reproductively modern folk and sometimes even describe themselves in these terms, many do not. Kalthum, for one, was proud that she belonged to a clan of prolific parents. What is significant, however, is that both discourses—that which glorifies reproductive control and that which glorifies reproductive efflorescence—look to the realm of reproduction for the determination of value.

Other people fall in between these two positions. Manal, a Druze mother of seven, did not see the issue in terms of stigma, but rather as alternative strategies: "I wasn't lucky enough to be sent to school. Our clan didn't educate girls. I'm not educated and I don't work. That's why I want a big family. If I were from a family that sent me to school, maybe I'd want fewer. Everyone has their way." However, Manal is in the minority—the dominant voice delineates one strategy as right and the other as not even a strategy, but rather an ignorant default mode.

Still, along with powerful deployments of reproductive stereotypes, some less dominant voices claim that there are no reproductive differences between clans—at least not any more. Most of the nurses I met at the MCH clinics believed that reproductive difference was distributed along clan lines, but Siham Bardarneh was one nurse—and a high-leveled one at that—who disagreed. She insisted that if one actually conducted a statistical survey, the differences between clans, and even between city, village, and Bedouin, would be found to be just a social stigma not supported by the numbers. Siham was not the only person sensitive to social stereotypes and clan-based assumptions, although she was in the minority.

Some people who were most clearly victims of the clan system in the past denied the relevance of clan today. At 86, Badriyyi, a former sharecropper and tobacco smuggler, was certainly not ignorant of clan history—she could tell endless stories about family fights and feuds, landmark intermarriages, important births and deaths, and much more. I felt that she was toning down some events of the past and omitting others for my sake, since her family's history was linked to mine—she and her family sharecropped on one of my grandfather's brothers' land. Moreover, her family had since intermarried with mine and some of them had begun to register our clan name at the Ministry of the Interior, thus attempting to merge themselves into our clan. Badriyyi had nuanced knowledge of kinship history, yet she was a strong opponent of clannishness. She told me:

Before they wanted to increase the family. The strong used to eat the weak. You needed children to defend yourself. If you had no family, you couldn't lift your head in public. Today there is a government and order and there is no big and no small, everyone is the same. Today there is the high life [ʿiz] and everyone lives any way they want. Before there wasn't any work [wage labor]. It's better that there is now.

Several people who belonged to less powerful clans in the past repeated this binary image of a scarcity-driven, lawless clan system in the past, when having children was key to survival or empowerment, and a lawful, egalitarian, more abundant present, when having children was up to the individual.

In Badriyyi's view of the past, childbearing and family/clan building were such an important survival strategy that she could not even conceive of anyone resorting to contraception then, except to avoid an "illegitimate" pregnancy. Although other women of her age had told me of different "traditional" contraceptive methods used during that period, when I asked Badriyyi about them, she was confused by the question. "Hanni Khury, the midwife,[16] used to collect roaches, grind them, and make suppositories from them to help women get pregnant. There was also a water pipe in Tiberias, just a pipe with water coming out of it, and women would go there and spread their legs and sit on it and sing, '*Hārūn hūrinny, ajitak ḥabbilny,*' 'O Harūn, harūn me, I came to you, impregnate me.'" She laughed very loudly at this lewd verse, while her daughter-in-law shushed her and tried to help me: "But she wants to know what they used to do if they *didn't* want children." Badriyyi said, "Which married woman didn't want children? There was no such thing." [17] In Badriyyi's vision of local history, the decline of clan significance in the village has led to the change in attitudes towards childbearing: "Today everyone depends on himself, and everyone lives any way they want." Thus the relative decoupling of clan and class, or family background and resources, has supposedly led to the freeing up (not necessarily a positive evaluation) of reproductive practice.

Badriyyi's view is far from dominant; the discourse of reproductive difference between clans is much stronger and more widespread. The criterion of reproductive modernity is clearly at play in most people's ordering and bordering of clans.

RELIGION

The dominant discourse of reproductive stigma also orders religion in the Galilee, despite a widespread embrace of secularism or, alternatively,

---

16. Note that the village midwife in 'Arrabi was Christian. Badriyyi is Muslim.

17. Although Badriyyi constructs contraception as a modern development, studies demonstrate that birth control methods were known and used in the region before the nineteenth century (Musallam 1983).

religious tolerance: Christians are frequently considered the most reproductively modern, followed by the Druze and Muslims. Clearly I cannot begin to offer here a comprehensive account of the complex, changing, and multivocal history of these three religions in Palestine. I only
roughly outline some of the larger, relatively recent transformations in
order to undermine any preconceptions about "ancient" entities, "natural" animosities, or "eternal" friction.

During Ottoman rule, Christians in the Galilee, as in other parts of
the former empire, had the status of *millet,* a tolerated or protected
minority. This system placed restrictions on Christian subjects of the
empire but allowed for considerable autonomy within the communities. With the rise of European power and influence in the nineteenth
and twentieth centuries, this confessional structure continued, only the
Christians were now to be protected—and privileged and preached
to—by the Europeans. Before the nineteenth century, the "Holy Land"
had been for a significant period of time a kind of terra incognita to the
West (Shepherd 1987: 13).[18] But in the nineteenth century, European attention to and influence in the region took a quantitative and qualitative
turn (Haddad 1970: 37) with "the struggles of various powers to secure
paramount influence" in the weakening Ottoman Empire (A. Hourani
1991: 275). In addition to European political and economic ambitions,
the growing Western influence involved a series of fluctuating interests,
desires, needs, and curiosities.[19] All of these European projects affected
the local population. The nineteenth century witnessed the rise in the

18. Although the number of foreign and especially European Christian missionary
priests in the Middle East as a whole started to increase in the seventeenth century, as
the papacy attempted to widen its influence in the area and to expand the number of Eastern Christians who accepted the authority of the pope as a side thrust of the Counter-
Reformation (Hourani 1991: 242; Haddad 1970: 17), the attention the Holy Land received in the nineteenth century was much more intense and variegated. Still, considerable
antagonism was created between Christians who recognized the authority of the pope and
those who did not in the seventeenth century.

19. In the early 1800s, a "modern crusade of knowledge" brought scientific explorers
and romantic travelers. In the 1820s, pioneers of militant Protestant activity arrived with
the hope that the sobriety of Protestantism would improve the Eastern Christians and established a number of institutions that became of paramount importance, such as schools,
experimental farms, and medical and other services. Scholars, clergymen, and "Scriptural
geographers" came seeking to establish the literal truth of the Bible, under threat by the
rise of the secular sciences, especially geology. In the latter half of the nineteenth century,
the rise in millenarian Christian beliefs brought missions to convert Jews, which then resulted in the involvement of wealthy Western Jews in the fate of their coreligionists in
Palestine who were being pressured into conversion. European museums and societies
combed the land for archeological finds, and expeditions of the Palestine Exploration
Fund surveyed the country (Shepherd 1987).

power of European consuls, who gained jurisdiction over foreigners and protectorates over religious minorities in the area,[20] and in practice often gained much more. Two parallel systems of law developed, one for local Muslims and one for non-Muslims, Europeans, and their protégés (Shepherd 1987: 108–109).[21] Although Christian Arabs in Palestine were considered "hopelessly Eastern" by most Europeans (Haddad 1970: 80), they enjoyed the status of a privileged minority during this period vis-à-vis the Europeans.

Note that while Christians in the Galilee are sometimes referred to as a single group, they comprise several denominations: the Greek Orthodox, the largest group, is followed by the Greek Catholics and Roman Catholics, and smaller groups such as Maronites, various Protestant denominations, Anglicans, and Copts (Rabinowitz 1997: 27).

After the fall of the Ottoman Empire, communal solidarity continued to "be manipulated by the French and British along sectarian lines." The privileging of Christians was reflected in the fact that they constituted a substantial percentage of the urban population of Palestine and "in all likelihood, they constituted a majority of the literate public" (Tamari 1982: 186, 187). Missionary schools, hospitals, and other charitable organizations served the wider community but benefited the urban Christians the most. Yet Christians were clearly a numerical minority in Palestine (unlike neighboring Lebanon) and were thus particularly attracted from early on to the apparent secular discourse of Palestinian and Arab nationalisms (ibid.; Haddad 1970: 86).[22]

As with the so-called *hamula* system, it is misleading to think of so-called communal or sectarian divisions as inherent, ancient ones. They

20. In the 1840s, for example, the Russians claimed to protect the Greek Orthodox communities (20,000 Arabs at the time); the French protected the Latin Catholics (around 3,000); and the British wanted to protect the Jews (27,000 by 1870). The Crimean War of 1853–56 increased the influence of France and Britain as they fought with the Ottomans against Russia.

21. European states used religious minorities as an excuse for increased political and economic influence in the region, but people and institutions not directly linked to states, especially missionaries, also had a wide impact through their various projects. While non-Muslims in the area welcomed the financial assistance they received and especially the opportunity to serve as middlemen, traders, and translators for the Europeans, they also resented the considerable interference in communal life (Shepherd 1987: 235).

22. Salim Tamari argues: "The *millet* system, at its best, provided a protective and respected position for Christians as a minority in a culture in which they did not properly belong as *citizens*. For them, Arab separatism became the cultural-linguistic mold in which they expressed their striving for a new homogeneous (i.e. secular) order. Ever since the literary renaissance of the 1870s and 1880s Christian Arab intellectuals educated in the liberal missions of Beirut, Damascus, and Nazareth gave the movement of Ottoman decentralisation a nationalist (pan-Arab) direction" (1982: 187).

have been created at particular moments in specific ways. After the British and not unlike them, Israel attempted to consolidate its power by "feeding and reinforcing confessional loyalties until they eclipsed national feelings" (Jiryis 1976: 197).[23] Hence "the government's preferences with regard to the maintenance of separate Druze, Christian, Moslem, Bedouin and Circassian identities, as opposed to the emergence among the non-Jewish minority of an overarching Arab or Palestinian sentiment" (Lustick 1980: 135).

In addition to the Muslim/Christian divide, the Druze have been particularly singled out from other Palestinians. Starting with the 1936 Arab rebellion, the Zionist strategy of searching "for non-Arab and non-Sunni Muslim communities within the region who could be brought into an alliance directed against Arab nationalism" led Zionists to develop their first links with Druze communities in Palestine and Syria.[24] Israel's continued cultivation of so-called natural and endemic animosity between the Druze and the Muslim majority "paved the way for the neutral or pro-Zionist stance which most Palestinian Druze took during the battles of 1947–49" (Lockman 1996: 251–252; Hajjar 1996: 3).

In 1956, Israeli government officials and "16 Druze leaders agreed upon mandatory conscription for Druze males, illustrating the deeply embedded lines of patronage running from state agencies through a narrow elite to the community as a whole" (Hajjar 1996: 3). A year later, the Ministry of Religious Affairs "recognized the Druse as an independent religious community [rather than a subsect of Islam], a communal status which the Druse never experienced under Ottoman rule" (Lustick 1980: 133). Since then Druze have been forced to register with the Ministry of Interior as being of "Druze nationality" rather than Arab. An independent judicial system for the Druze established in 1962 strengthened their religious and conservative structure (Lustick 1980: 206).

23. Israel's divide-and-rule policy has been implemented through, for example, the establishment of separate religious courts with jurisdiction over matters of personal status, including a separate court system for each of the Christian sects, separate schools and curricula for "Arabs" and "Druze" (thus defining Druze as non-Arab), different scouting organizations, etc. In addition, ultra-Orthodox and feudal figures were often supported and appointed by the departments of the Ministry of Religion as "imams, caretakers of religious facilities, qadis, marriage registrars, etc. to reward supporters of the government and to strengthen the position of traditionalist forces" (Lustick 1980: 206). Thus the conservatism of the various religious leaderships is partly a result of Israeli structural policy.

24. Some twenty Druze sheikhs who resisted participation in the Arab revolt of 1936 were killed by rebel commanders. This episode is not widely known or discussed in the Galilee because the current Palestinian nationalist emphasis on sectarian unity tends to "obscure any recollections of instances of sectarian conflict" (Swedenburg 1995: 90).

A separate Druze "heritage" was created and taught in Druze schools. Ramadan, a holiday celebrated by both Sunni Muslims and Druze, was designated as exclusively Muslim, while Nabi Sh'ayb was declared to be Druze and transformed into a major annual national-religious festival. Hisham, a Druze man from Sajur, told me: "Israel took away Ramadan from us and gave us the day of the prophet Sh'ayb. That's their policy of divide and rule. When in fact we are Muslims—we were the first to believe in the Prophet when he revealed himself. The others who didn't immediately believe him were the Sunni and Shi'a, and that's why they have to fast and pray daily."

In the difficult economic context of Palestinians in Israel, the military has become "an important source of employment and financial security" for Druze, as "more than 30 percent of all employed Druze individuals at any given time work in various branches of the [Israeli] security services" (Hajjar 1996: 4). According to Lustick, government efforts to deepen the divisions between Druze and other Arabs in Israel "have been accompanied by the extension of special benefits to the Druse community as a whole—part of an overall attempt to coopt the Druse on a communal basis." In addition to symbolic expressions of commendation for good citizenship, the military administration ended its rule in Druze villages in 1962, four years before it was abolished for the rest of the Palestinians. Other benefits include the selection of more Druze to run for the Knesset, more judicial positions in the Druze court, the designation of some Druze villages as development towns and thus an assignment of larger budgets, and "marked preference for Druse in hiring . . . [in] government ministries and Labor Party organs" (Lustick 1980: 210, 133, 211).

Nonetheless, there has been some resistance to this Israeli segmenting policy, in the form of conscientious objection to military conscription and legal battles to register nationality as Arab rather than Druze.[25]

---

25. The conscription of Druze into the Israeli army led to some protest (Tuma 1982: 309). Organizations such as the Free Druze and the Regional Initiative Committee, affiliated with the Communists, have been active in resistance. Some Druze men have refused to serve in the army, emphasizing their loyalty to the Palestinian nation. Nayfi Naffa' from Bayt Jan was accused of attacking policemen who were trying to search her home for her conscientious objector son. On the occasion of her court hearing, she was interviewed by the Arabic daily 'Ittihad:

In my opinion the issue is not the issue of my trial. The issue is the policy of "divide and rule." . . . We mothers, sisters, and wives must refuse the attempts to oppress and quiet us. . . . We must not be silent, for she who loses her son does not have the right to live. . . . In my town, Bayt Jan, there are more than fifty victims [killed while serving in the Israeli army]. . . . The mother cries and agonizes and curses, instead of tak-

Many Druze believe that Israeli discrimination against them and their villages "in terms of land confiscation, local municipalities, education, employment, discrimination in the army and the unfulfilled promises of full equality" are constant reminders of the Arabness of the Druze (Tuma 1982: 208). Alongside the "special benefits" and the segmenting attempts, Israel contradicts itself by discriminating against Druze as Arabs. The privileging of the Druze is thus "largely rhetorical . . . as evidenced by the rampant social and political discrimination that Druze share with the rest of the non-Jewish minority" (Hajjar 1996: 3). Druze have had more land expropriated per capita than other religious groups (based on the records of Israel's Land Authority, 1988–89 [as cited in Yiftachel 1991:340]). The advisers on Arab affairs in the various Israeli ministries, for example, are in charge of Druze affairs (Jiryis 1976: 201). And the army is not the melting pot that it's claimed to be; "although there are 'mixed units' of Jews and non-Jews in the border police, most non-Jewish recruits serve in a separate 'minorities unit'" (Lustick 1980: 94). Thus policy contradictions , among other things, have made Israel's segmenting goal less than a total success.[26]

Despite, or perhaps because of, Israel's segmenting policy, a strong discourse of egalitarianism is constantly asserted in the Galilee. Just as

---

ing control of the situation, instead of defending her son before he becomes a victim, and allowing him to go to jail. Let her pay the price for his refusal of service. If the blood of victims does not unite mothers, I don't know when they will unite their ranks. (June 8, 1995)

Nayfi Naffaʿ clearly considers herself part of the imagined community of the Palestinian nation, though other Druze do not agree. The devotion of sacrificing mothers and the spilled blood of their sons, in her view, should overcome this dissension and unite all Druze with Arabs.

In 1995 the head of the Druze Regional Initiative Committee, Sheikh Jamal Mʿadi, won the right, after a five-year legal battle, to return the word "Arab" instead of "Druze" to the nationality line in his personal identification card (which had been changed without his permission). Mʿadi called upon "every young Druze to insist on his right to register his true nationality" (ʾIttihad, Nov. 15, 1995).

26. Interestingly, the attempt to Druzify the Syrian Druze of the Golan Heights, conquered during the 1967 war, along the same lines as the Druzification of the Druze community inside the 1948 borders of Israel has failed much more dramatically. Lisa Hajjar argues:

The Syrian Druze of the Golan . . . did not willingly accept efforts to nationalize their sectarian identity, or see themselves politically as part of some "Druze collectivity" which would negate or override their status as Syrian citizens living under Israeli occupation. Even religiously, notions of sectarian identity in the Golan differ radically from those holding sway inside Israel; these Druze do not see their religion as an "other" to Islam, a view which arguably is shared by Druze in Syria and Lebanon. . . . The differing views on religious and national identity in these two communities derive from their differing modern histories. (1996:5)

clannishness is rejected as backward, so is religious favoritism or discrimination. One explanation is Glen Bowman's argument that "in situations of radical social conflict between a multi-sectarian community and a 'foreign' enemy, perceptions of the antagonism of the Other can generate new forms of imagined community within which communal differences are subsumed but not elided" (1993: 431). As Swedenburg observes, Palestinianness is often considered a more important part of identity than religion. One man who had participated in the 1936 revolt told Swedenburg, "There is no *din* [religion]. . . . My *din* is Falastini [Palestinian]" (1995: 89).

Egalitarianism in the Galilee is expressed both through religion and outside it. The Muslim acceptance of the people of the book is one expression of egalitarianism. So is the acknowledgment and celebration of a diverse and joined history. The majority of the Palestinians in the Galilee live in mixed communities and also imagine a mixed national community. Nationalism in the Galilee has largely been secular, and the leaders of the various movements have come from diverse religious backgrounds.[27] Even the recent Islamicist minority has largely called for social reform rather than an Islamic state. The shared beliefs and basic similarities of religious teachings are frequently presented as the reason for the lack of confessional animosity. Some of the people I interviewed described themselves as atheists; a few others were deeply religious; most were somewhere in between and considered themselves secular at some level. Palestinians pride themselves on diversity and modern secularism, even as they invoke God's protection, religious connections to holy sites of Palestine, or communal differences in other domains— especially the domain of reproductive stereotypes.

Certain boundaries are regularly blurred. This fluidity is apparent in daily life in the Galilee: in the statues of the Virgin Mary in the buffet displays of Muslim households, in the Christian clientele of a Muslim healer, in the number of unconverted foreign Christian wives of Muslim men. I was particularly struck by the momentary blurring of these boundaries as Galya, a Romanian Christian woman married in my village, threw a Muslim *mawlid* (*molad* locally) celebration recently to

27. For example, the local leadership includes the prominent poet and author Samih el-Qasim, who is Druze; Emile Tuma, Marxist historian of the Palestinian struggle inside Israel, who is Christian; Emile Habiby, longtime Knesset member and award-winning author, who is Christian; Tawfiq Ziyad, late mayor of the largest Palestinian city and Knesset member, who was Muslim; 'Azmi Bishara, Knesset member, who is Christian. Indeed, many of these leaders were Communists and professed atheists.

bless her newly completed house (over the objections of her Muslim-born Communist husband).[28] But side by side with this blurring, religious boundaries are occasionally emphasized, increasingly through the reproductive measure.

Note that growing up in the Galilee I have largely been considered Muslim by Muslims, while many Christians focus on my mother's Christianity, our celebration of Christian holidays, my Christian high school education, and my marriage to a non-Muslim (though he is only partly Christian.) While I was conducting my research, both Muslims and Christians (but not Druze) would lean over to me and tell me things about "them," the folks of the other religion, assuming that I wasn't part of them. This afforded me some, though frequently uncomfortable, access to discourses of religious difference.

RELIGION AND REPRODUCTION

The dominant discourse in the Galilee constructs Christians as reproductively more modern than Muslims and Druze. According to the Statistical Abstract of Israel, in 1995 Muslims were roughly 76 percent of Israel's non-Jewish population, Christians were 15 percent,[29] and Druze 9 percent. Since 1950 these percentages changed slightly (from a recorded 69 percent Muslims, 22 percent Christians, and 9 percent Druze) as a result of differences in fertility rates and emigration (Central Bureau of Statistics 1996: 43). Israeli statistics indicate that Christians have lower fertility and higher rates of emigration on average than Muslims and Druze. But even if reproductive stereotypes draw on statistically reported fertility rates, they go well beyond them in the glorifi-

---

28. Another incident that illustrates the intermittently fluid and rigid religious boundaries occurred when a Christian friend of mine, Wardi, described a visitor her brother brought home one day. The visitor, who worked for the UN, was blond and blue-eyed and "very handsome." When offered a glass of water to quench his thirst after a meal, he drank half the glass, then casually threw the remaining water over his shoulder into the garden. Wardi exclaimed: "When I saw that, I knew for sure he must have some Arab roots, some connection to Arabs. I asked him and actually he was part Bosnian. He was a Muslim. He was just like us, exactly. He still looked like one of those handsome UN guys, you wouldn't believe from looking at him that he was just like us." For Wardi, a Christian, to see her family's guest as just like her largely because he was Muslim demonstrates the fluidity of religious identifications in the Galilee. Only moments later, however, Wardi asserted how difficult it was for "us Christian girls to get married, because we have such a small group of [Christian] men to pair up with." The boundaries were instantly reerected in the realm of family formation.

29. Statistics for 1995 include a small Christian non-Palestinian population of Russian and Eastern European immigrants.

cation of the modern and control of reproduction as well as the denigration of the primitive and supposedly uncontrolled reproduction.

Muslims are considered the most reproductively backward partly because it is believed that their religion forbids certain measures to control reproduction. According to Lawahiz (aged 29), who is Muslim, "the Christians are a little bit higher, more civilized than us. They have fewer children. Muslims remain from a religious point of view forbidden to stop reproducing. Religious people say it's forbidden to cut off one's progeny [nasil]." Many people, like Lawahiz, understood Islam to forbid sterilization, while others believed it also disallows contraceptives. As Khadra from B'ayni said, "Religious people have more children because they believe that using medicine is like killing a child." Thus the dominant discourse places Muslims generally below Christians.

But according to others who have formally studied religion, this view of Islam is distorted. Khadiji, the MCH nurse from Sakhnin who is married to the lawyer son of a sheikh, describes herself and her husband as "religious Muslims but not fanatical. I mean we truly believe and we pray and all." She explained to me that contraceptives are not forbidden, but

> I found through my work that many religious people think that contraceptives are religiously forbidden. Even those who don't stick to their religious duties in most parts of their lives, when it comes to contraception, they say it's religiously wrong to use it and are afraid. We had to get a *fatwa* [Islamic legal opinion] and hang it in our clinic to convince women they're wrong.[30]

In Khadiji's view, it is not formal religion that forbids family planning, but "ignorant" people's misinformed beliefs. Her version of religious-based reproductive difference places "learned believers" as more reproductively modern than the "traditional ignorant folk." While Christians may be more modern than Muslims, "real Muslims" are more modern than those "who don't know anything about Islam."

Dalya, a trained religious teacher, explained to me that the belief that Islam forbids contraception

> is actually a very common misconception. The ignorant ones [al-jahiliyyin] look at the Muslim woman and don't understand her. A

---

30. *Fatwas* in Israel are issued by government-appointed muftis, a fact that to some extent undermines their legitimacy in the Palestinian community.

lot of people think that Muslims have a lot of children, they just constantly and carelessly make *bazir*. But let me tell you what the companions of the Prophet used to say: "We isolated [practiced withdrawal] while the Qur'an was being revealed *[Kunnā na'zilu wa al-Qur'ānu yanzilu]*, which is an indication that Muslims aren't just always making children.

Dalya pointed out that she has three well-spaced children and "my husband and I use withdrawal. It's all right to use any form of contraception, it's only forbidden to close the womb [sterilization]." When I told Dalya that another religious teacher told me that using contraceptives for more than four or five years in a row is forbidden, she answered:

Yes, some people have that belief, but other sheikhs give a different opinion. My husband is of the belief that you can have an IUD for as long as you want. But a woman shouldn't deny this blessing for too long. If a woman is healthy and she has money and everything, why should she totally stop having children? . . . Look, the Prophet said: "Mate and multiply, for I will be boastful of you on the day of judgment" *[tanākahu takātharu fa innī mubāhin bi-kum yawm al-qiyāmati]*.

Dalya had a more nuanced understanding of formal religion than most and was disturbed by the many lay misconceptions of it—concerning contraceptives, but also concerning women's status and polygamy.[31] She had detailed knowledge of the various schools of interpretation. She was "trained in the Hanafi way and my husband is Shafi'i. But it was difficult because each of us would give a different opinion *[nafti]*, so I decided to become Shafi'i like my husband." She thought that "perhaps some people get their misconceptions from the fact that Islam is somewhat similar to old times and old-time values, and they used to have a lot of children in the past. But that's not true. Islamic values

31. In regard to the equality of the sexes she said: "Some people believe that Islam discriminates because it says that women are deficient in reason and religion *[al-nisā'u nāqiṣātu 'aqlin wa dīnin]*, but this is not discrimination against women. It does not mean that men are better than women. This was said because woman cannot fast all of Ramadan because of her period. Also women usually work according to their heart, not like the man, who works according to his head. For example, if the lights suddenly go out at night, the woman will get upset and afraid and might scream or cry, but the man will immediately go and check the fuse box to see what's wrong. The Prophet (peace be upon him) said, 'Woman was created from a crooked rib *[a'waj]*, but this rib protects the vital parts inside, the heart and other organs, so it's necessary. Man can't do without woman just as woman can't do without man.'"

are different from traditional old values. It's a modern religion." Thus in Dalya's analysis, "ignorant" Muslims (whom she refers to as *al-jahiliyyin*) are reproductively primitive, but "true" learned Muslims are, on the contrary, careful planners of how to best use this blessing of God.

Buthaina is not herself religious, but she described learned Muslims as exemplary in their control of their sexuality and reproduction: "My sister and her husband are very strict. They only have two girls and they don't want any more children for a while. They only have sex once a week rather than every day, because they don't want to have too much sex." Similarly, for Nayfi from Kufur Kanna, proper religion spares women and their children the traumas of high fertility. Nayfi had eleven children and said, "What I went through I don't want my children to go through. Even though I wasn't very tired at the time from it. But they should take care of themselves, have a life. Islam tells us to have children, but each child must breast-feed for two years. I used to have a child every eleven months. Is this what God said? No, a woman must rest."

Many people who had some level of formal religious education knew that Islam does not ban contraceptives. Rather, in this view—a variation on modernist reproductive stereotyping—it is the misinformed masses of superstitiously religious people who are reproductively primitive. Nisrin, the social worker who talked about clannism and tribalism, had also received formal Islamic education:

The problem of family planning is part of the larger confusion of these times. People ask themselves, "Is Islam a way of life or not? Should I behave this way or that?" Our society is in a transitional stage. But really Islam is a total way of life, and it even talks about family planning. The situation of reproduction is still very bad here, especially since we're a minority in the Jewish sector. You know, quite often science and religion come together. For example, a hospital won't tie a woman's tubes without a medical reason, just as Islam requires. An important part of reproduction is sexual compatibility. I often tell this to women and they start shouting, "Hey, how can you talk like that!" I tell them sex isn't only for the husband, it's for you, it's your right to feel good. And yes, this is part of Islam. But most women only look at the parts of religion that they want to see.

Just as devout Muslims are often criticized (mistakenly, according to Dalya and Nisrin) for being reproductively primitive in comparison with more secular neighbors, devout Christians are seen as being more fertile and reproductively primitive than secular Christians because of the dictates of their religion. Lawahiz said, "Religious people in general, all over the world—Muslims, Christians, or Jews—have too many children." Within this framework, individuals who are "too religious" or communities that are perceived as being more attached to their religion are stigmatized as primitive reproducers.

As discussed in Chapter 2, the belief that God will provide for whatever children are born supposedly leads to the fatalism and uncontrolled reproduction of religious people. The "superstitiously religious masses" were inclined to be reproductively primitive because of their literal belief in *rizqa*, their fatalism and lack of family planning. In this way, too, people who are "too religious" are stigmatized by those who are "not too religious."

However, some "religious" people interpreted the belief in *rizqa* in ways that made it compatible with standards of reproductive modernity. According to Munir, a Druze man:

> Let me tell you, I don't want to argue with the men of religion and I am a strong believer. But if I want to take the *rizqa* saying, I don't take it literally or in a hard way *[shakil jamid]*. What it really means is that a human is born in a family and that family is responsible for providing the livelihood. And if you work hard, God will open for you the door of livelihood. So when a child is born, his livelihood is born with him because you take the initiative to find a source of support for this child. It doesn't mean that I can have a child and sit down and say OK, God, now send me a livelihood, like certain people do. That's not the meaning of it. I don't take it as a saying that leads to laziness and that I don't care—I'll have kids and God will care for them. That's my interpretation of that old saying. Or it might even mean that the state is responsible for this child. So I don't see it as a bad belief. The livelihood doesn't come from the sky, but from the earth.

Like Nisrin's interpretation of Islam's position on contraception, Munir's interpretation of the faith that God will provide is figured as thoroughly compatible with modern requirements of reproduction.

"Superstitious," "unlearned," and "traditional" believers are ridiculed by modernists for their allegedly exaggerated emphasis on the need to bear children. Mockingly, the Communist *'Ittihad* daily covered the rumor that the voice of a crying child was emanating from the wall of a childless couple's home:

> The residents of 'Ara are busy with a new rumor that the voice of a crying child emanates from the wall of one of the homes. . . . The old home belongs to Rihab and Mas'ud Abu-Shaykha (47 and 50 years old). They have been married for 28 years and have not been blessed with children. . . . This story has become the gossip of the town. . . . It has no scientific explanation. . . . Our correspondent reports that while he was at the named home yesterday he did not hear any crying of a child. The owner of the house said that the crying had stopped the day before! (June 20, 1995)

The author of this piece, like others who repeated the story, distinguished himself as a rational disbelieving modernist from the superstitious child-hungry couple. Probably the "masses" that "flocked" to hear the crying child held a different view—but they are not the ones writing articles for 'Ittihad.

The reproductive stereotypes attached to the different religions are related not only to edicts regarding reproduction and contraceptives but also to the varying degrees of supposed traditionalism of the communities, or their "developmental stage." For Katarina (36), resident of 'Ilabun, her family was more reproductively modern than Taghrid's because "the concept of clan power ['izwi] is not in the realm of our thinking. This is only among the Muslims. That's why they have more children."

According to Ghusun (54), who is Christian:

> Among Muslims mothers-in-law still have a strong influence. Among Christians, the young generation doesn't listen to the older one: each woman goes according to her own convictions. It really depends on your culture [thaqafi]. We [Christians] are more educated, drugs have entered their communities more, it's full of hashish smokers. . . . Muslims like reproducing more, they want a boy to carry the father's name. Muslims are more attached to religion than Christians. We don't have religious fanaticism.

Indeed, Ghusun and her husband had a long discussion over whether their child should prepare for First Communion because they are not religious. They finally decided that he should go through the process, because they didn't want him to feel left out or different from his friends. Yet their weak attachment to religion coexisted with a strong view of religiously based reproductive hierarchy. Thus their view of reproductive differences between Muslims and Christians is based on cultural rather than religious differences.

It is not only Christians who believe that Muslims are behind Christians in progress toward reproductive modernism. Zayni, a kindergarten teacher who is Muslim herself, said that "Muslims have more children than Christians and Druze. But it's not a matter of religious belief. No, the woman's awareness [she used the Hebrew 'eranut] determines things. And among Christians, woman's wit began developing earlier— it's not because of religious arguments." Similarly, Muna who is also Muslim and is a high school teacher, said that "Christians are much more aware. They give more time to each child and have fewer children. I know one woman who has two girls and doesn't want any more. Even in Sakhnin, the children of the Christians are given more time. They're smarter in the schools because the parents are interested and concerned and help, and most of the parents are more educated—both the mother and father. This is very clear in the case of the Nazareth schools." Yumna said: "Our Christian brothers in our villages are more aware in terms of number and their view of children. Why deny it? Christians' view of life changed before ours. I don't know why, maybe they mixed with foreigners more than we did, they're more educated, they used to study in the Christian schools, and they brought different opinions than the ones that existed." [32]

32. The criterion of education often enters this mélange: the educated group in society is often considered the reproductively modern group and the uneducated group as reproductively primitive. Ahlam, the preschool assistant, told me that an important reason why "our society has fewer children now than before is that we are educated, not ignorant, so we naturally have fewer children. The group that's not educated has the most children because they feel that life is a routine. Life today is like it was twenty years ago and like it will be in another ten years." Thus education is a sign of an investment in modernity and its narrative of reproductive progress. And education is often linked to particular groups and their reproduction: Christians are often considered more educated than Muslims and Druze and thus more reproductively modern, city people more educated than villagers or Bedouins, etc.

Reproductive modernity also manifests itself not only in numbers but also in the style of reproduction. According to Nuhad, who had dropped out of college a year before she was to complete her bachelor's degree, "Among our generation in Haifa it's impossible to find more than four children in a family, among the educated and uneducated. But educated people take longer till they have children; we do it right away. They wait and prepare themselves economically and psychologically."

The question of how many years of schooling and what type of schooling make you educated are disputed. Ahlam, for example, only finished tenth grade and considers herself educated. Badira, who is pursuing a degree in English and education, does not consider people like Ahlam educated. She was very proud that, unlike her sister Haniyyi, who has three children and is a housewife, and her other sister Su'ad, who got pregnant immediately after marriage, she went on for postsecondary education and that she and her degree-holding husband stuck to their plan to wait three years after marriage to have a child. Moreover, for some people religious training is not considered a significant sign of education, and degrees in the humanities are not as substantial proof of education as a degree

Druze are often considered as falling somewhere in the middle of the Muslim–Christian reproductive continuum. As Riad, who is Druze, told me, "Mixing in the army changes young Druze men, they see the Jews and their life and learn from it—that's why their mind-set is different than their parents'. As a result, they don't want as many children." In another version of this ordering, Ghusun said that "the Druze are just as bad as the Muslims when it comes to family planning, if not worse. Druze boys serve in the army and they get a salary so they like to have a lot of boys."

Strong opinions about reproductive stereotypes seemed to be more common in places where Muslims, Christians, or Druze lived together. Fatmi, originally from 'Arrabi and married into Dayr Hanna, both of which have a Muslim majority and a Christian minority but no Druze, repeatedly voiced her opinion on the ranking of Muslims and Christians reproductively but said, "I don't know about the Druze." This despite the fact that the next village down from 'Arrabi and Dayr Hanna—a ten-minute drive away—is Mghar, which has a large Druze community. Many Muslims and Christians who did not live in a village with Druze in fact claimed to have no opinion on this issue. Perhaps the separation of the Druze communities—both self-imposed and state-imposed—has at times prevented them from being part of the larger community that is placed and ordered by the binary gaze of reproductive hierarchies.

As mentioned above, in addition to the generalized Muslim-Christian-Druze division, each community has its "too religious" and "not too religious" faction, and Christian communities may also be divided along denominational lines. For example, tensions sometimes arise between the Greek Orthodox and the Catholics, but today these boundaries are less pronounced and stable than those between the Muslims, Christians, and Druze. I did hear a few Greek Orthodox Christians ridicule Catholics for their edicts against contraception. Also within the Christian community, reproductive hierarchy is often related to the community's environment: Christians who live in villages or cities where they are the majority are more modern than Christians who are a minority in their community. Ghusun said, "When Christians are a minority in a town, they like to increase their offspring." Similarly, Georgina believed that her parents were more strict with her when she was growing up,

---

in the hard sciences. Still, level of education, religion, clan, and urbanity are interwoven into a powerful web of reproductive hierarchy.

and had more traditional views about children and reproduction, because Christians were a minority in her town: "It depends on the environment; here in 'Ilabun they're all Christians, so they let their girls do many things. In other mixed places there's more danger, so the Christians behave more conservatively."

QUALIFICATIONS, COUNTER-DISCOURSE

As with clans and towns, the strong discourse of modernist reproductive hierarchy is mirrored by a weaker traditionalist hierarchy. Some people believe that the abundant reproduction of the "too religious" is better than the small families of those who are not, or that Muslims and Druze are better for having more children, since they are not corrupted by the West, as Christians are. In the local Islamic movement's weekly, Walid Abd-el-Latif warns that "We have almost become like Jews and Christians. Is it because of fear of people or of women (do you fear them, for God is more worthy of your fear if you are believers)" (*Sawt ul-Haq wal-Hurriyyah,* June 30, 1995). In the same paper Khitam Dahli, a religious teacher, provides an excellent example of this antimodernization yet totally modern discourse; she simply reverses the hierarchy:

> A religious man came to the Prophet (peace be upon him) and said: "O Prophet, I love a woman of high rank and wealth, except that she cannot have children. Shall I marry her?" And he told him not to. Then the man came to him a second time and the Prophet told him not to, then a third, so the Prophet told him: "Marry the friendly fertile one [al-wadūd al-walūd] for I am increasing the peoples in you.' . . .
>
> Those who frighten women from having many children are either ignorant or wrongdoers, and they must not depend on a few special cases and generalize from them to all women. Pregnancy, birth, and breast-feeding are vital processes that activate the woman's female glands, so that they perform their duty in the best way, and thus the femininity and the beauty of the woman is complete after marriage. . . . Dear brothers, why have we become afraid of large families? Is it because of following Western thinking? Or is it fear of hunger? God is great, God is the Generous Provider.
>
> My Muslim brother, our perspective should not be a material one, a perspective of wasters/luxuriators [mutrifīn], all we care about is much food and clothing for a few children. This perspective is not for the devout Muslim . . . the large family is stronger than the small family because it is better able to work and earn and produce, and in most cases it is more successful in trades and crafts, even though it suffers in the beginning from lack of money.

It is extremely unfortunate that intellectual subordination controls many Muslims, and they followed their way of living, for in Western countries they do not have many children and are satisfied with one child or two. Not because they do not like children but to exaggerate their luxury. And the West wants the Muslims to follow their way in limiting offspring, because high reproduction among Muslims has come to strike fear in the minds of many Western leaders, and this issue has become an international conspiracy on Islamic offspring, for fear of the day when Muslims take control of the leadership of the world once again.

Finally, my brothers in God, I call upon you to be big families like the families of our children [sic] and our grandfathers, growing on the teachings of our great religion and sunna of our Prophet, and let the West do as it may. (May 1996)

The anti-Western traditionalist nostalgia of this piece, its rendering of authenticity, its alleged hatred of modernity and luxury but not of money, can be found in similar form among some Christian fundamentalists. But this counter-discourse is less dominant in the Galilee. For one thing, the *Voice of Truth and Freedom* has a much smaller circulation than the modernist *'Ittihad*. The small-family position is much more widespread. A review of fifteen articles on the Cairo International Conference on Population and Development in *'Ittihad* demonstrates a tone sympathetic to family planning and strong opposition to the Islamic countries' positions at the conference. The editor asserts that the conference resolutions are a "victory for the mind and reason" that will allow humanity "honorable reproduction," even as he is aware that Western countries tried to use the conference to enforce a new world order (Sept. 5, 1994). Another title states: "Call for Investment in Humans Most Important Principle in Existence" (Sept. 7, 1994). This modernist discourse is more dominant in the Galilee.

Many religious people, of course, are ambivalent about what they understand to be religious injunctions. Nuhad and her husband became born-again three years ago:

Our parents were Communists, but the Lord made miracles that medicine doesn't explain. I am born-again and our preachers tell us to have children. There's a verse in the Bible, "Go forth and multiply" (she used the Hebrew words: *pru ve rvu*). You have the fruit of the Lord and glorify the Lord through your children. But I don't believe in this because *pru ve rvu* was said two thousand years ago. It's true that the believer, the one who depends on God, is not afraid even if he has twenty children. And maybe, for sure God will open doors for him. But at the same time, we must make some calculations.

Nuhad thus has complex and contradictory feelings about reproductive modernity.

And as with clans and towns, a strong discourse of reproductive difference coexists with a less often voiced egalitarian one. According to Rawya (aged 21), from Dayr Hanna (who is Christian), "The number of children people have has nothing to do with religion. In Syria there are more religious people than here and yet they have family planning commercials on TV. Today there's nothing similar between people, each person goes according to his own opinion." Khaldiyyi, who is Muslim, also believed that there were no differences and in the importance of the interweaving and similarity of the religions:

> As a child, our house in Nazareth was between the churches. Ever since I was a child, there was no difference between Muslims and Christians. When my son nearly drowned in Tiberias, I made a vow that if he survived I would take him to the church, and indeed he did get better and I took him to the church and Abu Ibrahim [the priest] rang the bells for him. But my father-in-law is traditional, he would object if he had the chance. We are the same. Imm Nayif [who is Christian] and I are the same age and I had nine and she had nine. My children have two or three children each and so do hers. I lived in Haifa for fifteen years and I know the communities very well. I feel there is no difference.

Moreover, the Muslim-Christian-Druze distinction is not entirely stable—conversions do occur, although they are rare. Some of the fear of "mixing" emanates from the fear of the breakdown of these boundaries. Rabi', who is Druze, told me: "In Sajur there are only Druze, but if you go to Rami, it's terrible, there's so much mixing. You can't tell the Druze girl from the Christian girl. The same dress, the same behavior. You pass by a group of girls now and you don't know what they are. One of the Christian leaders there said he wants to make all the Christian girls wear crosses so you can tell them apart."

To my mind, the subtext here is the fear of a man's falling for a woman of the "wrong" religion. There are several cases of such intermarriage. Rawda Ballan, a sister of a friend of mine who is Christian, married a fellow college student who is Muslim. Their families objected initially, but eventually the families reconciled and the relations are now more or less normalized. Interestingly, the marriage of Arab men, mostly Muslim, to Christian foreigners is rarely considered a problem in the religious sense, and is much more common than Muslim-Christian marriages within the Palestinian community. Perhaps the foreignness and modernity of the brides remove them from the realm of local sectarian competition.

A strong discourse that orders groups within Palestinian society by measures of reproductive modernity places Christians over Muslims and Druze, learned believers over ignorant superstitious masses, "not too religious" people over "too religious" people. If occasionally the order is reversed in moments of antimodernization zeal, the measure of reproductivity continues to hold. Changing attitudes toward religion, shifting relations between different denominations and newly acquired "authentic" born-again religions are all negotiated today through reproductive hierarchy.

ARAB AND JEW

As might be expected, the use of reproductive stereotypes in the Galilee extends to the construction of concepts of the local and the foreign, the Arab and the Jewish, the inside and the outside. The reproductive modernity and primitiveness that are constantly deployed to order city, village, Bedouin, clan, and religion can be seen also in the delineation of Arab and Jew, but with a difference. The exclusionary nature of Israel, as a Jewish state, has weakened Palestinians' attraction to a modernist discourse that places modern Jews over backward Palestinians, thus strengthening the antimodernization narrative in this instance.

Overall, the language of modernization theory and population studies about the Third World has largely been taken up by people within that world. In the case of city, village, Bedouin, clan, and religion, the discourse that sorts people as reproductively modern or primitive is unmistakably dominant in the Galilee. This pro-small-family discourse largely accepts the superiority of the modern over the primitive, controlled reproduction over uncontrolled reproduction, the urban over the rural, the Christian over the Muslim, and so on. A counter-discourse of antimodernization nationalism and romanticized traditionalism does exist, but is marginal and muted. Only occasionally do Galileans express the pro-big-family view, which accepts the categories and measures of modernization but simply reverses their order to make the modern, the urban, the Christian inferior. This is not exactly the case, however, with the categories of Jew and Arab. Here expressions of alienation and disaffection are more pronounced. This antimodernization narrative is partly an expression of modernism's *failure* to fulfill its promises and to assimilate everyone into its fold. This failure is even more pronounced when it comes to the modernist discourse on Arabs versus Jews.

Many Palestinians have accepted and incorporated the designations of West as superior to East and Jew as superior to Arab, but many others have reversed them. The attraction of this particular modernist discourse is weakened by Zionism, which clearly distances and repels Palestinians. A Palestinian can aspire to be more modern, urbane, secular, even Western, but the racialized discourse of nationalism does not generally allow him or her to aspire to be Jewish.

If even the poorest person can still have the local equivalent of the American dream, many Palestinians find it difficult to have an Israeli dream. While modernization has a homogenizing appeal, Israeli nationalism does not. Zionism has never carried the promise for Palestinians of "integration as a reward for acculturation" (Khazoom 1999: 1).[33] The overwhelming and blatant discriminatory practices of both state and individuals against Palestinians make it hard for them to imagine, much less to achieve, the assimilation of their identity.[34] Even when they do try to become assimilated, they are often rejected, as in the case of a Palestinian man who changed his name to a Jewish version (from Yihya Rahim to Yihi'el Rihamim) to disguise his background, but his "real" identity was quickly discovered by his Jewish employers, and they fired him (*Kul ul-'Arab,* June 14, 1995). Thus the antimodernization discourse is more dominant in the construction of Jew and Arab than it is in the other social categories.

CREATION OF ARAB AND JEW

The Jewish–Arab conflict is not a "natural" ancient animosity but a product of recent history. Both Israeli and Palestinian nationalisms, like many others, are relatively recent creations. In fact, the very separation

33. This is unlike, say, Zionism's combined message to Mizrahim: that they are "not Western and culturally advanced, but that the Ashkenazim would teach them how to become so"—that is, the powerful lure of a transformation option (Khazoom 1999: 30). Mizrahim are in the end allowed to be Israelis, albeit "Israelis with a problem" (Motzafi-Haller 2001: 700).

34. Smadar Lavie suggests that this self/other dualism has allowed Palestinians to "mend some seams in the ruins of their culture" while Arab Jews are unable to do so because "the ambivalence immanent in their multiple subjectivities interferes with their attempt to establish their own linear narrative of oppression vis-à-vis the state" (1992: 90).

of Arabs and Jews into two distinct groups is a modern project, initiated early in this century by European Zionists, who essentialized Jewish identity as properly Western. Through its history of "saving" the Oriental Jews from the grips of their "natural Arab enemies," [35] often against their will, and its attempt to civilize them as proper Jews through the erasure of their Orientalness, Zionism created a rigid duality: "The Mizrahi Jew was prodded to choose between anti-Zionist 'Arabness' and a pro-Zionist 'Jewishness.' For the first time in the history of Oriental Jews, Arabness and Jewishness were posed as antonyms" (Shohat 1988: 35).[36] Israel "was based on a complete overhauling of the ethnic identities of the population over whom it was to have jurisdiction," both European and other (Massad 1996: 54). In addition, the formation of Arab nationalist collectivities is linked to the removal of the Arab Jewish communities from their midst and the exclusionary (non-Jewish) bases on which they were largely ultimately consolidated (Behar 1997: 69). Although I do not care to compare and generalize about the degrees of religious chauvinism of the various strands of Zionism and Arab nationalisms, it is safe to say that most build upon a Jewish-Arab separation.[37]

According to Ella Shohat, an Arab Jew herself, it is important to dispel a Zionist historiography that consists of "a morbidly selective 'tracing the dots' from pogrom to pogrom" (1992: 27). In doing so it is also important not to romanticize the history of relations between Jews and other communities in the Middle East. Tensions, conflicts, and violence based on familial, regional, or religious politics are hardly unknown to the area. But conflict based on nationality, that Jews are not Arabs and Arabs are not Jews, is a modern phenomenon and one that has developed in much more violent, larger, and more consequential ways.

The separation of Arab from Jew involved the Ashkenazi Zionists' arrogant belief in their "qualitative and cultural superiority to the Palestinian Arab people and the Arab Islamic community, including those

35. Ella Shohat writes: "This selective reading of Jewish history hijacks the Jews of Islam from their Judeo-Islamic history and culture and subordinates their experience to that of the Ashkenazi-European shtetl, presented as a 'universal' Jewish experience. . . . The master narrative of universal Jewish victimization has been crucial for the Israeli 'ingathering' of peoples from such diverse geographies, languages, cultures and histories, as well as for the claim that the Jewish nation faces a common historical enemy in Muslim Arabs" (1992: 27–28).

36. Amitav Ghosh argues that, "the idea that individuals owe loyalty to a single political entity is relatively recent, and probably connected with the comparably recent birth of the nation-state" (New Yorker, June 23, 1997, 116).

37. As Shiko Behar points out, both Zionists and anti-Zionists accept the premise that Arabs and Jews are two separate groups (1997: 68).

Jews who came from Arab countries. Even the 'progressives' who oppose racism can be characterized by their paternalistic attitude towards
the inhabitants of the area" (Giladi 1990: 3). The Ashkenazi establishment saw Arab Jews as savages, primitives, despotic, and backward,
sometimes genetically inferior, brought to Israel as the Africans were
brought to the United States, to be civilized.[38] Their Middle Easternness
was perceived as threatening to drag Israel into unnatural Orientalism
(Shohat 1988: 31–32). Ben-Gurion, for example, said, "We do not want
Israelis to become Arabs. We are in duty bound to fight against the spirit
of the Levant, which corrupts individuals and societies, and preserve the
authentic Jewish values as they crystallized in the Diaspora" (quoted
in ibid.).

Amitav Ghosh's *In an Antique Land* highlights the beginnings of the
modern project of separating Jew from Arab. Ghosh studied the documents of the *geniza* (storage chamber) of a synagogue in Cairo, which
were written in Judeo Arabic, "a colloquial dialect of medieval Arabic,
written in the Hebrew script," and a language that is itself a hybrid
(1992: 101). By excavating the rich stories of Cairo and its *genizas,* he
attempts to inscribe an interlaced past that did not rigidify "many of
those boundaries that are today thought to mark social, religious and
geographical divisions" (278). While his reconstruction of this interlaced past may be overly romantic, it helps undermine assumptions of
the naturalness of contemporary divisions.

By 1898 the *geniza* that was the source of this other history was emptied of its documents by Orientalist scholars and mostly transferred to
libraries and collections in Europe. Ironically, these documents "went to
countries which would have long destroyed the Geniza had it been a part
of their own history." In Egypt the dispersal went unnoticed and the
documents' removal "only confirmed a particular vision of the past." In

---

38. Ironically, the Ashkenazi attitude toward the so-called Oriental sects strongly
echoes the racist European view of the Jews. Moreover, Zionism's

> commitment to West European culture . . . denies the actual origins of most European
> Jews. The culture of the rural, poor, and squalid shtetls of Eastern Europe is replaced
> subtextually in Zionist discourse by the cosmopolitan cultures of Berlin and Paris from
> where relatively few Jews originated. It was by assuming a European "gentile" or as-
> similated identity that Zionism could market its colonial endeavor as one of spreading
> European Jewish identity in ways never thought possible. Views that used to be at-
> tributed to assimilated German Jews about East European Jews and their "backward"
> culture were now used against "Europe's others" in general, whether Jewish or gentile.
> (Massad 1996: 55).

A similar point is made in Lavie 1992: 87.

the silent emptying of the Cairo synagogue, Egypt, "which had sustained the Geniza for almost a millennium . . . was left with no trace of its riches: not a single scrap or shred of paper to remind her of that aspect of her past. It was as though the borders that were to divide Palestine several decades later had already been drawn, through time rather than territory, to allocate a choice of Histories" (ibid.: 95).

Like the *geniza,* an emblem of a rewritten past stands in the center of my hometown; a small shrine to a holy man named Hananya. Imm 'Abid and other old people recall a time when they used to bring sick babies, hopes, illnesses, and woes to the shrine: "We didn't know that Hananya was Jewish. How would we know? We just respected him as a holy man." Imm 'Abid and her contemporaries, not unlike the characters Ghosh finds in the *geniza* documents, lived in a world where today's boundaries did not yet hold such sway over the imagination. Having reclaimed the shrine as exclusively theirs, religious Jews today occasionally visit the site in large tourist buses that have difficulty navigating the narrow streets of 'Arrabi, to which they would otherwise never go. And the people of 'Arrabi have more or less accepted this gating off. According to Imm 'Abid, local people stopped going to the shrine because "the sheikh told them it was forbidden to go—Muslims mustn't worship graves. But today people don't even believe in God anymore, not to mention in the power of Hananya. They don't have time for this anymore. . . . Those days are gone."

The new divisions not only came to separate Arab and Jew but also erased any *memories* of hybridity. A new history of Arabs and Jews as bounded and separate was created within the Zionist project and partly accepted by both sides of the new Jewish/Arab divide. Yet this project of constructing separate identities has not been without weaknesses. As Shohat points out, historically certain Arabs and Jews have tried to distinguish between Jews and Zionists, so that the struggle is conceived of as between Zionists and anti-Zionists rather than between Jews and Arabs. This resistance to a simple Arab/Jewish divide, however, did not hold up—"The situation led the Palestinian Arabs, meanwhile, to see all Jews as at least potential Zionists. With the pressure of waves of Ashkenazi-Zionist immigration and the swelling power of its institutions, the Jewish/Zionist distinction was becoming more and more precarious, much to the advantage of European Zionism" (Shohat 1988: 35). Given that Zionism equates religion with nationality, it is not surprising that "many Palestinians call their oppressors 'Jews,' a name their oppressors chose for themselves and on whose basis they justify their oppression of the Palestinians" (Massad 2000: 58). Moreover, the "cultural massacre" that occurred through the Ashkenazi Zionist assault on Oriental Jewish culture has partially "wiped out millennia of rooted Oriental [Jewish] civilization" (Shohat 1988: 47), and Arab-Jewish history has been systematically denied by all sides (Behar 1997: 68), leading many Mizrahim to be "subordinated to the doctrine of European Zionism" (Chetrit 1997: 52).

The Jewish/Arab divide is challenged at some moments and emphasized at others. Some Arab Jews have insisted on their Arabness and linked their oppression to that of other Arabs; many non-Jewish Palestinians attempt to distinguish between Zionists and Jews, and do not predicate their struggle on racism or religious hostility but see it as an anticolonial project. There are exceptions, of course: the Palestinian Nationalist Charter states that "Jewish citizens who are of Palestinian origin are considered Palestinian if they wish to live peacefully in Palestine" (Hourani 1980: 225). In most parties' formal rhetoric, however, "the Zionist enemy" is invoked rather than "the Jewish enemy" (see, for example, sec. 19 of the Palestinian Nationalist Charter in Hourani 1980: 227; Swedenburg 1995: 146–147). Moreover, Palestinians' deep distrust of the Arab countries and of their perceived self-interested betrayals of the Palestinian people further disrupts a simple Jewish/Arab divide.

Palestinians living in Israel regularly challenge this divide. Their struggles have been to a large degree formulated not as "national independence" but as a quest for equality and civil rights, an effort not to establish their own separate state but to transform an existing state into one that is inclusive of them. Still these same Palestinians often advocate a separate state for Palestinians in the West Bank and Gaza Strip. The oldest parliamentary party that represents this goal, the Jabha (the Democratic Front for Peace and Equality), is a Communist-led Jewish Arab party. In its equality program, one of the main demands is for "a law that prevents any procedure and order in a government or private organization that includes nationalist discrimination in any area, political, economic, social, or cultural" (Tuma 1982: 314–315). At the same time, it advocates a two-state solution. Knesset member 'Azmi Bishara and his party clearly insist that their goal is to transform Israel into a state of all its citizens rather than a state for Jews (or a state for Arabs). At the same time, however, Bshara advocates Palestinian cultural autonomy in the Galilee.

Thus Palestinians in the Galilee bypass the insistence on the separation of Arabs and Jews at one level. But at another level and in different
contexts, this divide is very much present, and many Palestinians have
accepted the superiority (or inferiority) of the Jews as essentially foreign
or European. The context that concerns me here is that of reproduction.

REPRODUCING ARABS AND JEWS

According to the modernization paradigm, Jews are more advanced
than the Arabs in the area of reproduction. And the category of Jews in
general is often merged with foreigners or Westerners, as it is within
dominant Ashkenazi Zionism. One Palestinian columnist suggests this
merger in his term "American-Israeli" ('Ittihad, Aug. 4, 1995). Buthaina
believes that "foreigners don't reproduce like us. Their life isn't even related to our life here. There's a big difference between Jews and us because they have only one or two children, even if they're girls. They may
even have just one girl. They don't discriminate against girls. They love
to live, not like us. And they're content with a few." In Rawya's opinion,
the very reason for marriage in Jewish society is different: "The Jewish
woman doesn't marry for reproduction and children. She wants to continue working. They love life more than us. They like to rest more, to go
on trips, and spend more money than Arabs." Shihnaz also said that
"foreigners [and she included Jews in this category] like to organize their
homes and everything in it, the number of their children so each child
will have a room, and when they go on trips they'll all fit comfortably in
the car. Here we move and put [minqīm u minḥuṭ] and we build and we
don't care." Her tone said it was all right not to care.

Palestinians who live in close proximity to Jews, as in mixed cities,
are supposedly affected by Jewish culture and are often considered more
modern than other Palestinians. But even those who live in villages keep
in mind the mixed context of their lives. Samah (aged 28), who lives
in the village of Jish but who grew up in Kuwait, said: "We're living
among Jews. I can't name my son after his grandfather Abdulla—it will
affect his life. What, do people go backward or forward? What is this
'Abdulla'? If it were a nice name, why not, something light and delicate." In naming her children (Phillippe, Rabiʿ, and Manar), Samah tried
to accommodate herself to modern requirements; rather than old Arabic names she chose modern and foreign ones, lighter on the Western
tongue.

Yet the putative differences between Arab and Jewish reproduction do get a mixed review. The modernist paradigm that applauds the small families of Jews and their "enjoyment of life" is strong, but so is the anti-modernist paradigm. Many people believed that part of the reason for these differences was the development of individualism in Jewish society. Some saw it as good; others condemned it. Taghrid said: "Jews have fewer children than Arabs, as the different growth rates testify. Our conviction, upbringing, habituation, and our holding on to society make us have more children—each one wants to increase his family. Jews, on the other hand, have personal independence. In some ways it's good and in some ways it isn't." Similarly, at a conference on "pregnancy termination" at the Israeli Family Planning Association, Dr. Elena Zeigler presented data on "the clear norms that Israeli women have for how to create a family," and stated that the principal reason for seeking an abortion—given 25 percent of the time—is "desire for independence." A Palestinian nurse sitting next to me commented: "Palestinian women would never say that." When I asked her, she said she wasn't sure if she thought that was good or not.

As with the other categories of difference, the counter-discourse asserts that Arabs are better for having more children, in this case the romantic discourse is more pronounced, perhaps because assimilation into Zionism is even more difficult than assimilation into consumerist or modernist culture. According to Ghadir from 'Ilabun, "Jews don't have very many children, only one or two, because mothers aren't prepared to sacrifice for their children, and most of the Jewish women work." Interestingly, Ghadir had only one brother and her mother worked. She herself had only one child, was planning on one or two more, and was looking for a job in the local school. Samah and Haitham, on the other hand, said they were aiming for six children and already have three. Samah from Jish—the same Samah who didn't want to name her first-born after his grandfather because "we're living among Jews," told me: "Our parents used to have large families to protect themselves. We do it for a different reason, for emotional reasons: we love children. I don't understand how these young people can dislike having lots of children. Do they have no heart? Maybe they've become like foreigners, totally self-absorbed [binshighlū bḥālhin]."

'Azizi (aged 64), from Kufur Minda, knew from her visits to her children in California that "there is no society in America. My son's neighbor in California is an old divorced woman and she has a different boyfriend living with her each time I visit, and it's totally normal."

'Azizi's daughter said, "That's the way their society is. Is it better that she remain a lonely widow?" 'Azizi insisted: "What are we, cows or goats? We still care about respect and marriage. I tell my son Wajih [who lives in California and has no children] that he can't continue to live like the foreigners, even if he is living among them. I tell him it's better to go out and buy a child than have no children at all." If Jewish and foreign men don't discriminate between girls and boys and don't burden their wives with many pregnancies, they do, in 'Azizi's opinion, go to ridiculous lengths in spoiling their women: "I heard of one English guy who didn't want his wife to be tortured with pregnancy, so he got a surrogate mother for his child, but when the baby was born, she refused to give it up."

In the understanding of yet other Palestinians, Jews and Arabs are al-most equal in their reproductive modernity—either because Arabs have managed to catch up or because some elements in Jewish society have held back Jewish progress. Here the conflation of Jews and foreigners is disrupted by a not uncommon, more nuanced view of Jewish society, which is seen as consisting of foreigners/Europeans, Eastern Jews, and religious Jews. Eastern Jews in particular are considered to be "like us and worse." Thus the divide that is highlighted is that between East and West rather than the one between Arab and Jew. According to the nurse Khadiji:

> There's a difference between Jews and Arabs, but within the Jewish community there's a big difference between religious and secular Jews. So there is a religious component—the religious Jews are more like the Arabs. Nonreligious Jews have a higher level of education. Most of them came from Europe, where there's a different level of civ-ilization. The Eastern Jews are also like the Arabs. I also think that the Ministry of Health didn't work enough in our sector—there was a lot of neglect.

Not only do many Palestinians join in the secular Jews' ridicule of reli-gious Jews' overreproduction, some self-proclaimed modern Arabs use the slur shakhshakhim, a slang term that ridicules Arab Jews for their Arabness. It was probably coined by a European Jewish comedian. How a dark-skinned Middle Eastern "fecund" Palestinian can ridicule these traits in an Arab Jew is one of the wonders of modernization and its powerful lure.

Yet at other moments, Palestinians see solidarity with Arab Jews. An article asks, "Were the Children of Palestine Kidnapped? A Revisiting of the Children of Yemen" (Fasl ul-Maqal, Sept. 24, 1997). Referring to the disappearance of Yemenite Jewish babies in the 1950s, whom many Yemenites believe were kidnapped and given to childless European Jewish parents to adopt, the author suggests that something similar may have happened to Palestinian children who went missing during the 1948 war. Here Palestinians and Yemenite Jews are united in their subjugation to the Ashkenazi Jewish establishment through their lost children.

Despite the presence of a pronounced antimodernization discourse, a modernization paradigm is still salient, testifying to the pull of the modern despite the push of Zionism. With the increasing modernization of Palestinian society and its integration into a global economy of consumption and desire, the aspiration to become like the Western Jews, sometimes bordering on self-hatred, is evident, even as it is challenged by Jewish and Palestinian nationalism and romanticism. Watching my cousins play with Rambo action figures and plastic guns, I often wonder on which "side" they see themselves playing in their world of pretend. My cousin Ashraf, who was 15 at the time, told me his favorite actor was Jean-Claude Van Damme. When I said I thought his films were racist, and that Arabs were always the terrorist bad guys, Ashraf said, "That's OK. I hate them too." Rana, another cousin of mine (aged 11), once told me and her aunts that she wanted to be in the army. One of her aunts said jokingly that she could do whatever she wanted in the Palestinian army, but "we'll shoot you if you join the Israeli army." I said I wasn't sure how many women were in the "Palestinian army" in the newly autonomous areas.

Rana said: "Yes, I saw one in Haifa."

Me: "You mean in the Israeli army?"

Rana: "Yes, she had blue eyes and long blond hair tied back and she was wearing an army suit and carrying a gun—she looked amazing [manzarha bijannin]."

CONCLUSION

Jane and Peter Schneider found that members of the upper and middle classes in Sicily began to decrease their family size before the lower classes did, and the result was "a growing tendency to look askance at 'reproductive others.'" The poor were seen as lacking in rationality and morality and dangerous in their sexual amplitude, as evidenced by their large families. These divergent patterns of family formation "nourished classist notions of reproductive stigma whose ideological significance endured for decades to come." Such negative evaluations of "other people's children" became "a tenacious new anchor for inequality" (1995:10).

Something remarkably similar has been going on in the Galilee. Divergent strategies of family formation have set the stage for a parallel process. As I have argued, the reproductive measure is a subjugated discourse that has resulted from a particular nexus of state policy, economic development, medicalization, and local dynamics. Although perhaps not unique to Palestinians in the Galilee, the emergence of this modernist reproductive measure is certainly striking in this case.

Population and modernization discourses globally have tended to center on the evolution from traditionally high and developmentally draining fertility to modern low and developmentally stimulating fertility (Greenhalgh 1996). For Palestinians under Israeli rule this binary opposition has entered daily life and shaped their negotiations of reproductive decisions. They now measure their own success and advancement by the same standards used by powerful groups in the state, in the economy, and in the medical establishment.

It is not surprising that Palestinian options for empowerment and advancement in the Galilee largely follow lines of power that they are subject to and at the same time try to resist. But as Sherry Ortner writes, we must recognize that resisters "have their own politics." Moreover, "there is never a single, unitary, subordinate, if only in the simple sense that subaltern groups are internally divided" (1995: 175, 177).

That this reproductive measure is mobilized both as an Israeli tool of subordination and redeployed in terms of anticolonial struggle does not mean that Palestinian discourses are simply reducible to a repetition of Israeli canonical terms, nor does "this truth of decolonization's 'impurity'" constitute grounds for the dismissal of its counter-discourses (Stein 1996: 117). Rather, it provides grounds for a better understanding of these efforts to undo marginalization, including their limitations.

Reproductive difference is not hegemonic or straightforward in the Galilee. The definitions and requirements of modernity in reproduction are shifting. The measures are flexible; there is no one-to-one correlation between, for instance, how many children a woman has and how modern she is perceived to be. In addition, reproductive practices are not the only measures of hierarchy used, nor is reproductive difference the only dynamic involved in reproductive decision making. As an 8-year-old cousin powerfully reminded me when he heard me asking why his mother wanted to have a certain number of children: "My mother had me because she wanted to love me." It is important to note that discourses of reproductive difference tell us more about the speakers' sense of stigma than about their "others" and their practices.

Moreover, if Palestinians frequently rank one another according to a modern/traditional reproductive binary, this does not mean that even people who strongly subscribe to this binary are incapable of making alternative, nondualistic representations. They often do. Palestinians can and do distance themselves from both the modernist and antimodernist versions of this difference—as my critical analysis here does. But the reproductive measure is a powerful and compelling discourse, one in which I too got caught up, sometimes constructing myself as a disciplined modern future mother even while I was critical of it. What is clear is that these deployments of reproductive stereotypes "are implicated in a wider set of relations of power" (Stoler 1991: 55). That people are playful, maneuvering, and creative should not be understood as negating this power structure.

In complex ways, discourses on reproduction structure a variety of social conceptions: the urban, the rural, the Bedouin, clan, religion. People are ranked according to these categories, which are articulated in terms of reproduction. A group of ideas, such as those about family respectability, the value of partnership in marriage, rural mentality, clan favoritism, degree of religiosity, boundaries of the nation, and family planning have coalesced (Schneider and Schneider 1995: 191). These discursive practices are flexible: "though one could reconstruct the meanings which are frequently attached to key terms—'modernity' is democracy, universalism, capitalism, nuclear family, etc., while 'tradition' is gerontocracy, particularism, communality, extended family— these terms could be extended to accommodate almost every possible contrast" (Eyal 1996: 400). The modern/backward reproductive opposition draws into its vortex an incredible array of social life and "nearly every possible social and personal characteristic becomes associated with one side of the discourses' dichotomy" (Khazoom 1999: 8).

However, this modern reproductive discursive regime does not define altogether stable structures. It vacillates between the debased primitive and the noble traditionalist, between modern enlightenment and modern poverty and anomie. But despite variations, oscillations, and exceptions, it can be argued that this "regime" has something of "a coherence of effects" (Mohanty 1995: 259). While it is not hegemonic, it has clearly come inside our homes.

FOUR

Modernizing the Body

Modernization is perceived as having altered the state of gender and the body. In fact, these changes are often perceived and constructed as the primary features of modernization. The increasing medicalization of the body, its commodification, and its penetration by "science" has led to new conceptualizations of reproduction and sexuality. Modernization of the body in the Galilee has involved a new "training" of sexuality through forms of consumption, sex education, and the medical control of reproduction. These transformations are enthusiastically praised and pursued at moments and criticized and shunned at others. Palestinians in the Galilee negotiate modernity as potentially producing positive effects on the body: improved beauty, health, fertility, and sexual awareness. But they also perceive negative effects: increased vanity, artificiality, medical invasiveness, and sexual danger.

NEW VANITY FOR THE NEW FAMILY

As with the "fundamental requirements of life" explored in Chapter 2, the fundamental requirements of the body have been changed by processes of commodification and medicalization. In this context, bodies, especially women's bodies, have been modernized. They are perceived, lived in, presented, and experienced in significantly altered ways. New knowledge, technologies, products, and desires have been introduced, shaping new bodies. Haniyyi, a close friend of mine from Kabul (a village in the Galilee), put it this way: "All our knowledge about bodies has changed—on the inside and on the outside. From the inside, now they know about biology, how everything works. From the outside, people have become more vain and care about their bodies more." Haniyyi, for one, cares for her body in relatively new ways:

> The first time I got pregnant, I was so afraid of gaining weight. And in fact I did get very fat. Wow, you won't believe how you hate your body, it's terrible. But I was very happy when I quickly lost weight while breast-feeding. The only problem I have now is that my breasts sag because they grew and grew each time I was pregnant and then they shrank again. If I hate looking at them in the mirror, then what about my husband? They're really causing me agony. I'm very happy with my weight now [54 kilos, or 119 pounds] but I have a problem with my stomach and breasts. I have a Cindy Crawford video and I do a lot of exercises. I'm also going to buy small weights to help my chest.

Not that Palestinians did not care for their bodies before the introduction of these new technologies and desires, but they cared for them in different ways. They construct new bodily care as a significant innovation. As suggested in Chapter 2, a Cindy Crawford standard of beauty is increasingly dominant, as are new methods of beautification, such as dieting and aerobic exercise.

Whether through magazines, door-to-door Avon ladies, consultants at pharmacies, TV, music videos, packaging, advertising, or promotions both locally produced and multinational, the modern body is a target of constant attempts at commodification and modification. In recent years there has been a boom in cosmetic products, plastic surgery, weight-loss centers, and dermatologists in Israel as a whole, and Palestinians were not excluded as potential consumers. Holders of debit cards—often of the middle and upper classes—receive catalogues by mail full of beauty aids, weight-loss pills, skin-lightening creams, and the like (see Figure 13). Many women have invested a great deal in these fads, even when they can barely afford them. Sawsan, a secretary friend of mine, bought a home electrolysis kit, a pair of rubber-insulated, sweat-inducing pants for weight loss, and a magnifying mirror with built-in light within the space of three months. After trying many diets without achieving her ideal body image, she saved up for several years and secretly had liposuction (see Figure 14).

Figure 13. Catalogues mailed to debit card holders feature ads for beauty and weight-loss products, including insulated rubber pants that will help you lose weight "effortlessly" (upper right).

Figure 14.   An advertisement for the nose jobs and liposuction available at the Doctor Center Plastic Surgery Center in Tel Aviv asks readers of an Arabic newspaper: "Are you looking for beauty and perfection?"

In this consumerist system, commodified standards of beauty are constantly changing: ever newer styles of makeup, haircuts, and clothing require continuous consumption. Thinness, however, seems to be a rather stable modern requirement. This modern ideal of beauty starkly contrasts with Palestinian ideals of only a couple of decades ago. When I met Sunbul, the lab technician from Kufur Yasif who married into "backward" Shfa 'Amir, she had had her stomach surgically stapled for two months and lost a quarter of her body weight. She could only drink fluids, and was planning to continue this drastic diet for several more months, until she returned to her prechildbirth weight. She reflected: "Before, people used to like fat women; they'd say, 'She's beautiful, she's all wrapped around [malfufi laf].' Today it's the opposite: they like women whose bones are sticking out." One of my girlfriends had an eating disorder in high school, although it was not identified as such by herself or our group of friends. She told a few of us how she would drink a glass of water with a high concentration of salt in it to make herself throw up after she had had a large meal. The "tyranny of slenderness" has been making inroads into the Galilee (Chernin 1981). Indeed, it has been argued that hyperthin bodies and hyperconsumption are "very much linked in advanced capitalist economies that depend upon commodity excess." As in other globalized locations around the world, consumption in the Galilee is increasingly paired with "the achievement of femininity and the appearance of an appropriately gendered body" (Urla and Swedlund 1995: 298, 281), even as the roles assigned to femininity vary from place to place.

Not everyone has been equally affected by the modernization of the body. For one thing, one's income level determines one's access to the long accumulating and mutating list of required accoutrements. Nuhad (aged 31) said she wished she could "take care of myself like the young girls do—especially my complexion—but I don't have the money or the time. Do you know how much those creams cost?" Nuhad has the desire for modern body consumption but not the purchasing power or leisure time to attain it.

Badriyyi, who was in her late 80s, had not caught on to this change when she told me that "women these days don't like to breast-feed. They're so silly, they're afraid of losing weight." Her daughter-in-law corrected her: "No, that's not why, they actually look for thinness today." But Badriyyi just dismissed her. The bombardment of images of skinny women had not reached her; perhaps because she was illiterate, was in poor health, and was losing her eyesight, she did not go to the mall, read magazines, or watch as much TV as her daughter-in-law did. One almost needs to be literally blind to elude the new inscription processes of body requirements.

I must admit to having what Mary Beth Mills describes as a "lingering sense that commodity consumption by working-class actors . . . entails a kind of complicity in their exploitation . . . the pursuit of commodities as markers of symbolic value or social status appears as a particularly insidious form of false consciousness in the face of capitalist hegemony." (I have this sense despite my own relatively privileged participation in these patterns of consumption and care.) However, I could not ignore consumption in my work—as many studies of non-Western societies that prefer to portray an exotic and isolated simplicity do—if only because it is ubiquitous among Palestinians in the Galilee and has involved striking transformations in a relatively short time. Moreover, "consumption practices are constitutive of [people's] sense of themselves as modern . . . commodities serve as important vehicles for the construction and contestation of identity" (1997: 40, 54). Consumption in the Galilee has not meant simple or overdetermined changes in the direction of Westernization or homogenization, but has resulted in specific new local modernities. Although Cindy Crawford has increasingly become a popular embodied ideal, this ideal has specific and local meanings in 'Arrabi and Sakhnin, different from, say, those near my house in lower Manhattan.[1]

Modern women in the Galilee are associated with vanity (*'ayāqa*) about their bodies, especially in connection with reproduction. As both Haniyyi and Sunbul highlight, many women today consider having children a strain on the beauty of their bodies. Recall that Haniyyi's concern was for how her husband felt about her postchildbirth sagging breasts, and that Sunbul had stapled her stomach to return to her prechildbirth weight. But rather than reflecting a self-centered move away from family, this concern about reproduction and its strain on women's beauty and bodies is thoroughly situated within a concern about the family in a new form, the modern family. Although vanity for the sake of the modern family was not necessarily part of the intended lure of the Revlon Consumer Products Corporation, it certainly does not harm its sales, either. Commodified body care in the Galilee becomes significant in changing local family and gender ideals.

1. What this Cindy Crawford ideal means in lower Manhattan is also shifting and complicated, but is specific to the social dynamics of that location.

Samah (aged 28), who had three boys and lived in Jish, considered her vanity essential to sustaining her marriage and family:

> It's true that I breast-fed my children for only a few weeks. My husband doesn't like breast-feeding. He's really disgusted by it; a woman always smells sour, especially in winter with heavy clothing—you need to change clothes a lot. I used Materna [baby formula; see Figure 15] and the children were plump and healthy. Arab women don't take care of themselves, and so the men go around and look outside at young girls. I'm very afraid of this. The sex side is very important for the man. Here, the village women get fat and let their hair go wild and gray and they neglect themselves. They don't care where the man goes, and they don't discuss it with him. The woman's appearance is very, very important to the man. She should have seduction for her husband. She shouldn't let her body hair grow out. There is this woman, my neighbor, whose husband told her to lose some weight and she got upset. But in my opinion it's good he told her, this can create problems in the future.

Samah grew up in Kuwait. Her father had fled Palestine in 1948, but he wanted all of his daughters to marry back in his still-existing village in the Galilee. When she was 20, through the intervention of the Catholic Church (she is Christian), she was allowed to visit her relatives in northern Israel, and wound up getting married and staying for good. She emphasizes that her marriage is based on mutual understanding between herself and her husband. "When I chose a husband," she said, "I didn't look at money or houses. Maybe other girls who were deprived when they were young look for such things in a husband. I was looking for something else, for someone I could understand and get along with. We go on trips, I wear whatever I want, I go wherever I want—and Haitham doesn't listen to his parents. He listens to me." Although Samah knew Haitham for only two weeks before she accepted his proposal of marriage, she described her choice to me and our mutual friends as based on their modern, companionate relationship as a couple, independent of the extended family and the older generation. Samah characterizes many of her disagreements with her in-laws as a clash between modernity and tradition. "For example, if I wear short shorts, my mother-in-law tries to interfere. But Haitham doesn't listen to her. I chose my children's names, too, but I never decided anything on my own, I always make the decision with my husband."

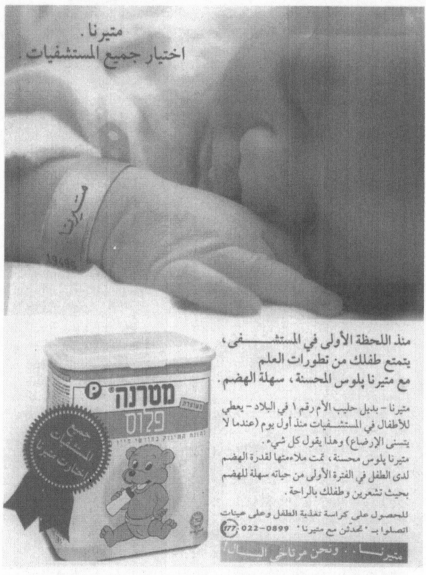

Figure 15. Advertisements for infant formula are distributed at the Ministry of Health's maternal and child health centers. This one reads: "Materna Baby Formula, the choice of all hospitals. From the first moment your child will enjoy the advances of science with improved Materna Plus."

Thus in Samah's view, her care for her body is linked to the maintenance of her companionate marriage. "Arab" and "village" women neglect their bodies, thus failing to keep their husbands' interest and undermining the monogamous companionate relationship. Modern women, on the other hand, work hard to keep up their appearance and remain attractive to their husbands. Indeed, Samah appeared very attractive to me, dressed in the latest local (yet not so local) fashions even when she was doing housework and not expecting guests. Like many women, she invoked a binary of primitive-neglected and modern-attentive bodies. She saw her modern attention to her body as being for the sake of her modern marriage and modern family.

Wardi (aged 46), a seamstress and aspiring designer who lives not far from Samah's village, also thought modern women were vain but was critical of them because, unlike Samah, she felt their vanity was not for the sake of the family. She told me she knew many young women who made important life decisions, such as whether to have more children, on the basis not of family interests but of what Wardi considered to be materialistic and selfish considerations, such as their weight and figure: "When I asked this one woman if she was ready to have a child, she said, 'Leave me alone, I don't want my body to change.' People prefer material things over children these days." Yet her criticism of vain modern bodies was complicated by what she quickly added: "In my case, after breast-feeding, my body always goes back to normal without a diet or anything."

Over and over I heard the concern that repeated pregnancy, child-bearing, and breast-feeding can take a toll on a woman's body. But this anxiety is usually construed not as antifamily, as Wardi projected, but rather as compatible with the modern family and in fact necessary for it. The ideal family is both couple-centered and *small*: it requires a woman to remain attractive to sustain the companionate marital relationship, and it makes attractiveness easier to retain because it requires fewer children. Hasna, Badriyyi's daughter-in-law, told me:

> Today life is different. Before, people didn't care how they dressed; they were only worried about finding something to eat. Now everybody is concerned with stylishness and elegance, diet and regimens. . . .
>
> After I had children, my breasts really shrank and sagged, and I gained some weight. I don't want to have too many more children for just that reason. Now I'm on a diet because I want to get pregnant again. After I have a baby it's very hard for me to get my weight back down. And your stomach bulges, your skin cracks with stretch

marks. My husband notices these things. Of course, this isn't the main factor in deciding to have more children. It's not a real reason. You think about it, but it's not a determining factor.

Vanity is thus a sign of modernity and class and is associated with, if not the main cause of, having fewer children.

In contrast to Hasna's evaluation that having children takes a toll on her body, Salam told me, "My body didn't really change much after I had children, just my face: I don't get as many pimples. I don't worry about gaining weight at all—in less than a month my body goes back to normal. I don't have any problems during pregnancy, I don't get fat or anything. When the doctor saw me in my ninth month, he wouldn't believe I hadn't had the baby yet." Salam had three girls and planned to have more children until she got a boy, even if it meant having ten girls. Although Salam's confidence in the resilience of her body was not the main reason for this decision, it did play a part in her willingness to have many more children.

Modern bodies are thus ideally young, molded, refigured, and modified by ever-changing products and disciplines. The new body care and consumption are ideally for the sake and upkeep of a happy couple-centered marriage and thus a modern, small family. These same transformations are criticized as vain, materialistic, and dangerous if they are not thus family directed. This is the social circulation of these products in the Galilee, even though these commodities and habits, mostly produced outside the Palestinian community of the Galilee, are not promoted as essentials of the new family (although certainly as modern and sexually desirable). But just as the television commercial for Reese's peanut butter cups extols the "many ways to eat a Reese's," so these new contexts of commodity consumption are certainly not disruptive of the power contexts that produced them. As we saw in Chapter 2, goods and ideas that flow through international networks tend to take on specific local significances in a subtle play of "indigenous trajectories of desire and fear with global flows of people and things" (Appadurai 1990: 5). In the insertion of body care and consumption into modern family planning in the Galilee we see these complex processes in play.

MANAGING NEW DANGERS, CONSTRUCTING NEW SEXUALITIES

The same people who enthusiastically embrace modernity simultaneously view it as threatening. These innovations are associated with sexual decay [inḥilāl jinsy] and perversion [inḥirāf]. In fact, at the heart of the discourse is an essential contradiction: the modern body is constructed as potentially controlled on the one hand (small families, precise scientifically controlled reproduction) and potentially out of control on the other hand (sexual immorality).

The new vanity concerning the body has been accompanied by a new sexual awareness of it. Part and parcel of the transformations that introduced allegedly scientific body modifications is a new biological knowledge of the body, including its sex organs. The combination of a new potential for beauty and sexual awareness is perceived as threatening. The availability and dissemination of sexual knowledge is evident in the barrage of sexually explicit images in the Galilee, especially in the Western media. Thus information about sex today, whether parents like it or not, is perceived as easily accessible. Fardos, who is in her early 70s, remarked: "Today's girls are so smart. You can't tell if they're married or not anymore. They all wear makeup. They go anywhere they want, and they know everything: they know more than married women about what's going to happen in the future." Widespread sexual knowledge—outside of marriage as well as in it—in combination with the new vanity about the body, calls for, in many people's opinion, a new method of control. One of these new management techniques is the provision of sex education, so as to control the new sexual awareness by firmly situating sex again within the modern family, thus ensuring the production of conjugal heterosexuality and legitimate children. This is not to suggest that education in sexuality is an exclusively modern phenomenon—clearly parenting, socialization, and the molding of sexuality existed in the past. But I point here to a specific type of sex education today, and the modern form of this management technique.

Safa' Tamish, a sex educator, has concluded from her experience that Palestinian parents are very interested in the idea of "proper" sex education for their children—although exactly what that consists of varies greatly. When she graduated from New York University with a degree in human sexuality education, her friends—Palestinians and others—taunted her that when she returned home with her degree, people would stone her all the way back to New York. But Safa' said, "A lot of my fears and stereotypes have been exploded because I've had such a warm reception all over the country.[2] Most parents feel that their children, es-

2. Note that Safa' has worked extensively with Palestinians both inside Israel and in the West Bank and Gaza. Safa''s construction of "the country" expands and contracts.

pecially adolescents, need educating. But they're not sure how to go about it. They're almost relieved when they think a sex educator can do the job for them."

Safa' made her first attempt at sex education when she was working as a nurse at a school where a 12-year-old girl got pregnant while "playing" with six boys from her class. Safa' said there was a lot of confusion and fear among the students at the school. She wanted to speak to them to explain what had happened. But the school principal objected because "we are a conservative society." Safa' told him: "When you have girls getting pregnant in your school and boys raping girls, this is not a conservative society." She persuaded the principal to call a parents' meeting to request their permission to discuss the issue with their children. The meeting was the first in the history of the school to be so well attended. Safa' said she told the parents "that the children are curious and they are going to get their answers about what happened to the girl from somewhere—from the streets or cafés or magazines. Isn't it better for them to be properly educated?" The parents agreed. Thus Safa' gave her first sex education class in response to what parents perceived as a perverse incident of young premarital sex, a symptom of modernity, and their desire to control and manage the sexual information their children received. Safa' was to explain to the students what had happened and give them "proper" information: she wanted to introduce "an objective scientific approach to 'sexuality' in order to enlighten youth" (Tamish 1996: 2).[3]

Many people I knew believed that the biology classes on reproduction in the standard curriculum of intermediate schools (and then again in high school for biology majors) were an important part of their children's sex education. When my research assistant and I asked many parents if they thought that their children knew about sex, they said yes— "they learned about it in biology class." However, unlike Safa''s sex education workshops (a few of which I attended and one of which I helped organize), these classes did not necessarily foster an open discussion about sex, nor were they meant to do so.

Even when biology teachers do not skip these lessons out of embarrassment, or ask members of the opposite gender to leave the class while the subject is discussed, the curriculum includes only a rather superficial description of sexual reproduction—the "reproductive organs"

---

3. This medicalized scientific orientation is evident in the title of Tamish's 1996 report: *Misconceptions about Sexuality and Sexual Behavior in Palestinian Society.*

are named in classical Arabic scientific terminology, the process of fertilization (but not intercourse) is described, and basic genetics are mapped. At some point the teacher is required to draw the male and female "reproductive organs" on the board, but rarely are they situated in bodies. I can remember the abstract floating womb on the blackboard and trying to guess what the teacher was drawing (a cow's head?). The curriculum has been slow to change. Still, there is a strong consensus among parents, including those who did not receive such an education themselves, that this basic description of reproduction is essential for their children. Thus intermediate school biology is considered a much-needed part of the new management of bodies.

Palestinian parents in the Galilee seek to provide their children with knowledge of the body as a requirement of modern life. Sex education is meant to manage children's bodies for the sake of the modern family, and to protect them from modern extrafamilial dangers. Like the new feminine vanity, sex education is firmly situated within the modern family. It is considered necessary partly because of the perceived heightened sexual dangers and perversions inherent in modern life. Girls especially need to know more about sex "in these times" than they supposedly needed to know "before," to protect them against "today's problems." Monira (aged 32), a housewife from Kukab who has two girls and one boy, told me:

> I think it's important to teach your daughters about sex and pregnancy. You know, it's really scary today. There are so many cases where young children are attacked. You know when kids hitchhike home from school. . . . I told my daughter never to ride with any strangers. My daughter is only six and I tell her not to get in a car with anyone. I told her to hit a boy if he touches her, and I explained to her where.

Similarly, Nayfi believed that Palestinian society was no longer safe for girls:

> Society has really changed. Although life used to be very hard, there used to be simplicity and safety—the boy works next to the girl. Today this little girl [pointing at her 7-year-old granddaughter], we're afraid for her to play with a boy in the street. Today there is rowdiness and hashish and young men and women dancing around in the street [bitraqwaṣū].

Haniyyi also told me: "Ninety percent of the young generation know how pregnancy happens, but that's very necessary and they need to know all the details. Some girls don't even know what rape is. How would they know to stop it?"

Note the emphasis on educating daughters as opposed to sons. Daughters are perceived to be more vulnerable to modern dangers, partly because of the possibility of pregnancy. Keeping girls' sexuality family-oriented and conjugal is considered to be largely the responsibility of mothers, while fathers are responsible for having those talks with their sons (although it is assumed that sons will learn more about sex on their own, gain more experience, and thus not require so much parental intervention).[4] Thus by regulating their daughters' sexuality, mothers are constructed as playing a key role in adjusting society to modern conditions. They are praised for raising aware modern girls, and blamed for failure to protect their daughters from the perversions of modernity. The image of the ignorant, old-fashioned mother is often evoked as a key stumbling block in the advancement of society. Nisrin the social worker told me:

> My estimate is that only 10 percent of girls who get married know what will happen on the wedding night. Especially girls who marry very young and those who don't have a close relationship with their mother, to have a free flow of information between them. These mothers were used to a system in which girls were grabbed from playing in the garden and told, "Come wash up, tonight is your wedding." Some of these newlyweds even reject their first child because of the emotional and physical pain and shock of marriage and sex. The mothers play a key role in this failure.

Muna, a teacher of physics, emphasized the role of mothers in providing this education:

> Especially today, the situation is not reassuring. They must tell girls about sex because there are a lot of problems. Before, girls used to find out some things from their friends, but today there's a close friendship [she used the English words] between mothers and daughters. Magazines teach these things, *al-Manbar* is full of stories about

4. The assumption is that young Arab men will gain sexual experience with Jewish and foreign women, or Arab women who are labeled prostitutes. It is also assumed that "normal" Arab women never have premarital sex, which is obviously not always the case.

rape. But not all girls know. Some girls aren't told before they get married—their mothers are too busy cooking—and so they run away when the groom tries to take off their dress. If girls know what ovulation [she úsed the Hebrew *biyuts*] is, they won't get pregnant. .

In these comments, sex education is an important part of proper up-bringing *[tarbiyi]*, intended to protect girls from pregnancy and rape si-multaneously; thus the issue of consent or desire is elided. In this con-text, uninformed consent is not considered valid consent at all. Proper sex education helps girls identify sex and thus (1) stop it, or at least avoid pregnancy before marriage, and (2) consent to it and perform it dutifully with their husbands. Sex education thus constructs and gives a girl the ability to refuse and consent, an ability central to proper family-oriented heterosexuality.

CONSTRUCTING NORMALITY AND PERVERSION

Sex education constructs normality as well as perversion. Over and over people told me that proper sex education prevents sexual deviance, especially homosexuality; no one who is properly raised would be "de-viant." Homosexual "perversion" is often seen as born of sexual igno-rance (lack of proper sex education) coupled with exposure to pervert-ing Western influences. Sex education thus has as one of its goals the creation of "proper" heterosexual subjects. However, the fear of mo-dernity's proclivity to produce homosexuals is less prominent than fear of its encouragement of premarital and extramarital heterosexual sex. In any case, sex education is intended to create straight, modern, proper conjugal sexuality.

'Abla Jabaly was part of a six-person team at the Ministry of Education in charge of creating the first "family and sex education" curriculum for Arabic junior high schools (Krainy et al. 1996).[5] Although the ministry claims that this curriculum will soon be comprehensively implemented, the funding and staffing situation suggests that a pilot program will be started in a few schools and that the rest will have to wait many years. This curriculum is thus part of the frontier of a sex education project, pioneered yet supported rather reluctantly by the Israeli government.

5. The Palestinian Ministry of Health has conducted some sex education in the West Bank and Gaza in universities and youth clubs to "raise the awareness of youths in the field of reproductive health, family planning and early marriage" (Shaaban 1997).

Ms. Jabaly, who had recently received a sex educator certificate from
the Israeli Family Planning Association, echoed the fear of modern perversions and the need for sex education to guard against them:

The Ministry of Education has had a sex education curriculum in
the Jewish sector since 1982. In the Arab sector we are reluctant. But
there are so many problems involving rape and killing. When right
here in Nazareth we have a homosexual rape of a thirteen-year-old
boy, and the man then kills the victim because he's so afraid of being
revealed, we can no longer ignore these problems. Also a five-year-
old child in Imm il-Fahim is raped and killed. There are so many as-
saults in the home. These problems are not confined to one sector
of society; all sectors have problems concerning sex—the village, the
city, all three religions. So beginning in 1990, the ministry formed a
committee to try to set up a curriculum.

Also, there has been an increased number of honor killings[6] recently—there has been a regression and an increase in the number of
murders, so responsibility needs to be placed on both the man and the
woman.

The media and television have had a lot of positive effects on us,
but they've had bad side effects too. Television has affected the social
side, led to social decay. We hear of cases where a father rapes his
daughter after watching a pornographic film.

Similarly, as part of its education and awareness campaign in the
West Bank and Gaza the Palestinian Family Planning and Protection
Association issued an AIDS-prevention poster showing a young heterosexual couple escaping what is labeled "sexual perversion" (an image
of two men smiling at each other) and "illegitimate sexual relations"
(a blonde woman, in revealing pink dress, smoking next to a man
who is touching her) (see Figure 16). The slogan reads, "Arm yourselves
with knowledge." Again the object is the creation of proper conjugal
heterosexuality.

The curriculum committee describes its book as "preventive" and
presents it to parents as a necessary corrective to the perverting influence
of modernity:

Because of the increasing spread of sexually explicit information and images
through media such as journalism, television, cable, and video, a large number of children in our society are exposed to assault. Our children fall under

6. Killings of women who had allegedly shamed their family by their sexual behavior.

Figure 16. This poster for the Palestinian Family Planning and Protection Association reads: "To prevent AIDS avoid . . . [clockwise from top] sexual deviation, use of used needles, contaminated blood transfusion, and illegitimate sexual relations"; "Arm yourselves with knowledge."

the influence of distorted information that pressures them in inappropriate ways and provokes them to ask questions that you and we find difficult to answer.

These licentious daily images contradict and conflict with the traditions and culture by which we raise our children. Therefore, we have found it appropriate to run a continuation course for schoolteachers on the subject of family life education and sex education so that they may provide our students with true facts in accordance with the dictates of the heavenly religions, and to correct wrong information they may have exchanged among themselves. (Krainy et al. 1996: 102)

TRAINING AND REFINING SEXUALITY

The sex education curriculum committee, like many parents who wanted to provide sex education for their children, sought to create new individuals—new future mothers and fathers (see Figure 17). Sex education was clearly placed within the context of the modern family. When I asked Ms. Jabaly if she felt there was a difference between the curriculum for Arab and Jewish schools, she replied that the most obvious difference was the more than twenty-year lag in the implementation of the program. She added:

In the Arab context, a sensitivity to conservatism must be maintained: we need to respect Arab culture, and emphasize the need for postponing sex until marriage. On the other hand, I'm forbidden to say to the students, "Don't practice sex." Each person should behave according to the way he was raised by his parents. I just help him make a decision. The students can look for themselves at the consequences of our traditions here, and then they can look at the West—ask themselves whether it's positive or negative—and then they can decide logically.

This subject has no coercion in it; the freedoms of the individual are taken into consideration. We want students to gain feelings of confidence. We want to emphasize that each individual can make decisions, and be assertive, and have independent opinions. This generation no longer accepts simplicity. The things the father and grandfather say, the son no longer simply accepts. He wants to think, argue, and conclude for himself.

The curriculum is explicitly aimed at creating a new individual and promises to provide "education toward correct future fatherhood and motherhood." The declared goals of the program include "providing the student with accurate, modern, and scientific information concerning the sexual aspects of humans" as well as "enhancing the ability of the

Figure 17.   The cover of the Israeli Ministry of Education's sex education book
Adolescence and Us depicts future mothers and fathers. (Krainy et al. 1996)

individual to think independently with a concern for the feelings of others from a perspective of social responsibility, tolerance *[tasāmuḥ]*, and
respect for the different elements in a multivalue society" (Krainy et al.
1996: viii, 9). Ms. Jabaly explained:

> The curriculum isn't just about sex. Marriage isn't just sex, it's an en-
> tire very complicated new life. We encourage students to think about
> issues such as: How do I face life? How do I live with a partner who
> is different from me? These are things that our curriculum must ad-
> dress as well. . . .

We also teach about the secret habit [masturbation], that it's a safety valve for the sex instinct. Everyone in our society, including religious people, must know that they can't repress *[yitghū]* nature, but we can control and train it *[tahdhibha]*.

Sex education is thus part of a conscious effort to domesticate sexuality in a dangerous modern context, by producing proper heterosexual conjugal subjects. This view of the sex education curriculum was echoed by many parents. Yasmin (originally from Syria) told me that she wanted her daughter to "know everything" so she would know how to behave properly:

I told my daughter Muna everything early on. In fact, she reacted very comfortably when she first got her period. She was visiting at my brother's house in Greece and they celebrated and passed out sweets. Muna knew everything, and it's good for girls to know so they won't run into trouble. If she finds herself alone with a boy at school, she'll know how to behave and I will trust her.

Najah (aged 67), from Mishhad, saw the new openness about sex with girls as allowing her more control over her daughters—not the restrictive, prohibitive control that her father had over her, but ability to guide them. She was very happy that her daughters had learned about sex in school and from books and TV, because she no longer worried about them, but also because she could give them detailed advice on married life:

That way I don't worry about them, and I can talk to them and tell them everything, to advise them on how to make their husbands happy, how not to resist or disobey *[yi'ṣū]* them. I can talk with them frankly about everything and we're not shy at all. That way it's much easier. Not like before, when women were always shushing and shooing girls so they wouldn't hear. There's no such thing today. My daughter's fiancé [an Egyptian migrant worker] lives in our house and they go out together and I never worry about her at all—she's not shy with him or afraid, she doesn't find anything weird or difficult.

Najah contrasted this openness to what she saw as the bad preparation her mother gave her before she got married:

The first time I got my period, I wiped myself after peeing and there was blood. I thought I must have been cut or something. I came out of the bathroom and my face was all different. My mother saw me and asked me what was wrong. I told her, crying, that I wasn't cut or anything but I wiped and there was blood. She said, "You silly girl, this happens to all girls, it's normal." That was it! She didn't explain anything. Later on I heard her say to the other women, "She's only twelve years old and she's already a woman [ṣarat bālgha]." I didn't understand what that meant. . . .

When I got married they came and grabbed me from playing with the other girls and washed and dressed me. I didn't know what was going on. They hadn't told me I was getting married. When they sewed my wedding clothes, they measured them on my mother because they didn't want to tell me. When they left me in the room with the groom, it was as though you'd left me with a monster, I was so afraid.

Munir, a Druze man from Mghar, discussed some of these issues with Manhal, my research assistant. Their discussion further emphasizes the role of sex education in controlling information, preventing perversions, and creating proper conjugal sexuality, good husbands and wives, fathers and mothers, in a context of assault by modern influences:

MANHAL: What would you say to your son if he asked you, "Where did I come from?"

MUNIR: Not all my children asked me this question, but some of them did. I answered them honestly, in a language that they can understand. I said things like "From your mom's belly" or "Your mother and I made you." This is when a child is three or four. When I was asked, I didn't run from the question, I answered it honestly. Some fathers say, "Shut up, what is this talk?" . . .

MANHAL: Should the answer be different for girls and boys?

MUNIR: When they're young the answer should be the same for both sexes. Later on I might be more honest with my son than with my daughter because we can talk about things more openly. I feel that my daughter will be shy and she's closer to her mother; so she wouldn't ask me. It's difficult for the Arab daughter to ask her father sexual questions and for the Arab father to talk to his daughter. . . .

I try to give my children the values I'm convinced of. I'd like our society to be advanced and developed but I reject the degeneracy we see in the West. I see it as negative, not civilized. But if we Easterners or Arabs can develop without copying the West, on the basis of our own principles, we can become a civilized society that we can be proud of, not mental and moral baseness. Of course, this degeneracy is a crisis in the West, while in the East we're in the crisis of backwardness. They've gone too far and we're still too far behind.

Raja', a woman from Haifa, had a similar view on sex in East versus West:

ME: If you could change things in our society, what would you change?

RAJA':   I'd burn it all. Sometimes I don't like to say that I'm Arab, I don't like to belong to this backward people. Yes, we're developing on the outside, but not on the inside. Two out of every three girls here have sexual relations. This is not advancement. We learned a lot of negatives from the West. We want to be civilized. The young generation is more open, even though that might lead to deep decay. Here it's either white or black. There should be a middle ground. Everything needs changing. Girls today don't impress me—they think about sex [she used the English word] and their heads are empty. Here in Haifa it's totally messed up and dirty. It's good that the old is dying, but we're creating something even worse, more difficult. This new society is going to be indiscreet in everything.

Not that I think a woman's honor is between her legs at all, or in the hymen. Look, every answer I gave you has contradictions in it. I believe in two things at the same time: because I am a believer [she is a born-again Christian], I believe that the sexual relationship should take place with a person you love, someone who deserves this love and you want to live with all your life, to give him the most valuable thing you own, yourself. I also believe that a woman's honor is not between her legs. It can happen that one loved a man very much and something happened, but they left each other. From a religious perspective this is adultery, but she should be given a second chance [she used the English term]. A lot of my girlfriends in college thought they were going to stay with these guys forever, and they didn't think the guy would be that weak and leave them. They made a mistake.

I don't know if I can blame this rotten society, it has been put in very difficult historical situations and positions, but it has chosen wrong things in postmodernism ["postmodernism" in English]. To tell you the truth, the men who can understand you are the ones who are not educated, they give you your rights and you live with them safely—they're simple and very honest and don't express themselves in isms [English] and *at-syah* [Hebrew for "ism"]. They just say what's in their hearts and don't make false pretensions of being advanced.

Munir seemed convinced that the family was the best source of sex education:

MUNIR: Although I expect that my sons will get sexual experience before marriage, if I saw the need, I'd sit my son down and tell him, "You're approaching marriage, which involves two partners, a male and a female," and that sex is very important in the life of a family and how he should deal with his wife, in which manner, and how you can practice sex with her so that you get maximum pleasure and she does too. And because sexual compatibility is one of the factors of happiness in the family, it's important. . . .

MANHAL: What other sources do your children have for information on sex?

MUNIR: There are a lot of sources. The ones available in our society are friends, each of whom has his or her own sources. There are also books on sex, but girls still don't have access to those. But there's a medium that imposes itself on this situation, and that's television. Television could be a good sex educator or a destroyer. The question is what television, what channel, how do we watch it, and who watches it. Today there are satellite channels, there's a Turkish channel that has a program once or twice a week called *Tutti Frutti* in which girls go up and begin undressing and only leave on something very small, smaller than Eve's fig leaf. There are young men and adolescents who watch this. Is this a sex educator or destroyer? This has nothing educational in it. There are programs in Hebrew for Jewish children that to a certain extent are educational and honest, and in Jewish schools they read about sex, more than Arab schools, because our teachers, even our teachers, find it difficult to talk about sex with their students, especially with female students. So there are not that many sources and it could be good. The question is does it reach a point where a young man waits till his parents fall asleep and stays up till two in the morning and watches this program. What is the impact of this program . . . why does he want to watch it, just to have a good time and then at the end play with his hand, or is this going to add to his knowledge about a woman's body and the way it's made? Of course it will be seductive to him. . . . The question is does this give him a complex or resolve his complexes? It depends on the home he lives in.

MANHAL: Do you think it's better for boys to know about this or not?

MUNIR: A boy should know about sex, not about anarchic [he used the Hebrew *anarkhi*] sex or commercial sex or the sexual perversions that are present in the West or among Jews. In our society there is sexual perversion, but that's not what a boy should be educated about. We don't chaotically tell him this is a spring and this is the river, drink from whichever you want. No, you must drink from the pure spring, the correct spring. You must educate and train the boy to reach the point of understanding that sex is a basic act in life, but it's also a civilized act, not a bestial one. If a human deals with sex like an animal, then we're no different than animals. Sex is a partnership. If I don't like my partner or she doesn't like me, then sex is just one animal mounting another. Sexual pleasure is present when you sleep with a woman you love, or lust for, or are compatible with. We're not allowed to educate our children that sex is chaotic like this and animalistic and come-on. Sex is about refinement, so you develop it and make it into a civilized high act. It's not like depicting women as sexual [*'awra*], if you see her thigh it's *'awra,* her chest, etc. No. How you make sure that this act is understood as civilized rather than animal depends on the father much more than on the street. Because the street has everything.

MANHAL: What about girls?

MUNIR: I also think that in our society a girl should be informed about sexual perversions. The mother, not the father, talks to her, and this depends on the mother's level of awareness and education because then she can convey more, has the courage to convey more, and also she can inspect the type of things that a girl might obtain. She can inspect whether the daughter can obtain sources about sex that could ruin her. But to take care that her daughter gets proper sources on sex, that will benefit her in the future, for the next stage when she becomes a woman and engages in sex, so the mother should help her and give her as much as possible and teach her about her sex organs. It's natural that the girl should have some minimal knowledge for the married life she'll enter. So it's better for her to enter it with some awareness, training, than to enter it ignorant or with a negative perspective, with things that we consider perverse. The West started being backward in sex, and it did things that I don't think are necessary for you to enjoy sex, you don't need these things. You can enjoy sex more even without these things.

Note the prominence of television in the discourses on modern sexuality, in Munir's comments as well as in the curriculum committee's vision of social change. Television is seen as a central vehicle of modernization that has a corrupting effect *and* an educational potential. Unlike Munir and the curriculum committee, Suha saw television, even the late-night sex shows, as educational, at least for boys:

When a teenage boy gets curious, he can learn from books and magazines and from watching TV. The parents can buy him his own TV and put it in his room so he can watch and learn. Like my neighbor, her son is a teenager and she keeps on asking me why he gets up late at night after they've all gone to sleep so he can watch. She is so naive. They should get him his own TV.

Moreover, the corrupting influence of television is not always seen as due to the Western content of programming. Buthaina (aged 21), the girl who worked in the egg-sorting factory, commented on the impact of "Arabic films," mostly Egyptian:

ME: Do you think most girls know about sex before they get married?

BUTHAINA: But that's exactly what they're running after. They all want to get married so they can have fancy dresses and take them off and sleep on a big bed.

ME: Where do they know this from?

BUTHAINA: From watching television, and from girlfriends. A girl
           sees an Arabic film and starts wanting someone to love
           her. She starts wanting someone to kiss her and hug her,
           like she sees on television. Mothers don't tell their daugh-
           ters about sex, and if the daughters ask, it's shameful. So
           the girl sneaks and finds out, and they become too eager
           to do it. They don't know what marriage involves,
           they're just dying to get married quickly for the sex.

Television, like modernity itself, is considered a double-edged sword.

"WE'VE JUST STARTED"

Farid (aged 32), an unemployed former member of the Israeli police
force from Dayr Hanna, commented on the spread of knowledge about
sex in Palestinian society: "Today everybody knows about sex. Today
even a twelve-year-old girl knows more than four old ladies put together. In my generation we used to be shy. But today the picture is
clear." Still, according to 'Abla Jabaly, sex education is a long process
that has just begun and is far from complete. The picture is not quite
clear yet. She admits that she is still not altogether comfortable with her
professional title:

> I had a lot of difficulty becoming a sex expert, and even after my
> training, when they announced "'Abla Jabaly, sex expert" during my
> interview on television, I still felt a prick [nakhzi] inside me, that this
> is shameful. Doing sex education is not something simple, but a seri-
> ous personal struggle. It's an ongoing process for all of society.

I, too, had a hard time asking sexually explicit questions.

Buthaina believed that many girls knew about sex (and were too eager for it) but she also said there were still some girls who are "embar-
rassingly ignorant" in matters of sex:

> There are still some stupid girls who don't know anything. There's a
> girl who works with us at the factory who is engaged and she asks
> silly questions, like how does a woman know she's pregnant. She is
> so sheltered. My oldest sister was thirty-five years old before she got
> married, and she asked me, her much younger sister, if a kiss makes
> you pregnant. It's like a funny joke now, but she never used to go
> out and around, she was always home at her sewing machine. The

mother should teach her daughters, educate them. There is this girl whose husband divorced her because she wouldn't let him get near her. Her mother used to scare her about men when she was young to the point that she gave her a complex [*uqdi*]. Her husband tied her up on their wedding night and called his uncles to show them how she wouldn't let him touch her. This girl later showed us her arm all covered with cigarette burns; her husband would torture her because she wouldn't let him sleep with her. Now they're getting a divorce. These mothers and fathers are hopeless, they ought to be institutionalized.

Sex education is increasingly considered a modern essential, but many people still see society in general as far from that goal. Although many more girls receive sex education today, almost everyone has stories like Buthaina's about girls "tragically" left in the sexual dark. The few trained sex educators see themselves as pioneers and innovators. The push for sex education is relatively recent; the educational process is considered to be at the starting point.

Additionally, many modern parents are dissatisfied with much of the formal sex education available. Salwa thought that school nurses did not provide adequate sex education even when they sought to do so:

ME: How do most girls in the village learn about sex?

RAWYA: Mothers tell their daughters, or the nurse from the [MCH] clinic comes to the school and talks to the girls in the sixth grade about menstruation, so a girl doesn't suffer by herself.

SALWA: When I was in school the nurse explained to us, but I don't feel that this is enough. At the time we actually knew more than the nurse told us. She told us about cleanliness and blood, but nothing about the period of adolescence or anything.

RAWYA: They have biology classes, although they don't explain exactly how things happen. The priest also teaches the children some things. And kids might catch a film by accident and fill in the details.

SALWA: I don't think these are enough. I shouted at my sisters because they never explained anything to me and my mother is too old-fashioned and shy. I'm not prepared to be shy with my kids so that someone else from outside will tell them about it, and maybe give them incorrect information.

Although Salwa told me she was relieved that the school had a nurse and biology classes, she did not trust them to give her children a full sex education: "Our schools in reality don't address the issues adequately."

One of the big hurdles in sex education is the "prick" that 'Abla Jabaly admits to; in a society that is just beginning the process of sex education, such talk is still embarrassing. Khadiji is a nurse who occasionally lectures to high school students about sexuality under the rubrics of "family life" and "maturity" (she used the Hebrew *hitbagrut*). "Actually," she said, "I found that mothers encourage these lectures, because they themselves don't have a way of talking to their children about this subject. They don't know how to break the barriers of shame they've been brought up with even when they want to." This is reminiscent of what Safa' Tamish said earlier about parents' feeling a sense of relief when a teacher can take the embarrassing burden of sex education off their hands. Many parents told me they gave their children books about anatomy and had them read on their own. Even nurses at the MCH clinics, who are required to discuss family planning with their clients, tend to give printed handouts on the subject rather than talk face to face. Thus many people felt the need for sex education and openness about sexual information, but were too shy and embarrassed to talk about it despite their convictions.

Many mothers said they were particularly afraid that if they told their young children about sex, the children might repeat what they were told in front of other people in an inappropriate context and embarrass their parents. Rawya was one such mother:

> My daughter is eleven and she asked me how babies are made and I told her that the father sleeps next to the mother, and I told her that babies come out from below where pee comes from. But I'm always nervous that she will embarrass me in front of other people. Especially little kids, they might repeat some of the things you tell them in front of people. Eee, my neighbor's son the other day said in front of all these men and women, "A woman gives birth from below, from her ass. Right, Dad?" Now, isn't that embarrassing [*'azara*]? What are people going to think about parents talking dirty to the children like that? My son once asked in front of all these people, "Why do you sometimes close your bedroom door at night and sometimes not?"

This prick of shame especially haunts parents when they try to instruct children of the opposite gender. My childhood friend Suha was adamant about telling her daughter about sex but admitted to being unable to broach the subject with her son. She told me:

SUHA: At the time I first got my period, I had heard you talking about it, but I thought it was something bad. I stayed around the house for a week, afraid and always in bed, I didn't know that I should wear a pad. Then my mom caught me and asked, "What's this on your pants?" Then she told me, "Wow, Suha, now you're a young woman" and everything.

ME: What if your children asked you where they came from?

SUHA: Rasha [6] asked me and I told her exactly. I don't tell her silly stories like you come from my stomach, or we found you under an olive tree or anything like that. Often she sees me with a pad and once she asked what it was and I told her. I don't want her to be surprised like I was. Can you believe I didn't know where a woman gives birth from until after I was married?

ME: What about your son?

SUHA: I can't tell Laith, I don't know why. Isn't Laith four years old? Still I'm shy with him. Maybe his father will tell him.

While many parents feared their sex-educated children might blurt things out at inappropriate moments, many others feared being embarrassed by their children's lack of sex education; that, too, reflected negatively on them. Sexually ignorant children reflected the sexual ignorance of their parents. As Buthaina emphasized, only daughters of "aware mothers" are properly sex-educated:

> If a girl doesn't have information about sex, people will laugh at her and at the mother who doesn't have enough time for her. A girl must know. If a girl doesn't have any information and she is kissed, she'll want to kill herself [laughing]. When that happens, it's embarrassing ['azara]. There are girls who hide the fact that they menstruate from their parents, thinking they have something wrong with them. There was one girl who thought she was cut and she put iodine on herself.

Thus fear that sex-educated children will blurt out "shameful" things is balanced by fear that children without sex education will demonstrate the "ignorance" and "neglect" of their parents.

Most Palestinian parents thus engaged in some form of sex education for their children or counted on others to do so. It was widely considered a modern necessity, essential for producing proper, safe heterosexuality in a potentially treacherous new era. This is clearly not to say that forms of sex education and regulation did not exist in the Galilee before the embrace of modernization, but rather to elucidate the particular forms and contours of these contemporary discourses and practices.

Certainly there are parents who do not believe in sex education. Khaldiyyi, for example, did not feel it was appropriate to discuss pregnancy even with her husband, let alone her children.

> ME: Did your husband want you to have this last pregnancy?
>
> KHALDIYYI: My husband and I don't talk about that subject at all. I don't talk like other women: "I got my period" and "I didn't get my period" and "I'm going to get my period." I find that ridiculous. Never in my life have I talked like that in front of my husband. . . .
>
> ME: What would you say if your child asked you, "Where did I come from?"
>
> KHALDIYYI: You know, none of my children ask such questions. They don't talk this talk. Even though a lot of kids ask these types of questions, my children never did.

Khaldiyyi said it was not appropriate to tell children about sex because they would try it. But most parents disagree; Khaldiyyi is in the minority. Suha's view was more dominant: "Some people say there's a lot of freedom today and if a girl knows too much she can sleep with anyone she wants. But on the contrary, the girl who doesn't know can make mistakes because she doesn't understand what's going on." The belief that sex education is necessary protection in a dangerous new world was, in my view, more widespread.

SCIENCE AS SOLUTION

What is evident in this emphasis on sex education and domestication is the positioning of Science, with a capital S, as the solution to society's problems, especially its new perversions. Science is seen as an essential ingredient in society's adjustment to modernity and change. As Nuhad told me, "There's a lot of sex education these days because a lot of rapes are committed. It's better for children to know everything in the realm of science. The other day I read in a book that I must explain everything to my children." Nisrin similarly said:

> A mother should explain to her daughter about sex, but not incorrect things, like these uneducated mothers who tell their children they found them under an olive tree. In that case, maybe it's better not to say anything at all, because then the children will need so much convincing later that what their mothers told them is wrong. I think a child of ten and older should be told exactly where the doctor took him out of. Any younger and I'm afraid they'll talk in front of people. I would get this information from books—the writers of books have the knowledge of doctors. They tell you what you should say and when.

Nisrin, the social worker, told me: "How can our society advance when women still believe in myths like the one about menstruating women turning the yogurt or the pickles bad? Or that if a girl eats lemons her menstrual blood will dry up and she'll stop getting periods. How far are we going to get thinking like this, with no relevance to science or facts?"

Envisioning Science—book knowledge, doctors, "facts"—as a remedy is by no means confined to the area of sex education. Palestinians in the Galilee, educated or not, constantly refer to and draw on so-called Science as a source of legitimacy. People use what they consider to be scientific terminology to support their beliefs and statements. I was particularly struck by the constant references to X and Y genes in discussions about pregnancy and childbearing. There were frequent references to what were considered to be scientific concepts about the body, as in Salam's comment: "Because I kept on having my kids so close together, my female gene became overactive. That's why I kept on getting pregnant with girls. So now I want to wait a little bit before I have another baby, so my gene will cool off." [7]

Science is seen as, produced as, the ultimate social remedy not only in the context of promodernization but at moments of antimodernization as well. An old schoolmate of mine, Arij from Nazareth, told me: "I am very traditional. I support the old and well-tried system of marrying relatives. Some people are afraid of the genetic problems that might result, but today there is science and there is medicine and it can take care of all these problems."

7. More on boy preference in Chapter 5.

Perhaps people I formally interviewed tended to index their comments with science because of their perception that I was conducting a scientific study on family planning. But such references to science and its centrality go well beyond my interviews—they are ubiquitous.

The use of science, especially medical science, as referent and support extended to doctors, nurses, and pharmacists. These people had considerable influence outside their professional capacities in part because of their association with this source of power, Science. The pharmacist in my village was often referred to as an authority on issues beyond his pharmaceutical domain, and his advice and actions were often emulated because of his association with science. When one of the MCH nurses in Sakhnin got pregnant at age 43, I heard many people argue that "if a nurse who knows everything about science had a baby at such a late age, why can't we?" In fact, many of the doctors and nurses who have long tried to discourage women over 40 from having children because of the health risks strongly criticized the nurse. Her actions were seen as considerably more damaging to their efforts than other people's because of her link to science.

Even when men and women of science are questioned or attacked, the argument is frequently based on an appeal to science. Once when I was visiting a good friend from high school, her parents started asking me questions about my research. I mentioned that I was surprised by the number of people I met who believed that contraceptive pills can harm the fertility of a newlywed woman. I was about to comment on what a bad job I thought health professionals have done in dispelling such misconceptions when my friend's parents jumped in: "Yes, pills are very bad for women who haven't had children yet. Any doctor who gives pills to a newlywed is only doing it for the money." Their support for this claim is that my friend's father had personally overheard a well-known Scottish doctor in Nazareth, Dr. Mackay, telling a married couple that pills were terrible for young women. Even when my friend's mother and father—an arts and crafts teacher and a nurse, respectively—were criticizing doctors, their evidence and support allegedly came from a doctor. Science and medicine are powerful sources for truth-making.

MEDICALIZATION AND CONTRACEPTION AS IDENTITY MARKER

As mentioned earlier, Emily Martin argues that not only does medicalization enormously transform the physical processes of giving birth, but new cultural values become embedded in these processes as well (1987). In the Galilee, assumptions about the superiority of science and modernity are now embedded in conceptions and practices of sex and family. Moreover, scientific methods of contraception have become entangled in the construction of identities.

The appeal to contraceptive practice as a measure of identity is part and parcel of the use of reproductive behavior to situate a person in social hierarchies. A modernist discourse that uses family size and spacing, control of sexuality, and family planning as a standard of social distinction will certainly have much to say about contraceptives. Indeed, contraceptives play a key role in the social negotiations of identity. From the promodernization point of view, reproductive control and family planning, especially through modern medical contraceptives, are widely esteemed. From the less popular antimodernization perspective, natural reproduction and fecundity are valued. Palestinians in the Galilee often subscribe to one of these views and sometimes oscillate between them. But for all the gradations of opinion, reproduction and contraception are topics of concern to almost everyone.

STIGMATIZING "MISTAKES"

Identities and power in the Galilee are increasingly entangled with science, modernity, and reproduction: modern, advanced people have planned small families with the assistance of medical science and contraceptives, while backward, primitive people have unplanned, irrationally large families because they do not use contraceptives or fail to use them properly. Certain parents are thus labeled irrational and their pregnancies and births regarded as untimely and unplanned. This Galilee language parallels the modernization discourse of population studies, which assume that high fertility in the Third World is largely a result of ignorance, especially ignorance of contraceptive methods. As mentioned earlier, studies demonstrate that birth control methods were known and used in the region before the nineteenth century (Musallam 1983), long before the introduction of the IUD and the pill. Yet the modernization narrative in the Galilee today constructs contraception as an entirely modern phenomenon taken up by "advanced" people.

The emphasis on sex education and awareness is paralleled by emphasis on knowledge of contraception. In this light, "mistakes" become key markers of backwardness. Georgina told me: "It depends on a couple's background, on their level of culture. Women who are not educated and cultured have children by mistake. You know, I didn't think your cousin was the type that keeps on having one mistake after another. She didn't seem the type before." Thus certain pregnancies are labeled as "mistakes" and certain women (and men) as the backward type. As Nuhad said earlier, "Certainly it is natural that a human being makes mistakes, in certain cases. For example with the day counting [rhythm] method, it is possible to miscalculate a day or two. But I use a thermometer so that everything is accurate. . . . You need a woman who has awareness, then you won't have mistakes." An educated modern woman uses science to ensure that no reproductive mistakes occur.

Farid, the former policeman, told Manhal, "Among us Arabs, women get pregnant even if they're using contraceptives." He laughed. "We're famous for our mistakes." Once more Arab inferiority/superiority is seen through the lens of reproduction. In Farid's account, a backward Arab fertility mysteriously overpowers modern contraceptives.

Suha expressed sympathy for her mistake-prone sister-in-law, but constructed her repeated pregnancies as an unfathomable inability to manage her body:

> There are a lot of women who can't manage themselves. They keep on getting pregnant when they don't want to because they can't manage themselves, they forget pills, or they get pregnant on top of the method [IUD][8]—I don't know how that happens. My sister-in-law keeps on complaining about her children, and her husband tells her it's her own fault that she didn't manage herself. She used the day-counting method and somehow it didn't work. I just don't understand why it didn't work so many times. I felt sorry for her, but some women just don't know how to take care of themselves.

Unintentional and unplanned pregnancy is often considered a source of stigma. Salam told me:

> My sister-in-law has gotten pregnant by accident three times in a row. Each time, after the baby's born she's breast-feeding and she has to wait for her period so she can put in the IUD, and in that time she doesn't use anything and gets pregnant. Last time she cried so much because she didn't want it, she started trying to miscarry by exercising, but they told her maybe she'll just deform the child. I felt sorry for her, but some women just don't know how to take care of themselves.

---

8. The IUD is commonly referred to as "the method" *(il-wasṭa),* an indication of its popularity.

A mistake made by someone of educated background is perhaps more stigmatizing than a mistake made by someone who is "the type that makes mistakes." Rawan's sister-in-law, Salwa, got pregnant by mistake (according to Rawan) soon after she got married, while she was still attending teachers' college. Rawan told me how embarrassed she was when Salwa got pregnant. She said that Salwa had decided not to take the pill because her mother thought it would affect her ability to have children later. Salwa's mother, Rawan said, had these Stone Age beliefs even though she was a nurse at the Family Health Center. "What kills me is that her sister, who's getting her master's degree at the Technion [University], supported her. 'Yes, pills are harmful to newlyweds,' she said. I couldn't believe what I was hearing from these educated people." Rawan and her family were especially embarrassed because Salim, Rawan's brother (and Salwa's husband), had not yet built a house and established himself. Thus the family formed "by mistake" was cramped in the parents' household. Actually the entire family was delighted by the birth of the first child of a new generation. I do not wish to imply that people's embarrassment about mistakes made babies unwanted or resented. Nor do I wish to imply that the stigmatization of mistakes as unmodern is overdetermining of identity or status. Rather, I suggest that a modernist discourse on contraception and reproduction is a major means through which identity, boundaries, and power are negotiated.

Haniyyi defended certain mistakes: "Some women do get pregnant on top of the method. Some women even have their tubes tied and go on getting pregnant. You can't control that. There's a good percentage, probably 50 percent, of women who say they made mistakes, and it's true. When people make a few mistakes you can believe them, but if they have more than five children and they're all mistakes. . . ." Haniyyi thought that women could not be blamed for "real mistakes."

Thus according to the modernist narrative there are also fake mistakes: certain women only claim to have made a mistake when in fact they had wanted to get pregnant. According to this narrative, many women want more children but in a modernist environment cannot admit it, and excuse their unmodern pregnancies as mistakes. It is very common to hear statements like Salam's, that "the real mistakes are just 3 to 5 percent. The rest just say it." According to Munir, the reason for these allegedly fake mistakes is that "women are ashamed to admit that they want more children, so they say it's a mistake." Georgina, who had four boys and used an IUD, also did not accept mistakes as justification: "Mistake, that's just a word. This generation knows everything, they don't need to make mistakes. They learned at school and they are very smart. Some women say they got pregnant by mistake even though they weren't doing anything to prevent pregnancy. That's not a mistake." Thus most mistakes are inexcusable signs of the primitive in the modernist eyes of many Palestinians in the Galilee.

Nisrin, the social worker, told me:

> People need to adjust themselves to the times. If Arabs used to have so many children in the past, times are different today and they need to change. It's amazing how many women tell me they got pregnant by mistaken—mistake, mistake. This is an impossible situation. I really don't think they're real mistakes, not the majority of cases. Only 5 percent or so are real mistakes. . . .
>
> There is a pathology in women's psychology. And it really takes a great effort and personal strength to separate yourself, to stop identifying with this fertile model mother. It takes an incredible degree of self-control.

When I asked Nisrin if she thought there might be a problem with the way the medical establishment offers contraceptive information and services, she said: "In the MCH clinic they have everything in print, everything about the IUD and the pill and even coitus interruptus (which people call 'the method between the man and the woman') and the pros and cons of each one and its success rate. Every woman knows that there are pills, and that it's easy to get them. But maybe inside her, she wants children." Nisrin thus did not accept the excuse of mistakes, and saw women who continued to have children by mistake as pathological.

Khadiji did explain to me that "really, a lot of the blame lies with the gynecologists, they don't give enough time and attention to their patients. Many of them never explain to the women how the IUD they are inserting or the pills they are prescribing work or what the woman needs to do. So it's not her fault if she remains ignorant." An article in al-'Ittihad is headed "16% of Women Have Unwanted Pregnancies Because of Lack of Awareness" (May 1996).[9] In spite of these qualifications, mistakes are still considered signs of a backward woman. Similarly, Suha said that she had developed some "infections" when she last asked her doctor to prescribe contraceptive pills for her and "the doctor

9. The study discussed in this article actually finds that 16% of women between the ages of 16 and 25 being treated at a particular clinic reported having unplanned and unwanted pregnancies "because of lack of awareness."

told me, 'Pills I won't give you,' and that was it. She didn't explain to me what other options I had. If I weren't educated and aggressive, I'd have gotten pregnant. These doctors are just out to make money." Criticism of doctors, however, does not relieve their patients of the stigma of "too many" unwanted or unplanned pregnancies.

METHODS OF MODERNITY

Not just the use of a contraceptive method but its type is a measure of modernity. Withdrawal and the rhythm method were closely associated with mistakes since they were less "guaranteed" and were thus considered less modern. The IUD and the pill were praised as more modern and accurate. Sunbul said that women usually say they made a mistake when the man was planning to withdraw but "couldn't control himself." This method, with its high failure rate, is considered unmodern.

Lamis, whose husband used withdrawal for five years and who had only one boy, reversed the usual hierarchy of IUD over withdrawal by emphasizing the control required by withdrawal: "Only the wives of men who can't hold themselves insert an IUD. I don't need one. Unlike my husband, most men don't really care about their wives' pleasure [yinbisṭū]." By emphasizing her husband's degree of control and his care for her pleasure, Lamis stigmatized the IUD as a method for men who can't control themselves.

Contraceptive methods were often ranked by their degree of modernity. Sana' didn't know what her older sister, who had six children, meant when she said she used "a method between me and him" [wasṭa bayny u-baynu]. When I told Sana' that she probably meant early withdrawal, she laughed ironically and said: "Yuck. I can't believe my sister would do that. I've never heard of people today relying on that. Why would anyone use that when modern scientific methods are available?" Sana' preferred the pill, which she described as more modern than withdrawal.

Manal, an MCH nurse in Mazra'a, and her sister-in-law Karam also ranked contraceptive methods according to their cost and the degree of "attention" they required from the user.

KARAM: I just recently bought a packet of pills, and each packet costs fifteen shekels. So it turns out to be the most expensive method because you need to buy more each month. The IUD is cheaper. Some women say, "Why should I pay so much for pills?" They just choose the cheaper method.

MANAL: But the problem is that they have to pay the whole amount for the IUD all at once. And they complain about this too. More women use IUDs because it's the method most familiar to them, so they're most comfortable with it.

KARAM: The IUD is guaranteed, but not 100 percent. The pills are more guaranteed, but that's only if you remember to take them every day. I think most women think the IUD is more comfortable because they could forget a pill, and you know how these women mess up. With the IUD, they just get it inserted and they don't have to ask about it any more.

ME: But some women complain of problems with it, they get infections and hemorrhaging.

MANAL: Yes, after all it's a foreign object inserted into the body, and infections can happen if the woman doesn't clean properly. But of all the methods, it causes the least problems.

Implied in Manal and Karam's discussion, their tone of voice, and the fact that they both use the pill is a ranking of the pill and its users over the IUD and its users: the pill is more expensive, requiring a willingness to invest money in one's health; IUDs are used out of sheer familiarity, and they are helpful for women who would "mess up" and forget to take their pills.

Anna Lowenhaupt Tsing's work on Meratus Dayaks, a marginalized group in Indonesia, highlights the "instability of meaning and practice" of contraception. The meaning of contraceptive pills promoted by the Indonesian state was shifting:

> The pills I knew in the United States as artifacts of medical science had been transformed by Indonesian state discourse into an icon of bureaucratic order, and transformed again [regionally] . . . into the daily health-promoting herbal tonics of folk medicine, and again into nodes for Meratus acceptance of [regional] and state models of civilization. These interpretations coexisted uneasily, each threatening but never fully displacing others. (1993: 104)

Tsing does not portray these wider political developments "as imposed on a solid core of traditional social and cultural organization" where gender and fertility are assumed to solidly lie, unchanging and ahistorical (105). These meanings were constantly being negotiated by different Meratus people in both the present and past, and were linked to regional political changes.

In the Galilee too, as I read it, it is indeed political, social, and economic transformations and struggles that underpin the changing meanings and values of contraceptives. Shuruq, who has three children, told me:

They didn't explain anything about contraceptives to me at the MCH center. Explanations are for those who don't know anything, for women the nurse can see can't take care of themselves. There are many types of contraceptives in the world. Today there are books and everything. A cultured woman can read and she can decide. For example, before they used to use injections, now they don't recommend using them anymore. They barely exist. Only older women who are used to using them still request them. My doctor said that advanced, high [rāqyi] people in the world today use the pill, and the IUD is old-fashioned now.

The First World and its medical advances, books, facts, and science, the accelerating present and future, and where "we" lie in relation to them—all these things can be read between the lines of Shuruq's and many other people's discussions of contraception and reproduction.

However, the state enters women's lives to different degrees in different places. Martin suggests that the state comes relatively close to the bodies and lives of middle-class white women in the United States; according to Tsing, the state does not come so close to the marginalized Meratus women, but does affect them indirectly. The processes of medicalization, like those of consumption and commodification, have affected some women in the Galilee more than others, and not all women subscribe equally to the modernist hierarchy of planned pregnancies over mistakes, of new doctor-provided contraceptives over traditional or older methods. But this ranking has obviously become an important, if not hegemonic, measure of identity in the Galilee. Khadiji, the nurse and daughter-in-law of a sheikh, told me that my research absolutely required a look at contraceptives:

You should ask people about the type of contraceptives they use and how much they know about it and where from. A lot of women are afraid of the pain of the IUD because they don't understand anatomy and science. Still they don't think of the pain of not using an IUD, of being pregnant and delivering. Women also don't want to get an IUD because they say they don't want to open their legs in front of a doctor. But they forget that they'll open their legs even wider when they deliver the baby.

Thus contraception is clearly involved in plays of power, status, and identity. Sexual and reproductive control has today become deeply entrenched in the negotiation of power and identity in the Galilee. And it has become entrenched in ways that challenge us to examine the many categories of difference, including class and global positioning.

SCIENTIFIC ABORTION

Abortion is not nearly so polarizing an issue in the Galilee as it is in the United States, and it would be a gross mistake to associate it with the meanings and conflicts so familiar to Americans. Rather, its significance in the Galilee is in its "scientific application" to produce healthy modern families. Like contraceptives, medical abortion is seen as essential to family planning and hierarchizing, not because it is valued as a backup measure when contraception fails but because it is promoted as preventing the birth of "deformed" children and the production of bad families.

As Dalya and Fatmi (both Islamic religious teachers) explained to me, Islam permits abortion before the fetus has a soul. However, the fact that neither of these two teachers knew off the top of her head when "ensoulment" took place (each had to look it up) suggests that these ideas are not central in the everyday discourse on abortion. (Fatmi telephoned me a week later to tell me she had found out that ensoulment occurs 120 days after conception, not 90, as she had told me earlier.) Abortion is not a great focus of attention in the Galilee. But when it does come up, the issue of fetal deformities is often involved.

It is indicative that Katarina (who is Christian) said, "Abortion is permitted although I wouldn't personally do it. I fear God. Children are a blessing from God. You can't kill a soul. . . . But if the woman has a small fetus, or the fetus has something wrong with it, or the fetus is sick, then she has to get an abortion." Fardos (71 and Muslim) from Tamra told me that "God will show his wrath to those who remove a child [have an abortion]." But when I asked her, "What if the fetus is deformed?" she said: "If it's deformed it doesn't matter. It's better to remove it than for the mother to be tortured with it."

Janan, an MCH nurse from Sakhnin, said: "Abortion is acceptable if a woman has tests and it becomes clear that there's a problem with the fetus, but otherwise I'm against it. She should have made calculations in the beginning to not get pregnant, and if she didn't, she should continue the journey. I think it's religiously forbidden to kill it, it's a soul." It is striking that the issue of the soul frequently loses its relevance the moment the fetus is found to be deformed.

Another MCH nurse, Khadiji, told me: "I think abortion is allowed if it's known that the fetus is deformed—it would be a crime against the rights of the fetus to go ahead and have it. Also, I think a woman can have an abortion if it's an unwanted pregnancy because of social or economic crises or for health reasons and it's before twenty weeks. At the clinic we even got a *fatwa* [Islamic legal opinion] showing that this is religiously acceptable. We show the *fatwa* to the mothers—especially those with deformed fetuses."

People who go ahead with a pregnancy after being told the fetus has Down's syndrome are considered primitive. Most people interpret such actions (or inaction) as either a lack of trust in science, meaning that the pregnant woman does not believe in the doctor's ability to predict whether her child will have Down's syndrome, or a fatalistic trust that God will perform a miracle and cure the fetus before it is born. In both cases, the lack of faith in science and blind faith in God are looked down upon strongly. Iftikar (who is unmarried and has no children) told me: "We want to live, my dear. The mother and the child will suffer. The deformed child will then say to his mother when he's older, 'Why did you bring me into this world?' The other day I saw a girl who is paralyzed and she was crying and saying that to her mother. Her parents were first cousins. What is sinful is to give birth to a deformed child, not to abort it."

What becomes central then is *determining* the presence of a deformity in the fetus—an essential step in planning a healthy "natural" family. Lubna, another MCH nurse, explained to me the difficulty of convincing "backward," "silly" women of the importance of fetal testing:

> Our policy is to encourage all the older women to take the amniocentesis test early on. But few women take this "headwater" test, as they call it, because they don't want to tell their husbands that there's a possibility that something is wrong. One woman said her husband didn't want her to take the test and she gave birth to a deformed boy and then they made a big problem for our clinic. She said we should have told her. . . . We do everything to try to convince them. We even brought a *fatwa* from Jerusalem about abortion and testing that says that the mother must have tests to see if the fetus is healthy because

Islam calls for healthy reproduction. We also have a new video put out by the Health Ministry that I find very effective. But my clinic is one of the very few in the Arab sector that has a video player. So the woman becomes convinced that she should take the test. Then she goes to the doctor for consultation and she comes back having changed her mind because the doctor told her there's a one in two hundred chance that she might miscarry. The women understand that there's a 99 percent chance that they might miscarry because of the test. They drive me crazy. They just don't want to understand because they don't want to have the test.

On the other hand, I have women who want to miscarry and try to drink boiled onion leaves, or have a child jump on her back while she's lying down. That way she'll be rushed to the emergency room, it will be covered by insurance, and she doesn't have to apply for an abortion. I told them that's wrong and can cause internal bleeding and be very dangerous.

Women don't understand, they don't look to the long term, only to today. Another situation is if a pregnancy is over forty weeks, we must direct the woman to the hospital for tests. What do the old women say to her? "No, don't go, when the dish is done, it will come out on its own." We've had situations where the fetus has died inside the mother's womb. We try to teach the women to count the movements of the fetus in the ninth month. Sometimes, even though you've explained to the woman, she comes for an appointment and casually mentions that there's no movement. "Why haven't you gone to the doctor?" . . . They say they're afraid the baby will die! We have a long, long way to go in the Arab sector.[10]

Lubna seemed sure that she knew what was good for her clients, and was very passionate about trying to prevent the birth of abnormal babies:

There was one woman whose condition was very bad. She was thirty-nine years old. She came to me asking to remove her IUD so she could get pregnant. She's married to her first cousin and their children haven't been normal. I asked her, "Does your husband know you want another baby?" She said, "No I didn't ask him." So I told her I was going to tell her husband, and I did. Some people criticized me because

---

10. Note that Lubna here adopts the designation "Arab sector," used by her employer, the Israeli Ministry of Health.

they think she should be free to do as she likes. But I didn't force her to not have another high-risk pregnancy, I just encouraged her not to.

According to Barbara Swirski and her colleagues, "there is a marked difference in the compliance of pregnant Arab and Jewish women with recommendations for amniocentesis. In 1992, 16% of pregnant Arab women and 68% of pregnant Jewish women aged 37 years and more carried out the recommended procedure" (1998: 22). These varying degrees of compliance suggest varying degrees of medicalization and trust in medical establishments and procedures.

Khadiji told me that part of the problem is that women are told there is a *chance* of deformity, and they go around telling people that the doctors told them the fetus *is* deformed. Then when some of them go through with the pregnancy and the fetus turns out normal, "they say 'You see, the doctors were wrong. How can anyone know about an unborn fetus?' But in fact the doctor only told them there was a chance in their case." As Monira said, "Before, people didn't believe these tests where they tell you if the baby is deformed. In the beginning it was something strange; afterward we were convinced. But science has advanced and we now accept this."

There are, of course, many different views on abortion. Most people I spoke with said that it is a woman's right to do what she wants, to give birth to a deformed baby if she so desires. But most of them thought it was "backward" not to abort it. Georgina told me, "The doctors can't force the mother to remove a deformed fetus. They can only warn her. After all, she's the one who has to live with it. And in any case, if the pregnancy is unwanted, then in the end a woman's psychological situation affects the baby. If she's unhappy emotionally, this will stunt the fetus's growth or dry her womb up and she'll miscarry on her own anyway." Despite the variety of opinions, concern about what is referred to as "deformity" and its scientific predictors was widespread. This is yet another example of the infiltration of the medical sciences into the social processes of reproduction and family creation. Family planning and specifically the planning of healthy families with the aid of science are highly valued in the Galilee.

COUNTER-NARRATIVE

As I have emphasized repeatedly, the modernist narrative is dominant but not hegemonic. An antimodernist narrative is also strong and expresses unease and discontent with many transformations taking place in the Galilee. Alongside the idealization of science, medicine, and modernity is a strong critique of them as corrupting and corroding. As with sex education, modernity's perversions are inextricably linked to its advances.

In fact, a popular criticism of modernity is deployed through the construction of opposed binary bodies: mythically robust and natural premodern bodies versus weak and delicate modern medicalized bodies. This is best illustrated by a conversation I had with a group of elderly women from the 'Asli, a clan heavily stigmatized in the modernist hierarchy of family planning:

ME: Was life very different when you were young?

KALTHUM: Oh, yes, of course. A pregnant woman would go to the fields to pull out weeds, to harvest, all day long, and she'd go home in the evening and they'd simply place a hard pillow on the floor for her—one woman would hold her from behind and one from the front—and she'd just give birth. Just like that. Then the midwife would cut the cord. They'd make her *khwayya* [a special dessert for such occasions] to eat while she was resting and that's it. Then she'd go back to work.

Today it's a rare woman who gives birth well. We didn't use to go to any clinics or to any pictures [ultrasound] or anything. The healthy baby would come and the unhealthy would go. But take today, from the first month or the second: "Where are you going?" "To the clinic." "Where were you?" "At the doctor's."

ZAYNAB: I swear, the bottle you put in a child's mouth we didn't even know. . . . If the child used to get hungry we'd put a little piece of candy in a scarf and wet it and give it to the child to suck. The woman who couldn't find candy would make some dough and sprinkle sugar on it, wet it, and put it in the scarf. Life was very simple and there was scarcity. But today women can't keep the baby past seven months. We used to give birth naturally, from God. Today, honey, they're all early deliveries.

A woman in her [ninth] month would go to collect firewood, she'd carry huge bundles on her head and not care. Today there's no girl who can carry a huge bundle on her head even if she's not pregnant.

KALTHUM: Before, they used to move around a lot, they were much
               stronger. It was much better than today, we were so
               happy, because we used to be out in the wilderness, with-
               out medicines or anything, and all these illnesses of today
               we didn't know about them.

ZAYNAB: Girls today give birth to half of their babies deformed,
               and from the sixth or seventh month. Every month they
               go to the hospital and come back, go and come.

ME: Why do you think they're so weak?

KALTHUM: Before, the woman used to work harder than the man. To-
               day the man gets more tired. Women used to work with
               the men all day long and on top of that get pregnant. A
               lot of women died in childbirth, there were no doctors, no
               help. Today there's a lot of help. Before, people didn't un-
               derstand. Today, people have developed.

The feeling that "doctors help a lot" coexists with the belief that bodies
cared for by doctors are weak and reproductively inferior. For over three
hours these women emphasized over and over again that modern-day
women are reproductively weak, that it is rare for them to carry their
babies to term, unlike "the old days." Today's women don't work, they
sit at home and are pampered and their bodies are weak.

This critique of modernity vis-à-vis women's bodies and fertility coexists with the embrace of modernity and its pursuit. Kalthum and
Zaynab themselves told me that having experienced home deliveries
and hospital ones, the less natural deliveries at the hospital were easier
and in the end definitely preferable. Kalthum said that after her first
medically assisted hospital delivery, "I would never go back to the village midwife, no matter what." Thus there is a constant tension in this
deployment of binary bodies; the modern includes the good and the bad.

An article in al-'Ittihad similarly tells of a woman who had eleven
healthy children without setting foot in a hospital or a clinic, without
ever taking iron supplements, without seeing her fetus's heart beat on an
ultrasound screen. When her older daughters forced her to do all these
things during her twelfth pregnancy—to visit the doctors, who "love to
conduct tests and play with stethoscopes"—the pregnancy became
complicated, though the doctors were able to manage the complications
(Apr. 9, 1996).

A few neighborhoods over from Zaynab and Kalthum, Badriyyi, who
is even older than they by some twenty years, echoed their analysis of

premodern powerful bodies and modern weak ones: "Before, we used to do so much work and women would give birth in the fields. There was a woman who was coming home from the fields and gave birth on the road—isn't that a crime? But the children would come out better than they come out now. Now women are spoiled and have everything. So they don't want to have as many children, they don't want to make the effort and get tired." Part of Badriyyi's critique of modernity and medicalization is the reproductive "laziness" it fosters and the reluctance of modern women to have big families.

Khaldiyyi, who is significantly younger (she is in her early 50s), said: "I had easy deliveries. I'd be in and out of the delivery room in three or four hours. And easy pregnancies. I was so energetic. Today I find the young generation to be spoiled and silly—they complain so much. Once I had an operation [Caesarean] and three days later I was at the sink cooking and cleaning. I can't stand staying in bed. On the other hand, my neighbor had an operation and for forty days she was on her back with her hands folded behind her head. I don't like this."

It is not just elderly women fondly recalling the days of their youth who criticized modernity's weak and lazy bodies. Far from it; this discourse was deployed across generations. Karam, a 30-year-old woman, said: "Things used to be more natural and healthy before. Now everyone gets cancer. In 'Arrabi alone there are seventy cases of cancer. Before, we used to raise our chickens and goats and vegetables, all our food, without chemicals and needles. Today everything is artificial and bad for the body."

Modern bodies were seen as altogether different from premodern ones. The belief that young girls menstruate much earlier today than they used to, that the percentage of women who are infertile has increased, or that young women gain more weight during pregnancy were very common. Georgina (32) poked fun at her younger sister-in-law, who was pregnant for the first time: "She refuses to lift anything or do anything around the house for fear the baby will come down. What is it tied with, a little string? No, it's holding on with its hands and legs. Today's girls are so afraid and weak."

The outbreak of mad cow disease in England was an occasion for the expression and reinforcement of discontent with the artificiality of modern life. Kamal, who used to raise cows when he was younger, told me on the senior citizens' bus trip: "How can cows eat cows? Of course they're going to go crazy. The world has gone crazy altogether." Fear of contagion stopped people from even buying chocolates that might contain milk from England. Similarly, allegations that radioactive refuse from the nuclear plant in southern Israel had seeped into the water system aroused fear of technology and its inescapably deleterious effects on the modern body. But such critiques and fears of modernity were particularly audible at the intersection with the body—the medicalization of reproduction.

CONTRACEPTION AND THE NATURAL BODY

The simultaneous denigration and idealization of technology and medicine is expressed in terms not only of modern and premodern bodies but also of the perceived effects of contraception. The pill especially evoked fears of an invasion of the body by a foreign element, which led some women and men to favor the IUD, rhythm, or withdrawal, all methods they considered "more natural." Many people told me that in one way or another, the pill weakens the body [bihabbiṭ il-jisim]. Samah, the woman born in Kuwait, said she used an IUD because she's "afraid of the pill, because it makes you fat and it's all hormones." Ibrahim from Kukab commented:

> Everything you put into your body that's chemical has side effects. Doctors are sure that the pill has side effects; it's not a teaspoon of honey or a vitamin. God knows what the exact effects of these chemicals are. Science may have an opinion but it's not always accurate. A human being is complex, his mind and his body. So even specialists don't know the extent of the negative impact of even regular medicines, like an Acamol for a headache, not to mention contraceptive pills.

Sunbul, the woman from "modern" Kufur Yasif who was trained as a lab technician, told me: "Pills increase the risk [she used the Hebrew sikuy] of cancer. Hormones in the body will have side effects. I am against any chemical material entering the body." Sunbul preferred to use what she considered a "natural" method, the rhythm method, though she emphasized her "scientific" precision in using a thermometer and chart for accuracy of calculation. Sunbul held "nature" and "science" in a delicate balance.

One of the reactions to fears of the pill's deleterious effects is women's attempts to "rest" from it periodically so as to not let their bodies "take to it" [yūkhudh ʿalayha]. Side effects that women told me they experienced and anticipated included weight gain, acne, nausea, thicker body hair, moodiness, and difficulty in getting pregnant for a long time after they discontinued the pill because the womb "dries up." To avoid these problems, many women recommended occasionally "taking a rest." Suha did this for three months of every year, so that her body would not become "addicted" to the chemicals. This was one way to attempt to control the artificiality engulfing the body.

"Too much" fear of modernity and medicine, however, was frequently designated as irrational suspicion. Most complaints about medicine were themselves supposedly based on "scientific" evidence, on medical science's own admission of the possibility of side effects. The fear that the pill would destroy a newlywed's fertility was often considered a primitive superstition. Rudaina, an MCH nurse, explained to me:

> Our neighbor, Afif's wife, used birth control when she first got married because she was still going to school, but it's been three years since she stopped, and she hasn't been able to get pregnant. The pill didn't do anything. She had a problem from the beginning and didn't know about it. But you know how old women talk—they all blamed her for taking the pill, that it ruined her, when in fact she had a problem to start with. But now all the women in her family refuse to use the pill.

According to this modernism, fear of science should be based on science itself.

Shihnaz, who used an IUD, told me: "A lot of women use the pill, but look at Samera (her half sister, who is my relative by marriage and is sitting next to me), see how bad she looks from it. Muntazir the pharmacist told me they were bad for my particular type of body." But Samira said she preferred to use the pill, as artificial and insidious as it might be, for fear of what she considered the even more invasive IUD: "I'm afraid of the IUD. Many women say it hurts when you sleep with your husband. How can it not hurt? It's a hard piece of plastic inside of you! I'd rather have medicine inside me than that."

Many couples preferred the IUD over the pill because it was more "natural" and (often) did not involve chemicals in the blood. But many did not consider it totally natural either. Rawya told me:

> The doctors at the MCH clinics prefer IUDs because chemicals are bad for the body. Also the IUD is more guaranteed because you don't have to remember anything. But my sister-in-law had an IUD and she had so many problems with it. They had to perform surgery to remove it. So now all the women in the family are scared of it. There

was a boy who was born holding his mother's IUD in his fist. So you can't just forget about it. You have to get it checked every six months.

In trying to choose a contraceptive method, women (and to a lesser extent men) faced dilemmas constructed in this way, as a balancing of the advantages and dangers of medical science. Such decisions were often considered a matter of choosing between imperfect alternatives. Salam told me:

> I heard that pills make you get veins in your legs. They make you nervous and give you headaches. But the IUD also has its problems. They say it makes you fat, although for me it was the opposite: I lost weight. It gives you backache, and you menstruate for ten days. It's not good for the woman or her husband for menstruation to last so long. What else is there to do, though? The method between the woman and the man isn't good for either of them. They don't enjoy themselves—I never tried this method, actually I don't even know how it's done, but there are a lot of people who use it.

Similarly Muna, the physics teacher in Sakhnin, said: "The IUD is the most guaranteed thing, and it doesn't have sediments like the pill, but it can cause hemorrhaging. Pills, on the other hand, give you nerves and lower your blood pressure—I had difficulty breathing. With the day-counting method, a person might make a mistake, and sometimes ovulation [she used the Hebrew *biyuts*] happens early. So you have problems with each method."

Nuhad, who finally settled on an IUD, told me:

> All the methods are harmful. Both ways—the pill and the IUD—the woman gets a bad deal. Pills increase a woman's hair and exhaust her mental state. I used it for a short period—I gained weight and felt nauseous. It can cause cancer. But the IUD causes cancer of the uterus. The easiest way is for the man to do it [withdrawal]. But they often don't agree, and it's their right. We used it and I didn't like it—it isn't fair [she used the English "fair"] to either of us. If the man can't hold himself, then it doesn't work anyway.

Trust in the harmlessness of medicine was rare. Shuruq's statement seemed rather exceptional: "There are no longer any problems with the IUD, it doesn't cause inflammation any more. They used to say that the pill would make you fatter, but now all the new medicines don't make you fat or anything. They've improved the technology so it doesn't cause side effects. Medicine has really advanced." Many more women (and men) said there was a tradeoff between medicine and health, between accuracy, success rate, and modernity on the one hand and naturalness on the other, a tradeoff that they had to calculate for themselves. Moreover, bodies are seen to vary: some bodies are more vulnerable to modernity's artificial effects and some are unaffected. Thus each woman must figure out for herself what suits her body best. While the IUD was sometimes considered less invasive and artificially insidious than the pill, withdrawal in combination with the rhythm method was considered more natural than both the IUD and pill. But it was not totally natural either, because natural sex is often conceived of as involving the "quenching" or "watering" [yirtwy] of the woman's body, both literally and figuratively: wetting her with the man's semen and giving her pleasure. Lamis, for example, said: "I count the days of the month and from day eight to day twelve after my period my husband spills outside. I heard that those other methods harm your health—pills give you veins and stomachaches. But still, on the days when he finishes inside it's better; I don't get a backache. It's not good without coming inside. Every method has its side effects."

Many people in the Galilee mentioned the importance of "quenching" on the permitted days (according to the rhythm method), for it prevents dryness in the womb and pain in the back. Yumna warned that "with spilling outside, one needs to be careful. There is no freedom in it. The man gets side effects from trying to hold himself back so much. The woman feels like she hasn't reached a climax that people reach, because she hasn't finished the sex act to its end." An article in a popular Arabic magazine says: "There is no doubt that the inevitable result of using artificial measures is the rise of tension in the woman's bodily order, whereby she increasingly feels anxiety, restlessness, discomfort, and boredom when she does not satisfy her sexual instinct. . . . These results have been observed especially among those who have chosen withdrawal as a contraceptive method" (Manbar, 1995). Muna similarly told me: "Some people like to have the man ejaculate outside, but that's a problem. I have a friend whose husband never spilled inside for six years. This is tiring psychologically for the woman; she gets dryness and infections." Thus although withdrawal is considered natural in comparison with the pill or the IUD because "no foreign materials" enter the body, it is unnatural and harmful in other ways. In some sense, the IUD and pill can be considered more natural because they permit quenching, even though they also involve foreign objects. According to Mustafa:

We also used the IUD. Methods like the condom decrease sexual pleasure for the man, a natural part of family life. Pills have health side effects on the mother and on the newborn, so we didn't like to use them. My wife wanted to use the pill but I suggested the IUD, because it's better than other methods. Of course, there had to be agreement between us, since she's the one who's going to be carrying it inside her. I never tried it on my own body, but my wife had few problems. The best thing about it is that you can practice sex naturally and you have a high degree of certainty that fertilization will not occur.

Thus the IUD in this sense is more natural than withdrawal because it allows the free flow of sex and semen.

Ideas similar to those concerning withdrawal are associated with the condom—that it prevents the natural flow of the man's semen and the woman's natural quenching, perhaps even more than withdrawal. Ghusun told me that "condoms are no good because there isn't enough sexual contact [used Hebrew *maga' mini*], and the man has to stop and put it on; the taste of things is gone. It's not good for the man. It's tight and constrains him and makes him nervous. It's better if he spills outside; he's more free and it's more natural."

However, condoms are also widely associated with modernity's supposedly perverse non-family-oriented diseases. Samah told me that the condom is only for young men who want to "go wild" with foreign women or men who travel a lot, and that "most women would say, 'I'd never let my husband use a condom,' because that would imply that he had a disease, or that he was afraid because he slept with another woman outside." 'Abid told Manhal:

Condoms are spread throughout the world because of AIDS. It decreases a man's pleasure. The sex act is no longer natural, something artificial enters into it, even in the mind-set of the man or the woman. There's an artificial abnormal *[shādh]* factor involved. In addition to its biological effect, it has a psychological effect on both. It's not used much among families, but it exists in free sex *[al-jins al-mutaḥarrir]* among young men who go outside and practice sex with Jewish or foreign women. Most of it is fear of disease, they don't care about fertilization. Inside the family they prefer different methods. Thinking about sex in the Arab family hasn't reached the level of condoms, because family life, even though it has sex, is still holy and pure. So we haven't gotten to these things, maybe to our good fortune. It doesn't exist and I don't see it existing any time soon.

Thus condoms carried the stigma of modernity's extrafamilial "perversions." Suha told me that even though the MCH brochures have information about condoms, Arab doctors and nurses never suggest using them; "They'll tell you about every method but that one. I once told my husband, 'Let's use this,' and he started shouting [she is laughing] that it's disgusting [qaraf] between a man and his wife." Muna said: "We used the condom once, but Arabs don't like barriers because they affect the sexual process. It makes it tepid, cools it off. It's mostly used for being loose [sayābi]." Farid told Manhal that "condoms are not used in our society. It depends on the client [zbūn]. They made it for foreigners. I'm not going to explain in detail so Rhoda doesn't get a complex when she hears this tape [laughing]. But it's not made for Arabs." Even I must be protected from hearing about condoms' modern perversity.

But while they carry the stigma of modernity, condoms also carry its distinction of science and control. One of my former classmates, Kawthar, said:

> The condom is the best method. It's the most guaranteed. The doctor told me that pills aren't good for me. It took me ten months to get pregnant when I first got married. I don't have an abundance of hormones. She told me that pills will affect me a lot, and even though she's Jewish, she told me, "Make one baby after the other [Kawthar used the Hebrew ta'asi yeled ahare hashini] and then rest." There is also the method of spilling outside, but there's no guarantee in it. So I suggested the condom and my husband was interested. We've been using it ever since, and it's the best of all the methods science has created.

Thus the condom can be a sign of science and modernity as well as unnatural and dirty.

Note the widespread frankness concerning sexual pleasure. Most of the comments on the pros and cons of withdrawal point to its deficiency in terms of sexual fulfillment for women as well as men. This matter, too, is tied to issues of modernity and identity: ironically, old-fashioned women, although conceived of as out of control where reproduction was concerned, were also considered ignorant of sexual pleasure and supposedly performed sex as a duty to their husbands, while modern women were seen as in control of their reproduction and more frequently sexually fulfilled. This attitude is evident in Munir's comments on withdrawal:

> I've used this method too. If you can control yourself, it's 100 percent guaranteed. But if you can't control yourself, any leakage and that's

it. Its bad side is that at the moment of climax you have to withdraw. To a certain extent it reduces your pleasure. The whole goal for the man is to finish inside the woman. But when you have to withdraw, you enjoy yourself a little less. But that's what's available. Not only for the man, but the woman prefers to have the man finish inside too. So it puts a damper on the pleasure of both. In Arab society, unfortunately, there are some women who have never reached a climax at all, because if a person doesn't have the sexual awareness or high culture to know that he has a partner in sex, then his wife will never experience pleasure. A man is able to reach a climax much more quickly than a woman. So if he doesn't deal with the woman as though she has a right to reach a climax and only cares about himself, then he finishes inside or outside, it doesn't matter.

Thus sexual pleasure, too, is embedded in "sexual awareness" and "high culture."

Note that both withdrawal and the condom are controlled largely by the man, with the cooperation of the woman, while the pill and the IUD are controlled by the woman and her doctor. This control is seen as a potential source of power. The control over use of the pill and the IUD permits some "old-fashioned" women to have more children than their husbands want. As many people pointed out, these unmodern wives could stop taking the pill or remove the IUD and claim a mistake. Similarly, male control of withdrawal allows some "primitive" men to force their wives to have more children. On the other hand, modern men and women ideally "consult" each other, try to reach an understanding, and agree upon contraception, rather than manipulate each other through control of it. Muna told me: "Some men don't talk to their wives at all about this. What kind of marriage is that? My husband and I always discuss this because he says, 'It's not up to the woman to stick the man with another child.' It's his life, too. And he wants it to be as organized as possible." Here again we see the companionate relationship at the center of the valued modern family.

PLANTING THE SEEDS OF MODERNITY

Just as contraceptive technologies have been inserted into daily life in the Galilee through constructions and negotiations of their meaning, assisted conception has also been endowed with local significances. As Marcia Inhorn notes, such technologies are not "immune to culture" but get appropriated in complex ways (1998: 2). The introduction of medically assisted conception has opened up a new field where medicine, modernity, and reproduction fuse in the Galilee. As noted earlier, Israel has more fertility clinics per capita than any other country, three times more than the United States (Kahn 2000: 2), although Palestinians' access to these clinics (like their access to other medical facilities) is clearly not equal to that of Jews. In any case, "planting" *(zari')*, as it is generally referred to here, like modern bodies, is the subject of much praise and condemnation. In line with the sentiment that science can solve any problem, planting is considered an important new invention that helps men and women achieve the important goal of parenthood and family. Planting is also, however, regarded with much suspicion as potentially undermining the very foundation of society and family. As Nuhad put it, "All this planting and surrogate motherhood technology, it's all stuff from America that's going to destroy the Arab society *[ykharrib bayt il-'arab]*."

A central component of this fear of planting is its potential "mixing of offspring." The term "birth control" *(tahdīd in-nasil*, literally "limiting offspring") usually refers to contraception and population control, but it takes on a literal meaning for Lawahiz: the specification and exact identification of offspring. Although Lawahiz is unmarried, she feels strongly about it:

> I accept the idea of planting, but not from a man other than the husband, because birth control is important. You must guarantee that the child is from me and my husband, otherwise I'd stop loving the baby. Adoption is a possibility for infertile couples, but it's not the same feeling as having your own. If you're going to go ahead and adopt, it should be from someone you know, otherwise there'll be suspicion and rejection.

Such fear and suspicion of planting as well as of anonymous adoption[11] point to a strong feeling of genetic determination and biological belonging—a type of "grassroots eugenics" (Tober 1998). Kinship and love here are configured as rooted in the blood or genes.

Yasmin, who grew up in Syria, thinks "it's great that they came out with this planting thing. Couples with infertility problems no longer

11. Najdiyyi also rejected anonymous adoption when she told me that "Arabs don't give children up for adoption. Jews adopt because there are so many bastards, they have so many bastards to fill the world. For Arabs, if you have a child, why would you sell it?"

have to go without children. But the planting needs to be from the husband or else the child will be a foreigner. Planting from outside goes inside the body—it's like adultery." Thus mixing of sperm and egg that are not from a husband and wife is tantamount to actual sex between the persons who produce the sperm and egg. The sperm and the egg and the genetic material in them, with the spread of science and medicine, have become invested with identity.

Dalya, the Islamic religious teacher, told me:

> Islam has allowed planting, but the seed must be from the husband. It's legal. But there is always the fear that the seed can be changed. There was a case recently in the Islamic newspaper about an Italian woman who had twins as a result of planting and one of them was white and the other was black! Apparently they mixed up and gave her another man's sperm.

This example is a dramatic illustration of the fear of miscegenation in planting. Patricia Williams comments on a similar case in the United States, where a white mother sued a sperm bank for the "tragic" mistake that caused her to give birth to a black boy; she asks what such an event tells us about the "supposition that it is natural for people to want children 'like' themselves" and "what constitutes this likeness?" (1991: 226).

Nuhad felt that planting from another man is

> a decision that the woman has to make. I personally wouldn't do it. Some people consider it adultery. Moreover, the man wants something from his flesh and blood. This is also true of adoption. There will certainly come a time when the child grows up when you realize you've done him an injustice by not allowing him his real parents. He will want to know who his real mother is. Perhaps his mother is an adulteress. . . . That's what he's going to think. I know one sister who gave birth to a baby for her sister—when the girl grows up she's going to have problems. This is selfishness on the part of the parents.

Again, Nuhad emphasized the idea that belonging requires a tie of "flesh and blood."

This is not to imply that before assisted conception was available or the science of genetics had been developed, paternity (or maternity) was insignificant. Rather, the "scientific" pinpointing of identity in sperm or ova has reinforced and given new expression to links between paternity and maternity on the one hand and identity, tradition, and Arabness on the other.

My former elementary school math teacher, Sobhiyyi, had fertility treatments after fifteen years of marriage and had a baby boy. She never considered adoption because she was religious and interpreted the Qur'an as forbidding it. She said: "Even if I took in an orphan to care for, when he gets older, he must know who he is. If I am the adoptive mother, I will be forbidden to him and his sisters would be too—he'll have to live in the house like a stranger." She emphasized that she wanted a child "for my loins [min ṣulby]. I don't want to get attached to a child, and wear myself out over him, only for him to grow up to be a stranger." The idea that genetic parenthood is the only means to attain true intimacy is strong for Sobhiyyi.

Moreover, my teacher was against using a sperm donor for assisted conception because "in religion it's illegal to mix, because then the child is illegitimate, a result of adultery. You don't know where this sperm is coming from. It's forbidden to mix offspring. This is true in Judaism, too. I'll give you this article written by the chief rabbi forbidding mixing. Surrogate motherhood is also forbidden, because some of the blood of the woman and her heritable traits will enter the child."

Many people told me they did not or would not approve of planting another man's sperm because the child would be a bastard, a result of adulterous unknown intermixing. Muna said, "The husband will always feel that this is not his son and that the son won't have affection [yḥinn] for him as a father." Jana, the nurse who got pregnant in her 40s, said:

JANA: It's better for planting to be from the woman's husband, because otherwise she could go through all the troubles of pregnancy and childbirth and upbringing just for an outsider [barrāny].

ME: What about adoption? Do you think it's a good option?

JANAN: It's OK—it's better than them staying without children at all.

ME: Why is adoption OK but fertilization from another man not?

JANAN: In the case of fertilization from another man, it could cause trouble in the future. The husband could say one day, "This isn't my son, I don't want it." But in adoption, especially if the child is very young, there's not that much difference from a real child, and the woman also is relieved of the torture of pregnancy and childbirth.

Planting has gotten a bad reputation because of the fear of "mixing." Recently there was a rumor in Nazareth that a politician's son had a fertility problem (supposedly his testicles were undeveloped) and his wife claimed she had had two children by planting. Later it was revealed that she was having an affair with a neighbor and her two children were products of "mixing" and adultery. This incident gave a new meaning to assisted conception and did not do much good for the reputation of planting. My teacher Sobhiyyi told me:

> People think planting involves mixing, taking sperm from outside. A third of our society thinks this way. I tried planting for a while. I had to do it four times, without success. At first I kept it secret. I didn't like to talk about it to anyone because I knew what they'd be thinking. No one actually criticized me to my face. Later I started explaining to guests exactly what my fertility therapy was. I suggested that there should be a center for this subject, an association of families that have an infertility problem, to educate people and change society's views on the subject. Planting doesn't have to involve mixing. I very much regret the fifteen years of marriage that went by before I tried planting.

Khadiji, the nurse I have mentioned many times, also had had planting done:

KHADIJI: My husband and I have reached a degree of contentment with our situation. Of course, if there are children, life is always better, but lack of children wouldn't affect our relationship.
We believe that planting is fine as long as the sperm and the egg are ours. Otherwise I don't consider it acceptable religiously or even morally. And of course I wouldn't accept a surrogate mother.

ME: Would you accept adoption?

KHADIJI: Yes, we've thought about that, and as a last resort we would adopt.

ME: What is the difference between adoption and sperm or egg donation?

KHADIJI: It's in the process of fertilization itself. I'm getting IVF [she used the English abbreviation for "in vitro fertilization"] treatment right now, but I don't tell people because they don't understand, and they start making accusations about the source. In the West, this is routinized. Even Israeli health insurance covers the cost of IVF for the first child, then partially for the second.

Monira similarly told me that "most of those people who get planting don't admit to doing so, so that people won't start spreading rumors and suspecting that it's from another man, because that would be considered shameful."

This fear of scientific methods of producing babies was far from total. Many people did pursue medically assisted conception, some even when it did involve "mixing," although they rarely revealed that fact. Taghrid, the Bedouin woman from 'Ilabun, said, "It's fine if the sperm is from another man, because it's a shame to deprive the mother of offspring." When the emphasis is on motherhood, mixing becomes acceptable. And the view that adoption, especially of a baby of unknown origin, is not the right way to build a family is also disputed. Ghusun reminded me of the old saying "Rearing beats milk" (ir-riba ghalab il-liba). She also thinks that "planting is fine even if it's not from the husband. It's better than remaining childless, even though people might gossip. Here in our village there are already two or three cases. People and relatives go and congratulate them just as if they had children normally." Georgina also said: "Planting is good. Even if it's not from the husband, it doesn't matter; a woman wants to feel her child inside her."

These attitudes contradict but do not negate the dominant view of planting and science as bad mixing, based on "scientific" ideas about genes and identity.

TOLERANT MODERNITY

The negotiations of contraceptives, abortion, and assisted conception suggest a bricolage of modernity in the Galilee. They trace a worldview that is rather eclectic. Indeed, "tradition" is often tolerated rather than excluded outright. At the same time that medical science is highly fetishized and pursued, traditional medicine is often tolerated as "harmless." It is considered acceptable to resort to it after scientific medicine has failed, but not in place of it. Thus tolerance of herbal medicine, religious healing, and ritual protection coexists with a strong insistence on "universal" yet "Western" medical science. Yumna said that desperate people, especially infertile women, "grab on to ropes of air, they're usually tired from medicine and they won't lose anything by trying something else, so they are persuaded and go."

This attitude is dramatically and crudely reflected in the explanation an elderly man from my village supposedly gave for his religiosity: "I pray to God every day, five times a day, because if there is an afterlife, I've guaranteed myself a place in Eden. If not, he can go stuff my prayers up his ass."

Muna, who emphasized her modernity to me repeatedly and in many ways, also did not hesitate to accompany a friend who had had several miscarriages on a visit to a healing sheikh:

When people try medicine for so long without results, they turn to traditional ways. I went with my friend to a sheikh because the doctors didn't know what was wrong with her. The sheikh started reading on her mother's name. He knew things about her life that she hadn't told him. He told her she needed to lock her back *[tʾaffil ẓahirha]*. He doesn't ask for money but she slipped some for him under his mattress. He told her she shouldn't eat the neck of an animal—it has a jinn in it and the fetus will fall if she eats it. In Ksal and Sakhnin they have these sheikhs. They frequently recommend this closing of backs for women who have repeated miscarriages. They also prescribe sleeping with your husband outside the house if you've recently moved to a new one.

The sheikh read prayers over Muna's friend to ritually "close her back" with a little lock and key, which she must keep in her brassiere until her child is born. Most of these healers are pious elderly men or post-menopausal women; they read prayers and write amulets to ward off the evil eye, cure diseases, help women carry pregnancies to term, and help them conceive.

Sunbul, the woman from modern Kufur Yasif who married into "backward" Shfa ʿAmir, said her mother-in-law "steamed" *(bakhkharat)* her two children—burned incense and recited the Qurʾan over the children to protect them from the evil eye. While Sunbul said she didn't believe in the evil eye, she allowed her old-fashioned mother-in-law to do what she wanted "because it comforted and reassured her. She also salted them to make them strong. I didn't want to upset her so I let her. And really there's no point in fighting about it—it's harmless." Despite Sunbul's background in chemistry and her emphasis on scientific precision in many aspects of her life, she accepted her mother-in-law's unscientific precautions. I knew many modern people who allowed their mothers and grandmothers to "steam" their children "so all the possibilities are covered," both scientific and traditional. My mother, too, adorned me and my brother as infants with the charms against the evil eye that my relatives brought as gifts. When I left for college, she slipped one into my suitcase.

Yet when I spoke with a family friend about the details of such traditional means to protect children and grandchildren—placing a blue eye pendant on a child, washing an infant in sweet-smelling myrtle (a Druze custom), giving a baby boy something of his father's *(min ʿathar abū)* the first time he is taken out—he cautioned me against telling the Americans about "these silly things." I must be sure to tell them, he said, that if a child falls ill, no one he has ever met would rush him to a sheikh rather than a doctor. People believe in medical science and depend on it.

Many people struggle to reconcile medical science and tradition or religion, arguing for their compatibility. Fatmi the religious teacher told me: "According to the Qur'an, the infant should sleep on its side. Nurses' recommendations keep on changing—a few years back, they used to say that infants should sleep on their stomachs. Then they did more research and changed their minds and said they should put the baby on its side. The Qur'an has always said that sleeping on the stomach is the sleep of the devil. God is always right." Khadiji, on the other hand, who is also deeply devout, said she would breast-feed her children for a year "even though the Qur'an says it should be for two years. But research [used Hebrew *maḥkarim*] indicates that after one year the mother's milk isn't that beneficial and that the child needs other sources of nutrition." Both Khadiji and Fatmi told me that in the end they would listen to a doctor before they would listen to a sheikh, despite their religiosity.

Imm ʿAbid lamented the passing of a time when women would gather at the saints' tombs in the village: "People used to go and make vows to the saints—to conceive a boy or to cure a baby. . . . But today people don't even believe in God anymore, not to mention the power of a saint. They don't have time for that anymore. No one goes these days, only a few old ladies give offerings. Those days are gone." Imm ʿAbid recently donated money to fix one of the walls that had collapsed around the nearby saint's tomb—she believes the saint has blessed many in her family as a result and allowed her to live ninety-odd years.

Nira Reiss notes that historically Arab peasants in Israel "had a medical pluralist and eclectic attitude," but that "traditional practice was evidently most persistent with regard to pregnancy and birth." She cites 1943 British government statistics: "about 2% of births among Muslims occurred in hospitals compared to 86% of births among Jews"; general hospitalization rates among Arabs and Jews were closer (1991: 47). Yet this alleged persistence of tradition is something that Palestinians themselves do not necessarily remember or emphasize. A good case in point is midwifery. The British mandate government first tried to regulate and supervise midwives by requiring annual permits to practice, although they offered midwives little training. Later the state of Israel encouraged medical control of births by disbursing maternity payments, as mentioned earlier—a check sent to every woman who gave birth in Israel, but only if the baby was born in a hospital or was taken to a hospital immediately after birth and was thus registered. Home births and non-doctor-trained midwives were made illegal. Yet this medicalization of birth has not been widely perceived as coercive. My aunt, who had seven children at home and the last two in the hospital (starting in 1962), did not know there was a law against home deliveries, and in fact did not feel that her transition to the hospital was coerced. Rather she thought that people made the switch on their own, because they became more "aware" and the services became more accessible. My uncle explained that it was a matter of the availability and affordability of hospital services and their accessibility after "means of transportation became available." [12] My aunt told me that hospital births are naturally more comfortable for the woman: "In the hospital she lies on a bed two days, three, maybe even four. They used to say she was 'drinking soup' because the woman would be so pampered. And on top of that, the woman guarantees her health and the baby's." My aunt, in fact, had one baby who bled to death because, according to her, "the midwife didn't tie his umbilical cord correctly. If there were hospitals then, that baby wouldn't have died."

CONCLUSION

Faye Ginsburg and Rayna Rapp point to the frequently contradictory results of medicalization: it can be simultaneously empowering and disempowering. For example, "new medical technologies that can enhance child survival, improve women's health and 'cure' infertility are also methods of surveillance and regulation" (1991: 314). This view certainly echoes that of many Palestinians in the Galilee. The infiltration of

---

12. My uncle's car was one of the few in the village in the 1960s, and he developed a reputation for good luck: "Women who ride with 'Ihmad il-'Abid give birth to boys."

science in health care is both embraced and feared, used but with caution and attempts at containment and control. Palestinians have come to express both their hopes and desires, criticisms and fears largely within the limits of this system. Their relations to science and medicine thus interweave issues of modernity, identity, health, and power. Attitudes toward specific technologies such as forms of contraception and assisted conception are rooted in a combination of a desire for "modernity," negotiation of identity, and physical experience of these technologies. These innovations are both praised and criticized. Palestinians in the Galilee gingerly negotiate these forms of modernity—combinations of scientific, medical, and economic transformations—by embracing what is constructed as positive (enhanced beauty, sexual awareness, health, and fertility) and condemning the negative (vanity, sexual danger and perversion, artificiality, and medical invasiveness). While they are in so many ways marginalized and powerless in the face of these forceful and overwhelming changes, they are calculating agents in others. Today the control permitted by modern reproductive techniques is widely perceived as a means to escape marginality, negotiate identity, and attain progress.

FIVE

Son Preference

The desire to have sons is central to family planning in the Galilee. While I have argued that aspirations for modernization constitute pressures to plan a small family, son preference enters this mix in complex ways: the modern family must be small, but it also must include a male child—heir, protector, and hope for the future. While "too much" emphasis on a preference for sons is considered primitive, in certain modern forms it is considered an acceptable and desirable requirement of the ideal family.

SON PREFERENCE AS BACKWARD

During pregnancy women are sometimes told that the size of their belly, the frequent movement of the baby, the specific foods they crave, or the brightness of their eyes are signs that the fetus is male—or that the same indications mean it is female. A few women claimed that after several pregnancies they could tell the sex of the fetus they were carrying. Occasionally certain persons were playfully sought out to predict the sex of the fetus: a severely mentally disabled man who roamed in one city, an old holy man who was blind and paralyzed from birth in another village. If these soothsayers predicted correctly, they would receive a box of chocolates from the mothers, especially if they had correctly predicted a boy. The idea that the body reacts differently to the presence of a male or female fetus—that, as Sunbul put it, "somehow they think the body differentiates between girl and boy fetuses"—is part of the discourse of gender differences that begin even before birth.

This discourse is looked down upon as primitive. Seen through a modernist lens, it is backward and unscientific. According to Sunbul, "A baby is a baby. There is no scientific basis for this guessing." Most women, even those who seek out fortune-tellers to predict the sex of their baby, concede that such predictions are merely a guessing game— a way of experimenting and dealing with the anticipation, or a way for women to tease or encourage one another. Only God or the ultrasound knows, depending on the orientation at the moment. The errors in prediction, the knowledge that it is just a game and "women's silly talk" are all points at which the fundamental sameness of boys and girls is asserted.

Son preference is constructed as backward, primitive, and undesirable. A cousin of mine who is the head nurse of the neonatal division at a hospital in Nazareth and a big fan of Nawal Saadawi, an outspoken Egyptian feminist doctor and writer, told me how upset she gets when women who have boys at the hospital get lavished with attention and have more visitors and gifts than women who have girls. Newborn girls and their mothers get less attention, and "girls with any sort of disability or disease at birth are rarely visited and sometimes even abandoned. These people are disgusting, their minds are still in the Stone Age."

Similarly, Iftikar told me that many old-fashioned men want to have a large number of children and especially sons because they want to "increase their seed." "This is an instinct for some people," she said, "just like in Darwin—a gorilla wants to inseminate as many she-gorillas as possible. My father wanted eight kids and do you know why? He says he wanted to increase his seed. God damn such a seed. Look at my stupid brothers, they *are* just like him." Iftikar here constructs son preference as a base instinct.

Nisrin, the social worker, told me that

even people you think are highly educated have the most backward ideas. The other day there was an inspector who said in front of me that he was so glad that he had only sons and didn't have to deal with girls and their problems. I was very upset and told him, "Why do even you have this backward view of girls, as though they were merely a source of problems, burdens, when in fact they are a very constructive part of society?" I try to stand up and say things loudly everywhere I go, in my work, at home, at weddings, anywhere—I always express my opinion and try to change things. There is tremendous discrimination against girls in the family, they get less of everything, even if they're the smarter ones and the ones who would go further if they were given the chance.

Kawthar assured me: "You'll be surprised how many people—educated or not—prefer sons, but the educated ones aren't willing to admit it." I heard highly critical rumors of several doctors and their wives who sought sex-selective abortions; they allegedly used their medical privileges to find out the sex of their fetuses and then continued to abort female ones until a boy arrived. There was wide social consensus that it was morally reprehensible to discriminate against girls *to that extent,* and that such behavior was particularly shocking in a doctor. Many people emphasized to me the fact that it was especially outrageous that these couples included educated doctors who still thought in such a backward way. Just as "mistakes" made by seemingly educated and cultured couples were particularly unacceptable, so was this group's preference for sons—an indication of the promodernization roots of this stigma.

Thus there is a significant discourse of sexual egalitarianism in the Galilee, sometimes based on modern or Western ideas, but expressed also in the languages of morality, humanism, and religion, whether Muslim, Christian, or Druze: "Aren't girls human beings too?"; "Didn't God create both of them?"; "Boys and girls complement each other—life requires both." Most parents told me they try to treat their sons and daughters "exactly the same," even though they might view their respective interests in highly gendered ways. Many people insist that they love their daughters just as much as they love their sons—"Aren't they both my flesh and blood? Didn't I raise them both?"—if not more, since the girls "love you back" more.

Many people recounted stories to illustrate the injustice of son preference. Basmi from Tab'un, mother of six, described how her mother tragically "died because she wanted a boy. The doctors told her that if she got pregnant again it would be dangerous. But she wanted a son so badly, and I came as the fourth girl. She died in labor. Our society is male *[dhukūry]*. In my opinion the boy doesn't do anything for the parents, even though people say the boy carries his father's name. This is a shame."

Even women who are stigmatized as primitive reproducers had their own moral tales of the dangers of son preference (although they did not always ground them in the desire for modernization). Kalthum and Zaynab, who told me earlier about robust premodern bodies and healthy natural childbirth in the past, also told me:

KALTHUM: God can punish. Between one contraction and the next, he can change a boy [fetus] into a girl and vice versa, with his almighty power.

ZAYNAB: There is this one man who had twelve girls and his wife got pregnant again so he told her to go get a picture and they told her it was a girl. She went home and told her husband that they didn't tell her what sex it was. He said, "How could that be?" She said, "You just want to know so you can remove it if it's a girl." He then forced her to remove it, and when they did the abortion, twin boys came out.

KALTHUM: Once I was visiting a patient at the hospital and we visitors started talking among ourselves. They told us about a surgeon whose wife kept on giving birth to girls until they were eight, and they called him father of the girls. They didn't have pictures at the time, so the surgeon said, "I'm going to open her stomach. If it's a girl, I'll remove her, and if it's a boy, I'll leave him in." He found it was a boy so he left him there and closed his wife's stomach back up. But when his wife finally gave birth, it was a girl. God changed the boy to a girl, with his almighty power.

ZAYNAB: People say this woman or that woman only gives birth to girls, but I think the woman's not at fault. The man gives XY and the woman XX. If the sperm that the man gives is X, it will be a girl. If it's Y, it will be a boy.

KALTHUM: The land that you plant with wheat will grow wheat—it's the same with the seed of the man.

Kalthum and Zaynab's stories punish men who want boys "too much," even as Kalthum told me, "Why would I want a girl? They have too many problems."

Another story I was told several times—supposedly it had appeared in the local press—is about a man who went to visit his wife in the hospital after her child was delivered. When he found out that she had had yet another baby girl, he hit her. The man was then suddenly blinded. When I looked for the story in the newspapers, I found an article in a tabloid about a young woman who was hospitalized after her husband beat her because she had given birth to a third daughter. But no mention was made of a mysterious blindness befalling him (to my disappointment), even in the tabloid.

Thus there are widespread criticisms of son preference, grounded in science, "civilized culture," and logic, as well as religion and "human sympathy." Not only should the birth of a girl not be denigrated, but the mother should not be blamed. Many people insist that the sex of the baby is purely a matter of chance. Although men, especially "before," claimed it was the wife's fault, and a man could take a second wife to bear him sons, a popular proverb says, "What the shit puts in, the wife delivers," or "What your dick put in, your God created" (illy ḥaṭu zibbak khalaqu rabbak). This old saying lives on today and has been reconstructed with widespread scientific medical knowledge of genetics, as Zaynab's comment brings home. "Science" leaves no doubt that it is not the woman's fault if a girl is born. Indeed, the "science" of sex determination has become a topic of great interest as I argue below.

PRAGMATISM, NOT IDEOLOGY

The degree to which men and women present themselves as preferring boys varies in the Galilee, but often correlates with how modern they consider themselves or their audience to be. When I asked men and women, boys and girls, why some people prefer sons, I was often answered in abstract third-person terms: "*They* want an heir"; "*It's believed* that boys continue the lines of their father"; "*People* think that girls get married and leave them, while boys continue to live with them"; "*They* think boys belong to their parents, while a girl will soon belong to another family." Less frequently would someone say, "I prefer boys because I want to continue my line." More often I heard, "I want to have a boy not because of my own beliefs but because of family pressure"— pressure from mothers-in-law, husbands, or more fertile son-bearing sisters-in-law. Thus many people distance themselves ideologically from primitive son preference even when they are trying to have a boy.

A common method of distancing oneself from backward son preference is to depict oneself as a victim of a male-dominated society: it's the society that's backward, not me. According to my friend Salam, who has three girls, she will go on having children until she has a boy, even if it takes her ten tries[1]:

> But it's not for me, it's for him. He doesn't say anything, but I can tell without him saying it. Men want sons to leave behind, to carry their name. For me, these three girls are enough. It's very hard. I'm afraid of getting pregnant because I get depressed [she used the Hebrew *dika'on*). I don't like being cooped up. The first time is the hardest. When you give birth there are at least two months when you can't leave the house. I used to read about this depression but didn't believe it. Sometimes the women in the neighborhood say, "God feed you a boy." They pity me as though I were infertile or something. It makes me very uncomfortable. My youngest daughter will be two in September. I'm going to remove the IUD in two months, so my youngest will be around three and she can go to preschool. I don't want to get pregnant again but I'm forced to. And I tell myself it's better to do it now because later I'll be old. One woman told me about a way [to conceive a boy]. I don't believe in it but I'm going to try it anyway. Her husband has a Hebrew book that tells you how and they tried it and it worked for them. It tells you the day that the sperm [she used an inaccurate term, *manawiyyāt*] is more for the male. I'll get pregnant in June so I'll give birth at the beginning of summer, at least I can sit outside.
>
> Our society is envious of those who have boys—not girls—even if the boys are stupid and not smart. Our society is superstitious and discriminatory—and this enters into the smallest details of life. When they mix the henna at a wedding, they have a woman with lots of sons do it.
>
> A person is really affected by the people around you, and you're happy when they approve of you. I was so naive before I got married, I didn't know how important it is to be strong, how difficult it is to manage a house, a husband, a family. I was so silly I didn't know how hard it would be. You really have to be strong here and maybe I'm not strong enough.

1. This attitude is not necessarily due solely to son preference. Three couples I knew that had only boys continued to have children in order to have a girl. They did, however, stop at four or five children. One of the mothers acknowledged to me: "I wish I had a girl because it's a different experience raising girls. But there isn't really a lot of pressure from anyone to do this. My husband doesn't care."

Not unlike Salam, Muna also saw her desire for a son as a matter of sheer necessity in a backward society, rather than of her own ideological belief. She gave birth to a boy after three girls.

A woman who has a girl is not considered good. My mother-in-law and sisters-in-law never used to help me around the house until I had the boy. Now they're tripping over themselves being helpful. I am also an outsider [from another city]—my sister-in-law and I are the only outsiders in the family, and not having a boy is more difficult. I was forced to try to have a boy; otherwise, my life would be too hard here.

Indeed, I do not doubt that social pressure can be overwhelming—and as a married woman who had not yet had any children (let alone boys), I experienced it at firsthand. Each time I left the village to visit my husband in New York, I was told only half-jokingly, "Don't come back without your husband and a son."

Even if a couple is content with a few daughters, people around them frequently assume that the couple feel something important is lacking in their lives and pity them—perhaps one of the most difficult and insidious forms of social pressure that the mothers told me about. The wife of one of my cousins told me, "When I had my fourth son, the nurse at the hospital told me not to say out loud that I had a boy because the woman in the bed next to mine had her eighth daughter." My cousin's wife and the nurse automatically assumed the woman would be pained by this information. Still, even as Palestinians in the Galilee often construct themselves as victims of other people's pressure, many of the people applying that pressure similarly distance themselves from this societal problem. My cousin's wife describes herself as against son preference too.

While some women may be victims of a system that is stacked against them, they often also participate in the victimization of other people; therein lies the strength of such systems. Buthaina noted that "the prejudice against girls is the mother's fault, really—she's the one who instills love in her children for each other, and she could make her sons love their sisters if she wanted to." The active participation of women in son preference speaks to the simplistic notion of women as victims of a male-dominated society. Gendered forms of discrimination, including son preference, are practiced by both men and women. According to Shihnaz, wives often continue to insist on trying to produce a son even when their husbands "don't mind." She told me the tragic story of a relative who "was told by the doctors she'd die if she had another child. But she insisted on trying again to have a boy, even though her husband told her it was all right. She then died together with the baby." Shihnaz told me this story of self-sacrifice not without a hint of admiration for the woman, but also condemning her for caring so much about having a boy. Abu Riad, who claimed to help women conceive boys with a "scientific formula," told me that it was the women's desire more then their husbands' to come to him, and when the husbands refused, the wives would keep after them until they persuaded them to seek his assistance.

It was repeatedly suggested to me that the women are often more traditional and dependent on social approval than their husbands. Zayni told me, "It's almost like a mathematical formula: if the man is educated and the wife isn't, they'll still have a lot of children. If they're both educated, they won't." The reason given for women's supposed excessive traditionalism was their structural vulnerability to the consequences of deviating from dominant social values; thus they were forced to participate in constructing and enforcing those values.

Still I knew several couples who actually stopped having children after three girls, despite social pressure, because they felt strongly that three was the number they wanted—their desire for a small, planned family overrode their desire for a son. Close friends of my family stopped at four girls and decided to live in a neighboring Jewish city, partly to avoid the social pressure to try to have a son. Ironically, eighteen years later, while the wife was going through menopause and thought she could no longer have children, she unexpectedly found out that she was six months pregnant with a healthy boy. As one of their daughters told me, his birth has greatly changed the family's relations with the community back in their village: "My relatives used to visit us only on holidays. Now we can't get rid of them. Just because there is a boy. They make me laugh."

MODERN SON PREFERENCES

The modernist narrative concerning son preference was produced through common forms of personal distancing from "backward" bias, but also through rationalizations of acceptable son preference. Modern frames such as economic rationality, nationalism, universalism, and science are used to construct modern forms of son preference.

Preference for sons is often constructed as a practical matter of economic necessity in a backward society—part of a rational economizing family planning strategy in a context that favors boys. In a patrilineal system "that you and I can't change," it is thus only rational to want a son. In an economy where more men are employed and are paid more than women (again things we as individuals supposedly cannot change), boys make perfect economic sense.

Similarly, because girls "in our society" do not generally inherit property (although all three religions sanction inheritance by daughters), sons are therefore important.[2] As Muna told me: "We live in a society where men inherit. I don't think that's right, but I can't deny that this is the case. So if you want an heir, you have to have a son. A man without a son will soon be forgotten; when he dies, his land will be divided up among his male next of kin, the home will close up, and all memory of his name will be erased. In the absence of a son, all of the parents' efforts seem pointless." Aspirations for economic advancement in this context require sons to mark that wealth and to carry it forth. Boys are thus essential for solidifying class status, or for aspirations to transcend it. In a vision of history as passing through boys' names and gains, where girls are marginal (but necessary) intermediaries, sons are essential for inscribing oneself in memory, history, and the material world of things.

Moreover, in the context of scarcity and poverty, girls are seen as potential burdens in dual and interrelated ways—they are economic liabilities and they threaten a family's reputation. Salim from Nazareth said that

> some parents are worried because today there are so many girls who can't find a husband—they call them "left-over girls" [bāyrāt]. And if a girl is uneducated, she'll be economically and socially dependent on her brothers or must work at a low-paying job in a factory or in seasonal harvesting, which is not so respectable. This is not a position anyone would want for their child. So parents worry more about girls, and this translates into son preference.

According to this line of reasoning, it is objective economic and social conditions that favor boys, rather than any ideological belief in their superiority. Salim added that "even when a girl is married, the parents still have to worry about her, and make sure she's getting along with her husband, that he's not treating her badly, and that he doesn't divorce her." Girls in this way are posited as structurally weaker than boys. As I was repeatedly told, a son can supposedly take care of himself in any situa-

2. For more on inheritance, see Moors 1995, although it focuses on a region in the West Bank.

tion he is thrown into—he is physically strong, can earn an income doing anything, and doesn't have to worry about his sexual reputation.
Girls, on the other hand, are considered vulnerable—they easily suffer
injustice, they can be abused, and respectable sources of income are hard
to come by for the uneducated. Moreover, a girl's sexual reputation, unlike that of a boy, can easily be "destroyed": "a girl is like a glass, throw
one rock at her and she's broken." These constructions of girls' economic and social vulnerability and boys' resilience are deployed in rationalizations of modern boy preference.

Thus, in a self-perpetuating cycle, parents expect and generally receive more economic and social support from sons. Especially when resources are limited, "it makes more economic sense" to invest in boys.
Nisrin the social worker told me:

> In many of the poorer households, boys get the better pieces of meat,
> the nicer clothes, fewer household responsibilities, and more services
> and attention from their sisters. And it's mothers that insist on and
> oversee this unequal distribution. As a result, many girls fall behind
> in their homework because they're given so many household duties.
> They are also sometimes taken out of school to care for their younger
> siblings or a sick parent. Boys are almost never required to do this,
> although they are often encouraged to drop out of school to get a job
> and earn an income. Then when the family needs more money, the
> girls have to work at bad jobs. And people start calling them "factory
> girls."

Iftikar, after her years at an egg-sorting plant, told me: "I hate girls
because I know exactly what it's like to be one and it's terrible." Given
the existing "objective" conditions, Iftikar would rather have a boy. In
a particularly moving moment, she told me:

> Do you know how humiliating it is—I've been working and bringing
> my pay to my father for eight years, and I've practically raised my
> younger siblings, and yet my brother's baby boy, who hasn't done one
> thing for the family, is more important than me. They already have
> plans for him and a savings account—which they use my money
> for—and they have no plans for me except to marry me off. That's
> why I hate girls.

Iftikar admitted that she wouldn't mind having two or three boys and
one girl; "then she's something special and spoiled." She said she wanted
to change the nature of the relationship between mothers and daughters.

Thus, despite her clear practical preference for giving birth to boys, Iftikar was ideologically against it.

There are more limited opportunities for employment for women than for men in the Galilee. Although this boundary is being pushed, teaching and nursing are the most commonly cited appropriate "feminine" professions. Better educated and "better employed" girls enjoy more mobility than factory workers: their comings and goings are less suspect and less closely scrutinized. I have enjoyed this class and educational privilege myself. Such daughters are seen as more resilient, with more potential, a possible asset—especially if there are not too many of them. Many people agreed with Georgina's statement: "Today, what do unmarried girls have to worry about? They wear whatever they want, have a car under their butts, they take trips, even travel abroad. What worries do they have?" Georgina is obviously talking about a particular class of unmarried girls. Thus boy preference is attenuated in more affluent contexts. But Georgina still saw the same girls as potential societal burdens and misfits because they still have a "deep-down feeling of something missing because they haven't fulfilled their biological potential of being wives and mothers."

Part of the economic rationality of son preference is the expectation that sons will support their parents in old age. However, many women pointed out to me that in fact sons do very little for their parents; it's girls who really take on the care of elderly parents. Since the script posits women as more emotional, caring, and nurturing—and since economic nuclearization of families is in full swing—fewer and fewer sons are living up to their parents' expectation of support in their old age. Karam told me, "My brother wouldn't even know what my mom and dad needed even if he wanted to help them. He's a man and he doesn't even know what his own house requires, he doesn't come over to their house and realize it hasn't been cleaned in a week, or that their refrigerator is iced over and empty, not to mention actually grabbing a mop and doing something about it."

One narrative that contests the economic rationality of son preference came from a woman from 'Ilabun who had two teenage daughters and was not planning to have any more children. She told me that her sisters-in-law would have to spend a great deal of money building houses for their sons so they could get married, and paying for the weddings and expenses, while she wouldn't have to build any houses or pay for her daughters' weddings, *and* she'd get to boss around two sons-in-law and make demands. While some people dismissed this economic evaluation as sour grapes, many admitted that boys *are* a bigger expense, although the return is (at least expected to be) higher as well.

The economic rationality of son preference is thus contested. People often emphasize the key economic roles that women have played in many families. Some women have demanded and legally obtained their share of their father's property. Other women have adopted the Western-style hyphenation of last names. Even in the mythically backward past, some families used to be referred to by the mother's name. Implied here is a criticism of the mother's unwonted exercise of power, but also an acknowledgment of her central role.

Genealogy determined by male inheritance is paralleled by a genealogy of names. Among Palestinians, married adults are often referred to as Abu (father of) and Imm (mother of) X, X being the man or woman's firstborn son. That son is then frequently expected to give *his* firstborn son the name of the child's paternal grandfather, thus paying respect and keeping that name alive, recycling it through alternate generations. My girlfriends often tease me by calling me "Imm David," since my husband's father's name is David. The handing down of names is supposed to parallel a distribution of wealth. But just as the "unmarried girls with cars under their butts" are exceptions, there are women and men who choose to challenge this system or reinterpret it (within limits). For example, my grandfather Abdil-Qadir was well liked and two of his sons named children after him, but so did one of his daughters as well. My cousin Wafa' insisted on naming a son after her own father rather than her husband's. Other women have refused to give their sons their father-in-law's name (such as Samah, who didn't like the old-fashioned name Abdulla in the context of a modern Jewish state). Similarly, some self-proclaimed progressive men who have no son have asked to be called by their daughter's name. A doctor in my village insisted that people refer to him as Abu-Layla—until his fifth child, a boy, was born. Thus names and titles, like son preference, are to some degree sites of power play, push and pull.

While criticism of "primitive" son preference is widespread, a moderate "liking of boys" constructed in modern terms is also widespread. This liking is positioned at a distance from "base instincts," "traditional old-fashioned desires," and "irrational discrimination."

The doctor who finally had a son after five girls celebrated his birth with an ostentatious display of son preference by having both a religious *molad* celebration and a party in a banquet hall. When I asked him why he did not have this kind of celebration when his daughters were born, he said, "It's only natural to want children of both sexes. And after four girls, we were happy to have a boy, that's all."

Indeed, I heard this reason more than once, that everyone wants to have the experience of raising both boys and girls, supposedly a neutral desire for variety and color in family life. Kawthar said, "We want boys but we want girls too. We like to have some of each kind [*jins*]." Note that this supposedly egalitarian argument posits that raising girls is basically different from raising boys.[3]

Another context in which son preference emerges as modern and compatible with modernity is that of nationalism. As I argue in Chapter 1, the emerging literature on nationalism, gender, and sexuality suggests that many nationalisms are formed by powerfully gendered and sexed duties to the nation (Parker et al. 1992; Mosse 1985; Wilford and Miller 1998; Chatterjee 1993). Thus as a more or less internationally common and acceptable set of discourses and practices, nationalism with its built-in male bias is evoked as a valid modern framework for son preference. Thus Palestinians, men and women, often express their preference for sons as part of their duty to their besieged homeland and identity—a component of nationalism's political arithmetic. Women's main concern in life, in this view, should be the making of men, whom they breast-feed "the milk of glory, honor, and courage" (*Sawt ul-Haq wal-Hurriyya*, June 17, 1995). Boys can stand up to the Israeli state, its police, its bureaucracies, its individuals. "Palestinians want boys because they're the backbone of the nation," a teenage girl told me. Part of the complex and changing motivations for and expressions of son preference is the belief that giving birth to a boy is an important contribution to the nation. Thus son preference gains much backing from the realm of modern nationalist discourse.

Another modern framework in which acceptable son preference is constructed is that of universalism. According to this view, the whole

3. Raising girls is often constructed as a pleasurable experience. According to Georgina, "Raising a daughter is more sentimental and emotionally rewarding for the mother. Girls are fun to raise, especially when it's an only daughter, and the family can afford to give her the attention—mothers enjoy dressing their daughters up in ruffly pink dresses, buying them ribbons and bangles, watching them learn to dance. These are silly things, but they're fun." Manal similarly told me that "boys are picky and moody [*miqtīn*]—they don't eat well and make trouble. Badira's girls are just like boys. Girls are different, they don't like to play in dirt, they like to show off their beauty. They see their mothers putting on makeup and they want to do it too. There is a saying that 'raising boys is like cutting hard stone' [*tarbiyit iṣ-subyān mithil qarṭ iṣ-ṣuwwān*]. But we treat our children the same—my husband, Ilyas, wants to order a piano and a computer for our daughter. People today are very concerned to educate their daughters."

world prefers boys, whether they openly admit it or not. It is part of the fundamental makeup of society and it is logical to prefer boys everywhere. Unlike "excessive," "primitive" types of son preference, this "moderate" son preference does not set us off in our backwardness, but joins us to the rest of the modern world. Kawthar said, "Even if there are some exceptions here and there, in Europe and America children take the father's name, and wives give up theirs. This is the way societies are." Anecdotal evidence of other societies' preferences for sons was often offered to support this universal claim. For example, Lamis, who is 24, has one boy, wants two more, and hopes she never has a girl, told me, "When I was in the hospital just after I delivered, the woman in the next bed was [European] Jewish and you should see how they were clapping and dancing around her because she had a boy, to carry on the family name. I thought it was just us, but it's them too."

THE SCIENCE OF PLANNING SONS

The economizing and modernizing pressures to have a small family combined with an appropriately modern preference for sons has led many people to try to *plan* sons. The many methods that women used in attempts to conceive a boy varied in popularity. I was told about several old-fashioned "traditional" methods. Salam's mother-in-law claimed that if a man really passionately loves his wife, if he really lusts after her, she will conceive a boy. Notice that the man is held responsible here. Another version is that the woman must come or "finish" before the man does to conceive a boy. A few women visit a shrine or get a sheikh to write an amulet. But methods that were perceived to be scientifically based were much more popular. Indeed, several of the people I interviewed hoped I could help them find such a method.

Yumna told me that a woman can sit in a warm tub of water with baking soda just before sex because the resulting pH balance in the vagina prepares the proper environment for male-coded (Y-bearing) semen. She also has a Chinese calendar that details the night of the year on which a particular horoscope will conceive a boy: "A nurse gave me this calendar. I hid it in the bottom of my closet because I don't want everybody to use it, only those who really need it. I made them photocopies of it and it has worked for them. It is scientifically proven." Taghrid said she had heard of calculation methods for sex selection but did not believe they were scientific—"the only thing I read is that if the man thrusts farther in, there's a better chance that the male semen will reach before the female ones, but it's only a possibility." Other "science-based" prescriptions include counting nights after the end of menstruation, even nights being those on which a boy is conceived; having intercourse during the last two days of fertility when the "egg" or the "female gene" is already dead; or trying to conceive after measuring the temperature of the vagina and ascertaining that it is 36°C (97°F). These methods were supposedly obtained from professors ("even Jewish ones"), doctors, and pharmacists.

Women and men repeatedly emphasized the scientific basis of these methods. Shihnaz told me that one method she heard about involves day-counting to determine when "the female egg dies while the sperm stays." In discussions of these methods, the ways in which the sex of the fetus is determined become central:

ME: How is the sex of the fetus determined?

GHUSUN: It's from the man.

SHURUQ: But it's is also from the woman, because it's in her that the pregnancy catches on [bimsik ma'ha]. So the pH balance of her womb is important too.

GHUSUN: But it's more related to genetics. As the old saying goes, what the shit puts in, the woman delivers. The woman has a feminine gene but the man, well, he has both.

SHURUQ: There are two people in two villages who work on calculations. For example, on the fifteenth day the female egg is dead, so you get a boy. But the man isn't an elephant, he might not reach that day.

GHUSUN: I don't believe in this way of making boys, but I've heard of it. It's up to God in the end. Before, people used to have the attitude that it's the mother's fault, as though she gave birth to a girl with her own hands, but from a scientific view it's from the father. I took biology classes, and I know this.

The pursuit of these sex-selection methods was very much part of the family planning agenda of modern men and women. Wafiq told me, "My wife and I waited a long time between the third and the fourth child because we wanted a boy so they would be two girls and two boys. I had heard that there's a way of making their ratio equal, so I waited till I was sure of this." Similarly, Ghadir, the mother of one daughter, said:

GHADIR: I want three children. My daughter can't go without a sis-
            ter—I want one more boy and one more girl. My husband
            agrees to this.
ME: What if the next two children are girls?
GHADIR: I'll go up to a maximum of four girls while I'm trying to
            have a boy and then I'll stop. But I wouldn't just get pregnant
            just like that anyway. There are doctors who do these
            things. Also our neighbor does calculations and I believe
            they work. A lot of people from outside the village come to
            visit him. And the Jews started admitting this thing now.
ME: Why wouldn't you have more babies than that?
GHADIR: Was I born so I can stay preoccupied with children my
            whole life?

Indeed, the most fascinating and popular methods of sex selection involved secret scientific formulas by which one could calculate the nights
on which a given woman would conceive a boy. Fayiz 'Ilabuny (Abu
Riad), in his early 50s, an engineer by profession, has such a formula.

Mr. 'Ilabuny spends much of his free time advising couples on how
to conceive a son. He himself has one girl and two boys. Both boys were
planned and achieved by his method. His daughter, Vera, had twin boys
by his method as well. He claims to have assisted in the making of a
thousand boys over the last twenty-five years—and one girl at the request of a woman who had three boys. On average, the families that
come to him have four girls or more, but there are also some that have
only two or three girls—"You know, now everybody likes to plan with
the method," he said. On average the women are on the older side, 35
or so, but some women come from the "first belly" to plan their pregnancies, especially people in his village who know him well.

He and his wife told me that "people have come from far and wide—
from the border of Lebanon in the north to Bir il-Sabi' in the south. . . .
And I have people from all religions come to me. I even had a Jewish
couple who came, both are doctors and the wife is even a gynecologist.
We get teachers, engineers, doctors." Abu Riad told me that he had
people come to him from my village—people I must know personally,
but who usually liked to keep their identities secret.

Abu Riad was surprisingly systematic about the advice he gave; he
made a card (he used the Hebrew word kartisiyah) for each couple and
kept it in a file under the woman's name. He insisted that he absolutely
never took money and refused gifts, and it was even costly to him, since

he often felt obligated to visit couples who had had a boy with his help and take a gift. He said that he required the husband to accompany his wife when she came to see him, after some embarrassing situations in which wives wanted to try his method without consulting their husbands. "One woman kept insisting that she had to come alone because her husband was abroad—how was she going to make a baby without him anyway?" Some husbands might object if they "didn't believe in such a thing, or thought it involved magic." He also requires the man or the couple to visit him in person at first, so that he knows whom he is dealing with. After the initial visit "they can phone and I pull up their card from the file and tell them what day to try this month."

Abu Riad insisted that his method does not involve magic at all—it is a scientific formula that requires certain information about the man and woman—birth dates, date of last menstruation, and so on. Depending on the month in which the couple want to make a boy, he can calculate the exact time when they should have intercourse. He clearly placed this method in the realm of modern medicine and biology rather than in the realm of what he called "traditional medicine." He told me that his brother, who is a pharmacist in Missouri, was very skeptical at first: "My brother kept saying that medicine hasn't reached this point and that it's impossible, until he tried it himself and it worked. The success rate is between 85 and 95 percent if it's done correctly—some people take the date from me but get pregnant before or after." He constructed his method as medical and rational; he compared it with what he said were current attempts in the United States to purify semen samples of all spermatozoa that were not "male-dominant." He told me that even doctors seek his assistance, and that on one occasion when he had to spend a considerable amount of time at Rambam Hospital in Haifa (a highly prestigious hospital), members of the staff recognized his name, were delighted to meet him, and gave him special attention. One doctor told him, "You are a doctor too. You are an Eastern doctor!" It seemed very important for Abu Riad to emphasize the scientific status of his method to me. And, he added, it is perfectly logical to seek out this kind of advice: "Just like if there is someone sick, he doesn't let himself die, he goes to receive treatment."

I asked Dr. Abu Riad why he thought so many people wanted to try to conceive boys. His answer was rather complex: "We are Arabs, and even among foreigners, the boy carries his father's name, so in the future his sisters can come and find the house open . . . an extension of memory ['imtidād dhikir]. A wife who has only girls will be cut out of the in-

heritance. It's true that the Qur'an says that the girl inherits half of what
the son inherits, and among the Christians it should be equal, but they
remain Arabs." (Abu Riad is Christian.) The more innovative part of his
explanation involves a scarcity argument: "In general, there are fewer
boys. If you look at society, men are the ones that go to fight in armies,
get in work accidents, car accidents—males keep on getting fewer, they
are more exposed to death than females. For example, getting a life insurance policy for a housewife is much cheaper than for a working
woman. And as long as there is a shortage, there is high demand." Thus
son preference is as rational and logical as an actuarial table. He added,
"Today people want smaller families. From an economic standpoint,
people today realize that what is important is the quality not the quantity. There is more care and attention to children and the mother . . .
look at the difference between my wife and me and my parents—there's
is a huge difference. Mothers have gone out to the realm of work [Abu
Riad's wife is not employed outside the home] and they don't have the
time to have so many children." It is the need to have a small family, the
desire to be modern, combined with the desire to have a boy that makes
Abu Riad's formula so famous and people so willing to try it. After all,
Abu Riad is proud of the help he is able to provide: "A family with six
girls and no boys is a tragedy—like eating food without salt. A boy
would bring happiness and brightness to the home."

Yet Abu Riad was aware of the potential abuse of sex selection. He
wanted to guard his formula and make sure that it did not become public knowledge—not because he profited from it in any way but because
he feared that it might get into the wrong hands: if everyone had the
ability to make only boys, that could jeopardize the human race. He thus
uses his secret wisely and guards it against such abuse. Like son preference in general, if taken to extremes sex selection is dangerous. However, the popularity of these "scientific" methods of planning a boy illustrate the importance of both small planned families and modern
forms of son preference.

COUNTER-DISCOURSE, COMPLICATIONS

Alongside strong condemnations of "backward" son preference is a less
dominant discourse that celebrates son preference as authentic. This
narrative claims the preference for sons to be part of the essence of
being Arab. Desiring sons and the attending gender relations here are
framed as being at the heart of what it means to be authentically Arab.

People told me: "Yes, our religion tells us that girls should inherit. And yes, it makes sense that girls should be treated equally. . . . *But* in the end we are Arabs and we can't deny it." When I asked people about the difference, if any, between the approaches of Arabs and Jews to reproduction, I consistently got the answer that Eastern and Orthodox Jews had many children "just like us," but that European or Western Jews were different. Western Jews supposedly often have only one child "even if it's a girl"; "They don't care if it's a girl or a boy." This assertion of reproductive difference between Arabs and Others was at different points viewed as positive and negative. According to the dominant pro-modernization perspective, this equalizing between girls and boys was a model to emulate. However, in the less dominant antimodernization version, the desire for sons was positive because Arabs loved boys, had traditions of strong men, and properly protected their women. The counter-discourse embraces more authentic and proper masculinity and femininity, unlike "corrupt" Westernized folk, whose girls are no longer feminine and boys no longer masculine. Yusif, a physical therapist who studied in Germany, told me: "I decided to marry my cousin back here because Arab women are still feminine. Although women in Germany have more equality with men, they have also lost part of their natural femininity and maternal instincts. Here boys are boys and girls are girls." An editorial in *al-ʾIttihad* similarly criticizes the "erasure of boundaries between the sexes" in American-Israeli culture (Aug. 4, 1995). Gender difference and their reproductive implications are central players in the politics of identity in the Galilee. Son preference, whether considered something to be proud or ashamed of, is central to notions of Arabness and sets us apart from, or alternately unites us with, the Western world.

Son preference, even in its popular scientific and modern forms, is not hegemonic. Nuhad from Haifa told me about "a guy at my office who had two girls and then used this method to make a boy. I don't go for these things. Whatever comes is good. I criticized him to his face." Indeed, Khadiji the nurse found sex selection morally reprehensible:

ME: Have you heard about sex selection methods?

KHADIJI: Yes, I've heard people ask about it, but it's not scientifically proved and it's totally unacceptable morally. I actually heard of highly educated people who have had abortions to get rid of a female fetus. Unfortunately, in our society there is a strong preference for boys. I totally reject this.

The story of my old math teacher who received in vitro fertilization illuminates the conflicting feelings many women and men in the Galilee express:

The fact that we didn't have children the first fifteen years didn't cause us any real or direct problems. Maybe because we're educated and our personalities are strong, we didn't allow anyone to interfere in our affairs. But we were always moody and we'd fight about any little thing. After I got pregnant we tried not to be moody, we were very worried about the fetus. And my husband spoiled me and relieved me and tried to allow me to rest.

We were of course very, very happy when the baby arrived—it makes a warm nest for us. My mother- and father-in-law began to treat me with more affection. They used to come to our house maybe once a year—now they always come to see the baby. They always respected me but the love has now increased.

Fathalla Nahhas is a doctor who does separation and semen selection [she used the Hebrew terms *hafradah* and *berur zera'*]. My husband and I refused to choose, because we wished so much to just achieve motherhood and fatherhood. From a religious perspective I think it's forbidden, but I'm not sure.

I always wanted a boy. I used to read verses such as those of Sayidna Zakariyya and Al 'Omran. Al 'Omran says, "O my Lord, grant me from you a sound boy," and this means without deformity. Also, "O my Lord, leave me not childless, you are the best of heirs."

A boy carries more responsibility than the girl and takes care of his parents when they're old, especially since there are so many diseases today.

I'd have been happy with a girl—it, too, would have been such a blessing. But we wanted someone to inherit from us. When we went on the pilgrimage several years ago and we closed the house, everybody started crying, there was so much crying, because if anything happened to us, mention of the name of the 'Aziz family would disappear. Now with our son, this is no longer the case.

While my teacher refused to choose the sex of her fetus on moral and religious grounds, she also found moral and religious grounds to justify her desire for a son. She wanted to continue the name of 'Aziz's family, even though it was a name she herself adopted late in life. She felt the love of her family because she bore a son, even as she lavished me—her female student—with encouragement when she chose me some twenty years ago for the national math competition. These subtleties and ambiguities are more characteristic of son preference in the Galilee than the notion of male-dominated society suggests. As Annelies Moors writes: "Acknowledging that women may take up partial, ambiguous and sometimes contradictory positions leaves open the possibility that women themselves can both be implicated in and resist such regimes of power" (1995: 260). Just as Palestinians are victimized by Israeli economic policies and yet construct their material aspirations from within that system, so women are victimized by a system of son preference yet often construct their aspirations from within it.

Despite son preference in the Galilee—whether modern or not—girls are loved and resilient. Female that I am, I was spoiled by my teachers, even in areas that were considered male, such as sports. I was allowed and encouraged to excel, and given many opportunities and privileges within the limits of my circumstances. And there are many women like me. Two good friends in New York are getting their Ph.D.s, Asil in anthropology and Sana in computer science (and they did not have the advantage of an American mother). They are excelling in their fields and have been encouraged to do so. Perhaps these women are exceptions to the rule, but it is essential to note such exceptions for a properly nuanced understanding of the rule of son preference.

Moreover, reproduction is a central site for these cultural works— their contestation and assertion. By constructing the desire for sons as a matter forced on individuals by a backward society, as economically rational, nationalistically logical, universally applicable, or scientifically achievable, Palestinians in the Galilee situate son preference squarely in the modern world.

Conclusion

The reproductive measure forms a profoundly influential worldview among Palestinians in the Galilee. Through reproduction Palestinians today navigate the vast, diverse, and interrelated terrains of nationalism, class, identity, health, the body, and gender. Indeed, reproduction serves as a deeply insightful "entry point to the study of social life" (Ginsburg and Rapp 1995: 1). It offers a unique window into and out of Palestinian society in the Galilee. Moreover, I suggest that what I have termed the reproductive measure may also be a window worth looking through to view other societies. By illuminating important links among reproduction, gender, nation, economy, difference, and the body, this approach may also offer a new perspective on life beyond the Galilee.

In my village of ʿArrabi, in neighboring Sakhnin, in Nazareth, and in other parts of the Palestinian Galilee, reproduction has become a central site for the negotiation of significant social concepts, including the feminine and the masculine, the household, culture, and nation. Differences in number of children, spacing of births, the sex of the child, the health of the fetus, child-raising techniques, household investments, and contraceptive methods have all become key in daily negotiations and re-creations of personal, collective, and national identity. In these processes, variations, inconsistencies, and exceptions abound. Yet certain systematicities can be discerned.

I have argued for an overall consistency that would be difficult to bypass, the consistency of a narrative of modernization and its intimate link to reproduction in the Galilee. Through the interrelated spheres of national identity, economic strategies, corporeal disciplines, social stratification, and gender relations, modernization has become profoundly entangled with reproduction. Together they create a complex and compelling web of new reproductive discourses and practices through which the modern and the backward are conceived and ranked.

Indeed, it is striking how powerfully modernization has transformed the lives of Palestinians in the Galilee. Promodernization and antimodernization define, shape, and limit the debates on gender, nation, class, and religion. These transformations have not affected all Palestinians equally or in the same way, but no Palestinian can ignore them. In the context of the Galilee, the state and its projects rub up against and mold Palestinian lives. The proximity of the Israeli state, its deep incursions and insertions into day-to-day life is a central factor in the salience of narratives of modernization (and of antimodernization) among Palestinians.

Israel itself is continuously struggling to secure its own modernity. Palestinian "backwardness" is called upon to play a key role in this struggle. Israeli national rhetoric and policy simultaneously produce and criticize "Arab non-democratic political structures, backward economies, traditional societies, bureaucratic inefficiency, and treatment of women to discursively locate Jewish Israel as the most western population in the region" (Khazoom 1999: 37). Israeli Jews engage in particular Orientalist practices and discourses "to separate themselves from the 'traditional' and the 'Oriental,' and thereby to constitute themselves as subjects of a 'Western' modernity" (Eyal 1996: 392). Through administrative policies, reports, and studies, the state constitutes Palestinians as the flawed and failed object of modernization.

Thus Israel's self-Occidentizing has relied on and necessitated the Orientalizing of its Palestinian population. Reproduction has been a pivotal arena for pursuing this project. Thus the state has specifically attempted to constitute Palestinians as the flawed and failed object of *reproductive* modernization. Their backward, Third World, Eastern high fertility has been constructed as not only the cause of their economic, social, and political lag behind the Jewish population (rather than discriminatory state policy) but also as highly threatening to the ethnically conceived state. A "national preoccupation over too many Palestinian bodies and too few Jewish bodies (and even fewer Jewish bodies of the right type)" guides an incredible array of state practices, from citizenship and immigration laws to population policy, land distribution and zoning, residential planning, municipal budget allocations, settlements, educational curricula, and data collection (Torstrick 1993: 260). All these policies are aimed at containing Palestinians and their fertility. My brief discussions in Chapter 1 of the Law of Return, Judaization plans, census counts, health insurance, and family planning policy only begin to capture the extent to which comparative ethnic political arithmetic permeates and fashions life in Israel.

This constitution of Palestinians as the flawed and failed objects of reproductive modernization shapes the parameters of their oppression in Israel, but also their visions of redemption. These state projects are coercive not only physically but discursively and organizationally; they "trickle down" in the Galilee. The modernization framework and its techniques are instruments of domination, but they also become instruments of liberation.

Palestinians obviously recognize and resist their exclusion and marginalization in Israel. As the state celebrated fifty years of independence in May 1998, the exclusion of Palestinians from these state memorials of victory dramatically symbolized a broader, longer history of marginalization. But Palestinians often challenge this marginalization through its underlying conceptual framework of modernization, the same framework by which they are subjugated. The Israeli system is exclusionary at many levels, but its modernization framework presents certain ruptures and opportunities for Palestinian engagement. These opportunities include family planning, in its economic, ideological, and social senses. Planning a family (whether small or large) is a point at which Palestinians can engage, emulate, contest, and challenge ethnic politics, economic transformations, medical interventions, and social organization—all changes that they cannot afford to ignore. The binary opposition of modern/backward forms the basis for Palestinians' negotiations of reproduction, but also those of nationalism, class, gender, and health. The standard they now use to measure success in all these fields reflects similar standards used by the powers that be in the state, in the economy, and in the medical establishment.

What I have termed the reproductive measure is both mobilized as an Israeli tool of subordination and redeployed as anticolonial struggle. However, this does not mean that Palestinian discourses are simply reducible to a repetition of Israeli canonical terms. The reproductive measure was not simply developed in the West or in Israel and imposed on Palestinians; Palestinians' appropriations of it have imbued it with new valence and significance. These appropriations, unintended consequences, and hybrid constructions have in turn confused Israeli productions in this arena, creating more of a zigzag process than unidimensional overdetermination.

To describe this situation as a discourse and counter-discourse is not to imply their equality. Dramatic disparities in power and resources exist between these institutionalized state projects and noninstitutional attempts to undo those projects. Moreover, "this truth of decolonization's 'impurity'" does not constitute grounds for the dismissal of its counter-discourses (Stein 1996: 117). Rather, it provides grounds for a better understanding of these efforts to undo marginalization, including their limitations.

Moreover, exploring the contestation and negotiation of shifting categories of personhood and community in the Galilee is not to present Palestinian identity as being in a special state of crisis, chaos, or decline. Contestation and negotiation are in fact standard processes in the construction of identity and the workings of power and are not unique to Palestinians or to the Galilee.

According to Betsy Hartmann, "Today, many Third World elites are embracing Malthusianism with as much, or even more, zeal than their Western counterparts" (1995: 37). While I argue that more than just the elite in the Galilee have taken up the flexible tool of the modernist reproductive hierarchy, Hartmann's statement does indicate that the situation I describe in the Galilee is not unique. Although the reproductive measure may be particularly striking in its degree of salience and in its scope in the Galilee—partly because of the positioning of Palestinians in the heart of a state with a strong settler colonial history and vision—it is not a measure exclusive to this region.

My analyses in the Galilee are thus relevant to family planning among Palestinians in other parts of Israel, and even in other areas where Palestinians live. But not having conducted an in-depth comparative study, I can only suggest that parallels to the Galilee may be found in the Triangle and al-Naqab regions, the other large concentrations of Palestinians inside Israel, as well as in the West Bank and Gaza Strip. Inasmuch as Israeli population policy constructs all Palestinians as the flawed and failed objects of reproductive modernization, it is likely that all Palestinians respond by resisting yet mimicking this framework in some ways.

However, there are significant regional variations to consider. The three main factors contributing to the emergence of the reproductive measure in the Galilee that I have discussed—Israel's population policy, economic transformations, and rapid medicalization—are all present in these regions but not uniformly so. For example, the forceful economic transformations I have described are brutal and appealing to different degrees in the Galilee, not to mention beyond it. Bedouins in Israel have overall been even more economically marginalized than other Palestinians in the state. Thus in the al-Naqab, where they are the majority, the new sensibilities of consumerism and the newly created desire for planned families are further from their grasp. The same can be said of most West Bankers and Gazans; their poverty (even in the eyes of the relatively poor Palestinians in the Galilee) probably dampens the seductive element in the planning of families and in modern consumption habits and desires. Similarly, the infiltration of science and medicine has been less extensive in the West Bank and Gaza as well as in al-Naqab. Israeli medical neglect and assault on local health services have perhaps lessened the spread of these "invasions" of the body. In addition, weaker educational systems, similarly neglected and attacked, and higher dropout rates are likely to weaken the molding of bodies and minds into more medicalized shapes.

In general, there are important disparities in Israel's policy toward its "problem population" of Palestinian citizens and the noncitizen Palestinians of its occupied territories and new "autonomous regions." These disparities have an impact on the contours of the reproductive measure. I have argued that reproductive practices and discourses have become important markers of self and other in the Galilee partly because they are a central framework in *Israeli* definitions of self and Palestinian other, which have then become mirrored by Palestinians' acceptance of this framework. Palestinians increasingly define themselves in terms of fertility and use reproductive control as a measure of modernity—or, alternatively, Arab authenticity. The tendency to value larger families over smaller ones while still accepting the basic modern premises is relatively muted in the Galilee but is continuously bolstered by the exclusionary nature of the state of Israel. This counter-discourse of romanticized traditionalism that reverses the terms of the argument is an expression of alienation and disaffection and of modernism's dramatic failure to fulfill its promises. In the West Bank and Gaza these "exclusions" and failures, to put it mildly, are significantly magnified. Thus the counter-discourse I described in the Galilee is likely to be even more pronounced after years of Israeli military occupation in the West Bank and Gaza.

Thus Palestinians there are more likely to stigmatize other Palestinians as reproductively corrupted and selfish. Fewer Palestinians in the West

Bank and Gaza distinguish themselves from others by denigrating them as Third World–like, driven by their reproductive instincts, while demonstrating that they themselves are rational and civilized by carefully planning their families. While supposed reproductive differences are likely to be important markers of identity in the West Bank and Gaza, the antimodernization version of this reproductive measure is probably more audible there than in the Galilee.

All of these differences should caution us against simple generalizations. Nonetheless, these various regions are certainly linked, their boundaries are porous to various degrees, and they are all considered parts of one overarching zone of identification—that of Palestine. Moreover, the permeating presence of the state of Israel can be felt—in diverse forms—in all of these areas. Thus I argue that the reproductive measure is worthy of serious consideration in these areas as well.

Moreover, although the demographic focus in Israel/Palestine is striking, the processes of economic globalization are sweeping, and the impact of medicalization is deep, the situation I describe is far from unique. My analyses will resonate for many readers familiar with other parts of the world where similar processes of state domination, economic transformation, and medicalization have unfolded. The links I make between these changes and the arena of reproduction may thus also resonate, and encourage others to pursue research in this direction in other places. These links may resonate especially given the global power and spread of population and modernization discourses that center on the evolution from traditional high fertility to modern low fertility (Greenhalgh 1996).

In the Galilee, the various trajectories of nation, gender, body, and class come together to create new conventions that establish agency—new reproductive conventions of agency. I hope this analysis will direct the attention of researchers studying other societies to the possibility of such forms of agency in their locales. Such a focus will further contribute to the disruption of the common and powerful stereotype of the passive and ignorant Third World woman. It will clearly unsettle the robustly circulating "conventional wisdom . . . that Third World people continue to have so many children because they are ignorant and irrational—they exercise no control over their sexuality, 'breeding like rabbits'" (Hartmann 1995: 6). Quite the opposite; my approach is likely to reveal that reproduction is precisely the arena through which many people around the world negotiate the overwhelming changes sweeping through their lives.

Bibliography

PUBLISHED AND UNPUBLISHED SCHOLARLY WORKS

Abdo, Nahla

1994   "Population Control and Global Development: Implications for Palestinian Women." Unpublished paper distributed by the Union of Palestinian Women's Associations in North America.

Abu-Lughod, Janet L.

1971   "The Demographic Transformation of Palestine." In *The Transformation of Palestine: Essays on the Origin and Development of the Arab-Israeli Conflict,* edited by Ibrahim Abu-Lughod, pp. 139–163. Evanston, Ill.: Northwestern University Press.

Ahmed, Leila

1992   *Women and Gender in Islam: Historical Roots of a Modern Debate.* New Haven: Yale University Press.

Anagnost, Ann

1995   "A Surfeit of Bodies: Population and Rationality of the State in Post-Mao China." In *Conceiving the New World Order: The Global Politics of Reproduction,* edited by Faye Ginsburg and Rayna Rapp, pp. 22–41. Berkeley: University of California Press.

Anderson, Benedict

1983   *Imagined Communities: Reflections on the Origin and Spread of Nationalism.* New York: Verso Press.

1991   *Imagined Communities: Reflections on the Origin and Spread of Nationalism.* Revised and expanded edition. New York: Verso Press.

Appadurai, Arjun
    1988   "Introduction: Place and Voice in Anthropological Theory." *Cultural Anthropology* 3, no. 1: 16–20.
    1990   "Disjuncture and Difference in the Global Cultural Economy." *Public Culture* 2, no. 2: 1–24.
    1993   "Number in the Colonial Imagination." In *Orientalism and the Postcolonial Predicament: Perspectives on South Asia,* edited by Carol Breckenridge and Peter van der Veer, pp. 314–339. Philadelphia: University of Pennsylvania Press.

Aretxaga, Begoña
    1997   *Shattering Silence: Women, Nationalism, and Political Subjectivity in Northern Ireland.* Princeton: Princeton University Press.

'Arraf, Shukri
    1985   *The Palestinian Arab Village: Structure and Land Uses.* Jerusalem: Association for Arab Studies. (In Arabic.)

Asad, Talal
    1975   "Anthropological Texts and Ideological Problems: An Analysis of Cohen on Arab Villages in Israel." *Economy and Society* 4, no. 3: 247–282.
    1994   "Ethnographic Representation, Statistics, and Modern Power." *Social Research* 61, no. 1: 55–88.

Atran, Scott
    1989   "The Surrogate Colonization of Palestine, 1917–1939." *American Ethnologist* 16, no. 4: 719–744.

Avgar, Amy, Janet Baumgold-Land, Sarah Magidor, and Lotte Salzberger
    1991   "Patterns of Contraceptive Behavior among Jerusalem Women Seeking Pregnancy Counseling, 1980–1989." Unpublished paper, Department of Social Work, Hebrew University of Jerusalem.

Ayush, Diab
    1994   "Towards a Palestinian National Population Policy in Palestine." Unpublished paper presented at the Palestinian Population Conference, Cairo. (In Arabic.)

Bachi, Roberto
    1976   *Population Trends of World Jewry.* Jerusalem: Institute for Contemporary Jewry, Hebrew University of Jerusalem Press.

Badarneh, Siham
    1994   "The Health Situation of the Arab Woman in Israel." In *Proceedings of the Conference on Health and the Status of the Arab Woman in Israel,* pp. 10–29. Haifa: Galilee Society and Israel Women's Network. (In Arabic.)

Bar Zvi, Sasson
    1991   *Jurisdiction among the Negev Bedouin.* Tel Aviv: Israeli Ministry of Defense. (In Hebrew.)

Behar, Shiko
    1997   "Is the Mizrahi Question Relevant to the Future of the Entire Middle East?" *News from Within,* January. Special supplement.

Boddy, Janice

1989   *Wombs and Alien Spirits: Women, Men, and the Zar Cult in Northern Sudan.* Madison: University of Wisconsin Press.

Bornstein, Avram

1998   "Give Me Your Identity: Palestinian Border Struggles in the West Bank." Ph.D. dissertation, Columbia University.

Bowman, Glenn

1993   "Nationalizing the Sacred: Shrines and Shifting Identities in the Israeli-Occupied Territories." *Man* 28, no. 3: 431–460.

Brennan Center for Justice, New York University School of Law; American Civil Liberties Union; and Puerto Rican Legal Defense and Education Fund

1999   Brief for Amicus Curiae in Support of Appellants. *United States Department of Commerce v. United States House of Representatives,* 525 U.S. 316 (1999), 98–404.

B'Tselem: Israeli Information Center for Human Rights in the Occupied Territories

1997   "The Quiet Deportation: Revocation of Residency of East Jerusalem Palestinians." Joint report with HaMoked: Center for the Defense of the Individual.

Caldwell, Lesley

1986   "Reproducers of the Nation: Women and the Family in Fascist Policy." In *Rethinking Italian Fascism: Capitalism, Populism and Culture,* edited by David Forgacs, pp. 110–141. London: Lawrence and Wishart Press.

Central Bureau of Statistics

1996   *Statistical Abstract of Israel, 1996.* Jerusalem: Hemed Press.

1997   *Statistical Abstract of Israel, 1997.* Jerusalem: Hemed Press.

1998   *Statistical Abstract of Israel, 1998.* Jerusalem: Hemed Press.

1999   *Statistical Abstract of Israel, 1999.* Jerusalem: Hemed Press.

Chatterjee, Partha

1989   "Colonialism, Nationalism, and Colonialized Women: The Contest in India." *American Ethnologist* 16, no. 4: 622–633.

1993   *The Nation and Its Fragments: Colonial and Postcolonial Histories.* Princeton: Princeton University Press.

Chernin, Kim

1981   *The Obsession: Reflections on the Tyranny of Slenderness.* New York: Harper and Row.

Chetrit, Sami Shalom

1997   "The Dream and the Nightmare: Some Remarks on the New Discourse in Mizrahi Politics in Israel, 1980–1996." *News from Within,* January. Special supplement.

Cohen, Abner

1965   *Arab Border-Villages in Israel: A Study of Continuity and Change in Social Organization.* Oxford: University of Manchester Press.

Comaroff, Jean, and John Comaroff
1990   "Christianity and Colonialism in South Africa." In *Customs in Conflict: The Anthropology of a Changing World*, edited by Frank Manning and Jean-Marc Philibert. Peterborough, Ont.: Broadview Press.
1991   *Of Revelation and Revolution: Christianity, Colonialism, and Consciousness in South Africa*. Chicago: University of Chicago Press.

Courbage, Youssef
1999   "Reshuffling the Demographic Cards in Israel/Palestine." *Journal of Palestine Studies* 28, no. 4 (summer): 21–39.

Cussins, Charis Thompson
1998   "Ethnography of Reproduction in the Post-Cairo Era: A Call for a Five-Year Moratorium on the World 'Population.'" Paper presented at the American Anthropological Association Presidential Symposium on Population, Philadelphia.

Davin, Anna
1978   "Imperialism and Motherhood." *History Workshop: A Journal of Socialist Historians* 5 (spring): 9–66.

Davis, Uri, and Walter Lehn
1983   "Landownership, Citizenship, and Racial Policy in Israel." In *Sociology of "Developing Societies" in the Middle East*, edited by Talal Asad and Roger Owen. New York: Monthly Review Press.

de Grazia, Victoria
1992   *How Fascism Ruled Women: Italy, 1922–1945*. Berkeley: University of California Press.

de Grazia, Victoria, with Ellen Furlough
1996   *The Sex of Things: Gender and Consumption in Historical Perspective*. Berkeley: University of California Press.

Dirks, Nicholas B.
1990   "History as a Sign of the Modern." *Public Culture* 2, no. 2: 25–32.

Doumani, Beshara B.
1994   "The Political Economy of Population Counts in Ottoman Palestine: Nablus, circa 1850." *International Journal of Middle East Studies* 26, no. 1: 1–17.
1995   *Rediscovering Palestine: Merchants and Peasants in Jabal Nablus, 1700–1900*. Berkeley: University of California Press.

Duden, Barbara
1992   "Population." In *The Development Dictionary*, edited by W. Sachs, pp. 146–157. London: Zed Books.

Escobar, Arturo
1984   "Discourse and Power in Development: Michel Foucault and the Relevance of His Work to the Third World." *Alternatives* 10 (winter): 377–400.

1988   "Power and Visibility: Development and the Invention and Man-
            agement of the Third World." *Cultural Anthropology* 3, no. 4:
            428–443.

Eyal, Gil
1996   "The Discursive Origins of Israeli Separatism: The Case of the
            Arab Village." *Theory and Society* 25, no. 3: 389–429.

Fahmy, Khaled
1998   "Women, Medicine, and Power in Nineteenth-Century Egypt."
            In *Remaking Women: Feminism and Modernity in the Middle
            East,* edited by Lila Abu-Lughod, pp. 35–72. Princeton: Prince-
            ton University Press.

Falah, Ghazi
1989   "Israeli 'Judaization' Policy in Galilee and Its Impact on Local
            Arab Urbanization." *Political Geography Quarterly* 8, no. 3:
            229–253.

Fargues, Philippe
1993   "Demography and Politics in the Arab World." *Population: An
            English Selection* 5: 1–20.

Flapan, Simha
1987   "The Palestinian Exodus of 1948." *Journal of Palestine Studies*
            16, no. 4: 3–26.

Foucault, Michel
1979   *Discipline and Punish: The Birth of the Prison.* New York: Ran-
            dom House.
1988   *Technologies of the Self.* Amherst: University of Massachusetts
            Press.

Franklin, Sarah
1997   *Embodied Progress: A Cultural Account of Assisted Concep-
            tion.* London: Routledge.

Friedlander, Dov, and Calvin Goldscheider
1979   *The Population of Israel.* New York: Columbia University
            Press.

Ghanadry, Samih
1987   *The Arab Masses in Israel: Panorama of Oppression and Na-
            tional Discrimination.* Nazareth: March 30th Press. (In Arabic.)

Ghosh, Amitav
1992   *In an Antique Land.* New York: Vintage Books.

Giacaman, Rita
1985   "A Profile of Life and Health in Three Palestinian Villages." Un-
            published paper, Community Health Unit, Birzeit University.
1997   "Population and Fertility: Population Policies, Women's Rights,
            and Sustainable Development." In *Palestinian Women: A Status
            Report.* Birzeit: Women's Studies Program, Birzeit University.

Giacaman, Rita, Islah Jad, and Penny Johnson
1996   "For the Public Good? Gender and Social Citizenship in Pales-
            tine." *Middle East Report* 26, no. 1: 11–16.

Giladi, G. N.
   1990.   *Discord in Zion: Conflict Between Ashkenazi and Sephardi Jews in Israel.* London: Scorpion.

Ginsburg, Faye, and Rayna Rapp
   1991   "The Politics of Reproduction." *Annual Review of Anthropology* 20.

   1995   *Conceiving the New World Order: The Global Politics of Reproduction.* Berkeley: University of California Press.

Goldscheider, Calvin
   1992   *Population and Social Change in Israel.* Boulder, Colo.: Westview Press.

Greenhalgh, Susan
   1996   "The Social Construction of Population Science: An Intellectual, Institutional, and Political History of Twentieth-Century Demography." *Society for Comparative Study of Society and History* 38, no. 1: 26–66.

Habiby, Emile
   1989   *The Secret Life of Saeed.* Los Angeles: Readers International. First published in 1974.

Hacking, Ian
   1986   "Making Up People." In *Reconstructing Individualism: Autonomy, Individuality, and the Self in Western Thought,* edited by Thomas Heller, Morton Sosna, and David Wellbery. Stanford: Stanford University Press.

Hadawi, Sami
   1991   *Bitter Harvest: A Modern History of Palestine.* New York: Olive Branch.

Haddad, Robert M.
   1970   *Syrian Christians in Muslim Society: An Interpretation.* Westport, Conn.: Greenwood Press.

Haj, Samira
   1992   "Palestinian Women and Patriarchal Relations." *Signs: Journal of Women in Culture and Society* 17, no. 4: 761–771.

Hajjar, Lisa
   1996   "Israel's Interventions among the Druze." *Middle East Report* 26, no. 3: 2–6.

Hammonds, Evelynn
   1987   "Race, Sex, AIDS: The Construction of 'Other.'" *Radical America* 20, no. 6: 28–36.

Harrison, Faye
   1994   "Racial and Gender Inequalities in Health and Health Care." *Medical Anthropology Quarterly* 8, no. 1: 90–95.

Hartmann, Betsy
   1995   *Reproductive Rights and Wrongs: The Global Politics of Population Control and Contraceptive Choice.* Boston: South End Press.

Holston, James, and Arjun Appadurai
 1996   "Cities and Citizenship." *Public Culture* 8, no. 2 (winter): 187–204.
Horn, David
 1994   *Social Bodies: Science, Reproduction, and Italian Modernity.* Princeton: Princeton University Press.
Hourani, Albert
 1991   *A History of the Arab Peoples.* Cambridge: Harvard University Press.
Hourani, Faisal
 1980   *Palestinian Political Thought, 1964–1974: A Study of the Main Documents of the Palestine Liberation Organization.* Beirut: PLO Research Center. (In Arabic.)
Hubbard, Ruth
 1995   *Profitable Promises: Essays on Women, Science, and Health.* Monroe, Maine: Common Courage Press.
Hussein, Juhaina
 1994   "The Health Services Available to Arab Women." In *Proceedings of the Conference on Health and the Status of the Arab Woman in Israel,* pp. 62–67. Haifa: Galilee Society and Israel Women's Network. (In Arabic.)
Inhorn, Marcia
 1996   *Infertility and Patriarchy: The Cultural Politics of Gender and Life in Egypt.* Philadelphia: University of Pennsylvania Press.
 1998   "Egyptian Mothers of Test Tube Babies: Gender, Islam, and the Globalization of New Reproductive Technologies." Paper presented at the annual meeting of the American Anthropological Association.
Jabbarin, Yusif
 1997   "The Politics of the Land Administration." Lecture at Galilee Society for Health Research and Services, Shfa ʿAmir, Sept. 29.
Jakubowska, Longina
 1992   "Resisting 'Ethnicity': The Israeli State and Bedouin Identity." In *The Paths to Domination, Resistance, and Terror,* edited by Carolyn Nordstrom and Jo Ann Martin, pp. 85–105. Berkeley: University of California Press.
Jiryis, Sabri
 1976   *The Arabs in Israel.* New York: Monthly Review Press.
Kahn, Susan Martha
 2000   *Reproducing Jews: A Cultural Account of Assisted Conception in Israel.* Durham, N.C.: Duke University Press.
Kanaana, Sharif
 1976   *Socio-Cultural and Psychological Adjustment of the Arab Minority in Israel.* San Francisco: R. and E. Research Associates.

1992   *Still on Vacation.* Jerusalem: Jerusalem International Center for
            Palestinian Studies.

Kanaana, Sharif, et al.
1984   *Birth and Childhood: A Study of Palestinian Culture and Soci-
            ety.* Jerusalem: In'ash Al-Usra Society. (In Arabic.)

Kanaaneh, Moslih
1996   "Peace and the Palestinians in Israel." *Magazine* (May, special
            issue for 50th anniversary of the University of Bergen), pp. 8–14.
1997   Transcribed TV interview with Abu Nasif [Fadil Jarad]. Un-
            published.

Kanaani, Ghada, and Nihaya Sih
1995   "Arrabat al-Battuf: One of the Deep Rooted Palestinian Villages
            Located in the Heart of the Galilee." *Promising Pens* ('Arrabi
            High School), Feb./Mar., p. 5. (In Arabic.)

Kapsalis, Terri
1997   *Public Privates: Performing Gynecology from Both Ends of the
            Speculum.* Durham, N.C.: Duke University Press.

Karkaby, Zahi
1994   *The Land—Motherland and Existence.* Haifa: Emile Tuma In-
            stitute for Social and Political Studies. (In Arabic.)

Kawar, Munther
1987   "Preventive Health Services." In *Proceedings of the First Health
            Conference in the Arab Community in Israel,* pp. 119–130.
            Nazareth: Al Hakeem.

Kemper, Steven
1993   "The Nation Consumed: Buying and Believing in Sri Lanka."
            Public Culture 5, no. 3: 337–393.

Khalidi, Rashid
1997   *Palestinian Identity: The Construction of Modern National
            Consciousness.* New York: Columbia University Press.

Khazoom, Aziza
1999   "Western Culture, Ethnic Stigma, and Social Closure: The Ori-
            gins of Ethnic Inequalities in Israel." Paper presented at the
            meeting of the Israeli Anthropological Association, Nazareth,
            March.

Kligman, Gail
1998   *The Politics of Duplicity: Controlling Reproduction in Ceau-
            sescu's Romania.* Berkeley: University of California Press.

Koenig, Israel
1976   "Top Secret: Memorandum Proposal—Handling the Arabs of
            Israel." SWASIA *North Africa* 3, no. 41 (Oct. 15): 1–8.

Krainy, Musa, et al.
1996   *Adolescence and Us.* Jerusalem: Israeli Ministry of Education.
            (In Arabic.)

Krause, Elizabeth
1994   "Forward vs. Reverse Gear: Politics of Proliferation and Resis-

tance in the Italian Fascist State." *Journal of Historical Sociology* 7, no. 3: 261–288.

Kretzmer, David
1990   *The Legal Status of Arabs in Israel.* Special Studies on the Middle East. Boulder, Colo.: Westview Press.

Lancaster, Roger
1997   "Sexual Positions: Caveats and Second Thoughts on 'Categories.'" *The Americas* 54, no. 1 (July): 1–16.

Lavie, Smadar
1992   "Blow-Ups in the Border Zones: Third World Israeli Authors' Groping for Home." *New Formations,* no. 18 (winter): 84–106.

Lavie, Smadar, and Ted Swedenburg
1996   "Introduction." In *Displacement, Diaspora, and Geographies of Identity,* edited by Smadar Lavie and Ted Swedenburg. Durham, N.C.: Duke University Press.

Lindenbaum, Shirley, and Margaret Lock, eds.
1993   *Knowledge, Power, and Practice: The Anthropology of Medicine and Everyday Life.* Berkeley: University of California Press.

Lockman, Zachary
1996   *Comrades and Enemies: Arab and Jewish Workers in Palestine, 1906–1948.* Berkeley: University of California Press.

Lustick, Ian
1980   *Arabs in the Jewish State: Israel's Control of a National Minority.* Austin: University of Texas Press.

Mackay, Runa
1995   *Exile in Israel: A Personal Journey with the Palestinians.* Glasgow: Wild Goose Publications.

Marcus, Abraham
1989   *The Middle East on the Eve of Modernity: Aleppo in the Eighteenth Century.* New York: Columbia University Press.

Martin, Emily
1987   *The Woman in the Body: A Cultural Analysis of Reproduction.* Boston: Beacon Press.

Masalha, Nur
1992   *Expulsion of the Palestinians: The Concept of "Transfer" in Zionist Political Thought, 1882–1948.* Washington, D.C.: Institute for Palestine Studies.
1996   "An Israeli Plan to Transfer Galilee's Christians to South America: Yosef Weitz and 'Operation Yohanan,' 1949–53." Occasional Paper no. 55, Center for Middle Eastern and Islamic Studies, University of Durham.
1997   *A Land Without a People: Israel, Transfer, and the Palestinians, 1949–1996.* London: Faber and Faber.

Massad, Joseph
1995   "Conceiving the Masculine: Gender and Palestinian Nationalism." *Middle East Journal* 49, no. 3: 467–483.

1996   "Zionism's Internal Others: Israel and the Oriental Jews." *Journal of Palestine Studies* 25, no. 4 (summer): 53–68.

2000   "The Palestinians and Jewish History: Recognition or Submission?" *Journal of Palestine Studies* 30, no. 1 (autumn): 52–67.

McCarthy, Justin

1990   *The Population of Palestine: Population History and Statistics of the Late Ottoman Period and the Mandate.* New York: Columbia University Press.

McClintock, Anne

1993   "Family Feuds: Gender, Nationalism, and the Family." *Feminist Review* 44 (summer): 61–80.

Merchand, Roland

1985   *Advertising the American Dream: Making Way for Modernity, 1920–1940.* Berkeley: University of California Press.

Mills, Mary Beth

1997   "Contesting the Margins of Modernity: Women, Migration, and Consumption in Thailand." *American Ethnologist* 24, no. 1: 37–61.

Minns, Amina, and Nadia Hijab

1990   *Citizens Apart: A Portrait of Palestinians in Israel.* London: I. B. Tauris.

Mitchell, Timothy

1988   *Colonising Egypt.* Berkeley: University of California Press.

Mohanty, Chandra

1995   "Under Western Eyes: Feminist Scholarship and Colonial Discourses." In *The Post-colonial Studies Reader,* edited by Bill Ashcroft, Gareth Griffiths, and Helen Tiffin, pp. 259–264. London: Routledge.

Moors, Annelies

1995   *Women, Property and Islam: Palestinian Experiences, 1920–1990.* Cambridge: Cambridge University Press.

Morris, Benny

1986a   "Operation Dani and the Palestinian Exodus from Lydda and Ramle in 1948." *Middle East Journal* 40, no. 1 (winter): 82–109.

1986b   "The Causes and Character of the Arab Exodus from Palestine: The Israeli Defense Force Intelligence Branch Analysis of June 1948." *Middle Eastern Studies* 22, no. 1 (Jan.): 5–19.

1988   *The Birth of the Palestinian Refugee Problem, 1947–1949.* Cambridge: Cambridge University Press.

Morsy, Soheir

1993   *Gender, Sickness, and Healing in Rural Egypt: Ethnography in Historical Context.* Boulder, Colo.: Westview Press.

Mosse, George

1985   *Nationalism and Sexuality: Middle-Class Morality and Sexual Norms in Modern Europe.* Madison: University of Wisconsin Press.

Motzafi-Haller, Pnina
  2001   "Scholarship, Identity, and Power: Mizrahí Women in Israel."
            Signs: Journal of Women in Culture and Society 26, no. 3
            (spring): 699–743.
Musallam, Basim F.
  1983   *Sex and Society in Islam: Birth Control Before the Nineteenth
            Century.* Cambridge: Cambridge University Press.
National Insurance Institute of Israel
  1996   *Annual Survey, 1995/1996.* Jerusalem. (In Hebrew.)
  1998   *Annual Survey, 1997/1998.* Jerusalem. (In Hebrew).
Offen, Karen
  1984   "Depopulation, Nationalism, and Feminism in Fin-de-Siècle
            France." *American Historical Review* 89, no. 3 (June): 648–
            676.
Ong, Aihwa
  1991   "The Gender and Labor Politics of Post Modernity." *Annual
            Review of Anthropology* 20: 279–302.
Ortner, Sherry
  1995   "Resistance and the Problem of Ethnographic Refusal." *Society
            for Comparative Study of Society and History* 37: 173–193.
Owen, Roger
  1982   *Studies in the Economic and Social History of Palestine in the
            Nineteenth and Twentieth Centuries.* London: Macmillan.
Palestine Red Crescent Society
  1993   "Towards a Palestinian Population Policy." Paper presented at
            the Palestinian Population Conference, Cairo. (In Arabic.)
Pappe, Ilan
  1988   *Britain and the Arab-Israeli Conflict, 1948–1951.* New York:
            St. Martin's Press.
  1994   *The Making of the Arab-Israeli Conflict.* London: I. B. Tauris.
  1999   *The Israel/Palestine Question: Rewriting Histories.* Edited by
            Ilan Pappe. New York: Routledge.
Parker, Andrew, Mary Russo, Doris Sommer, and Patricia Yaeger, eds.
  1992   *Nationalisms and Sexualities.* New York: Routledge.
Patriarca, Silvana
  1994   "Statistical Nation Building and the Consolidation of Regions in
            Italy." *Social Science History* 18, no. 3 (fall): 359–376.
Patton, Cindy
  1993   "From Nation to Family: Containing African AIDS." In *The
            Lesbian and Gay Studies Reader,* edited by Henry Abelove,
            Michèle Aina Barale, and David M. Halperin, pp. 127–138.
            New York: Routledge.
Paxson, Heather
  1997   "Demographics and Diaspora, Gender and Genealogy: Anthro-
            pological Notes on Greek Population Policy." *Southern Euro-
            pean Society & Politics* 2, no. 2: 34–56.

Peleg, Danny
    1997   "Palestinians and Health Insurance." Lecture at Galilee Society
                for Health Research and Services, Shfa ʿAmir, Sept. 25.
Permanent Mission of Israel to the United Nations
    1997   "Combined Initial and Second Report of Israel to the Commit-
                tee on the Elimination of Discrimination against Women: Re-
                sponse to Questions Presented by the Committee to the Delega-
                tion of Israel." Unpublished paper, July 21.
Peteet, Julie M.
    1991   *Gender in Crisis: Women and the Palestinian Resistance Move-
                ment.* New York: Columbia University Press.
Portugese, Jacqueline
    1998   *Fertility Policy in Israel: The Politics of Religion, Gender, and
                Nation.* Westport, Conn.: Praeger.
Povinelli, Elizabeth A.
    1994   "Sexual Savages/Sexual Sovereignty: Australian Colonial Texts
                and the Postcolonial Politics of Nationalism." *Diacritics* 24,
                no. 2/3: 122–150.
Rabinowitz, Dan
    1997   *Overlooking Nazareth: The Ethnography of Exclusion in the
                Galilee.* Cambridge: Cambridge University Press.
    1998   *Anthropology and the Palestinians.* Tel Aviv: Institute for Israeli
                Arab Studies.
Rand, Erica
    1995   *Barbie's Queer Accessories.* Durham, N.C.: Duke University
                Press.
Regional Committee for the Defense of Arab Lands in Israel
    1967   *The Black Book on Land Day, March 30, 1967.* Haifa: Ittihad
                Cooperative Press. (In Arabic.)
Reiker, Martina
    1992   "Constructing Palestinian Subalternity in the Galilee: Reflec-
                tions on Representations of the Palestinian Peasantry." *Inscrip-
                tions* 6: 115–133.
Reiss, Nira
    1991   *The Health Care of the Arabs in Israel.* Special Studies on the
                Middle East. Boulder, Colo.: Westview Press.
Rolph-Trouillot, Michele
    1998   "Globalization Then and Now: The Perspective of the World."
                Paper presented at the conference "Globalization from Below,"
                Duke University.
Rosenfeld, Henry
    1964   "From Peasantry to Wage Labour and Residual Peasantry: The
                Transformation of an Arab Village." In *Process and Pattern in
                Culture,* edited by R. A. Manners, pp. 211–234. Chicago: Al-
                dine Publishing.

Rouhana, Nadim N.
  1997   *Palestinian Citizens in an Ethnic Jewish State.* New Haven: Yale
            University Press.
Rudy, Preston
  1998   "Janitors Organizing California Cities: Globalization from Be-
            low as Local Transformation and Persistent Variation." Paper
            presented at the conference "Globalization from Below," Duke
            University.
Sabir, Yafa, and Rahel Mintz
  1992   *A World That Is Filling Up: Plant, Animal, and Human Popula-
            tion Groups.* Ramot: Tel Aviv University Press. (In Hebrew and
            Arabic.)
Sa'di, Ahmad H.
  1992   "Between State Ideology and Minority National Identity: Pales-
            tinians in Israel and Israel Social Science Research." *Review of
            Middle East Studies* 5: 110–129.
Sa'di, Ahmad, and Hatim Kanaaneh
  1990   "Poverty among the Palestinians in Israel, 1969–1988." Paper
            written for the Galilee Society for Health Research and Services.
Said, Edward
  1988   "Profile of the Palestinian People." In *Blaming the Victims,* ed-
            ited by Edward Said and Christopher Hitchens, pp. 235–296.
            New York: Verso.

  1995   *Peace and Its Discontents: Essays on Palestine in the Middle
            East.* New York: Vintage Books.
Salzberger, Lotte, Sarah Magidor, Amy Avgar, and Janet Baumgol-Land
  1991   "Patterns of Contraceptive Behavior among Jerusalem Women
            Seeking Pregnancy Counseling, 1980–1989." Unpublished pa-
            per, Paul Baerwald School of Social Work, Hebrew University of
            Jerusalem.
Sayer, Derek
  1994   "Everyday Forms of State Formation: Some Dissident Remarks
            on 'Hegemony.'" In *Everyday Forms of State Formation: Revo-
            lution and the Negotiation of Rule in Modern Mexico,* edited by
            G. Joseph and D. Nugent, pp. 367–377. Durham, N.C.: Duke
            University Press.
Schein, Louisa
  1997   "Of Cargoes and Satellites: Imagined Cosmopolitanism in
            China." Paper presented to the annual meeting of the American
            Anthropology Association, Washington, D.C.
Scheper-Hughes, Nancy
  1992   *Death Without Weeping: The Violence of Everyday Life in
            Brazil.* Berkeley: University of California Press.
Schneider, Jane, and Peter Schneider
  1995   "Coitus Interruptus and Family Respectability in Catholic Eu-

rope: A Sicilian Case Study." In *Conceiving the New World Order*, edited by Faye Ginsburg and Rayna Rapp, pp. 177–194. Berkeley: University of California Press.

1996   *Festival of the Poor: Fertility Decline and the Ideology of Class in Sicily, 1860–1980.* Tucson: University of Arizona Press.

Sha'ban, Dina

1997   "Reproductive Health in Palestine." Summary paper presented to the Intercountry Meeting on Women's Needs and Gender Perspectives in Countries of the Eastern Mediterranean Region, World Health Organization, Casablanca, Nov. 10–13.

Shafir, Gershon, and Yoav Peled

1998   "The Dynamics of Citizenship in Israel and the Israeli-Palestinian Peace Process." In *The Citizenship Debates,* edited by Gershon Shafir, pp. 251–262. Minneapolis: University of Minnesota Press.

Shahak, Israel

1989   "A History of the Concept of 'Transfer' in Zionism." *Journal of Palestine Studies* 18, no. 3: 22–37.

Sharoni, Simona

1995   *Gender and the Israeli-Palestinian Conflict: The Politics of Women's Resistance.* Syracuse, N.Y.: Syracuse University Press.

Shepherd, Naomi

1987   *The Zealous Intruders: The Western Rediscovery of Palestine.* San Francisco: Harper and Row.

Shohat, Ella

1988   "Mizrahim in Israel: Zionism from the Standpoint of Its Jewish Victims." *Social Text: Theory, Culture, and Ideology* 19/20 (fall): 1–35.

1992   "Rethinking Jews and Muslims: Quincentennial Reflections." *Middle East Report,* no. 178: 25–29.

1999   "The Invention of the Mizrahim." *Journal of Palestine Studies* 29, no. 1 (autumn): 5–20.

Simmons, Ruth, and Christopher Elias

1994   "The Study of Client-Provider Interactions: A Review of Methodological Issues." *Studies in Family Planning* 25, no. 1: 1–17.

Slyomovics, Susan

1998   *The Object of Memory: Arab and Jew Narrate the Palestinian Village.* Philadelphia: University of Pennsylvania Press.

Socolof, Robert

1997   "Abraham Fund Delegation Meets with Israel's Bedouin Community." *Abraham Fund Quarterly* 4, no. 1 (winter): 1, 6.

Sofer, Arnon

1989   "The Arabs of Israel—From Village to Metropolis." *New East: Quarterly of the Israel Oriental Society* 32 (125–128): 97–104.

Stein, Rebecca Luna

1995   "Remapping Israeli and Palestinian Tourism." *Middle East Report* 25, no. 5: 16–19.

1996   "National Itineraries, Itinerant Nations: Israeli Tourism and Palestinian Cultural Production." *Social Text* 16, no. 3: 89–124.

Stoler, Ann Laura

1991   "Carnal Knowledge and Imperial Power: Gender, Race, and Morality in Colonial Asia." In *Gender at the Crossroads of Knowledge,* edited by Micaela di Leonardo, pp. 51–101. Berkeley: University of California Press.

1997   *Race and the Education of Desire: Foucault's History of Sexuality and the Colonial Order of Things.* Durham, N.C.: Duke University Press.

Swedenburg, Ted

1995   *Memories of Revolt: The 1936–1939 Rebellion and the Palestinian National Past.* Minneapolis: University of Minnesota Press.

Swirski, Barbara, Hatim Kanaaneh, and Amy Avgar

1998   "Health Care in Israel." *Israel Equality Monitor* (Adva Center, Tel Aviv), no. 9: 1–32.

Tamari, Salim

1981   "Building Other People's Homes: The Palestinian Peasant's Household and Work in Israel." *Journal of Palestine Studies* 1, no. 41 (autumn): 31–66.

1982   "Factionalism and Class Formation in Recent Palestinian History." In *Studies in the Economic and Social History of Palestine in the Nineteenth and Twentieth Centuries,* edited by Roger Owen. London: Macmillan.

Tamari, Salim, and Ann Scott

1991   "Fertility of Palestinian Women Between the National Perspective and Social Reality." *Women's Affairs* 1: 155–185. (In Arabic.)

Tamish, Safa'

1996   *Misconceptions about Sexuality and Sexual Behavior in Palestinian Society: Proceedings of Workshops in the West Bank and Gaza.* London: World University Service.

Tober, Diane

1998   "'Grass Roots Eugenics' and Emerging Populations: Donor Insemination and the Alternative American Family." Paper presented at the annual meeting of the American Anthropological Association, Philadelphia.

Torstrick, Rebecca Lee

1993   "Raising and Rupturing Boundaries: The Politics of Identity in Acre, Israel." Ph.D. dissertation, Washington University.

Tsing, Anna Lowenhaupt

1993   *In the Realm of the Diamond Queen.* Princeton: Princeton University Press.

Tuma, Emile
    1982   *The Path of Struggle of the Arab Masses in Israel.* Acre: Dar Abu
                Salma Press. (In Arabic.)
United Nations Relief and Works Agency
    1993   "Knowledge, Attitudes, and Practices Survey of Palestinian Ref-
                ugee Women in the West Bank." Unpublished report by the Ma-
                ternal Health Project.
Urla, Jacqueline, and Alan Swedlund
    1995   "The Anthropometry of Barbie: Unsettling Ideals of the Femi-
                nine Body in Popular Culture." In *Deviant Bodies: Critical Per-
                spectives on Difference in Science and Popular Culture,* edited
                by Jennifer Terry and Jacqueline Urla, pp. 277–313. Blooming-
                ton: Indiana University Press.
Wiemer, Reinhard
    1983   "Zionism and the Arabs after the Establishment of the State of
                Israel." In *Palestinians over the Green Line,* edited by Alexander
                Schölch. London: Ithaca Press.
Wilford, Rick
    1998   "Women, Ethnicity, and Nationalism: Surveying the Ground."
                In *Women, Ethnicity, and Nationalism: The Politics of Transi-
                tion,* edited by Rick Wilford and Robert L. Miller, pp. 1–22.
                New York: Routledge.
Wilford, Rick, and Robert L. Miller, eds.
    1998   *Women, Ethnicity, and Nationalism: The Politics of Transition.*
                New York: Routledge.
Williams, Patricia
    1991   *The Alchemy of Race and Rights.* Cambridge: Harvard Univer-
                sity Press.
Wood, Davida
    1993   "Politics of Identity in a Palestinian Village in Israel." In *The
                Violence Within,* edited by K. B. Warren, pp. 87–121. Boulder,
                Colo.: Westview Press.
Yiftachel, Oren
    1991   "State Policies, Land Control, and an Ethnic Minority: The
                Arabs in the Galilee Region, Israel." *Environment and Planning
                D: Society and Space* 9: 329–362.
    1995   "The Dark Side of Modernism: Planning as Control of an Eth-
                nic Minority." In *Postmodern Cities and Spaces,* edited by So-
                phie Watson and Katherine Gibson, pp. 216–241. Cambridge,
                Mass.: Basil Blackwell.
Yisai, Yael
    1978   "Abortion in Israel: Social Demand and Political Responses."
                Policy Studies Journal 7, no. 2: 270–290.
Yuval-Davis, Nira
    1982   *Israeli Women and Men: Divisions Behind the Unity.* London:
                Change Publications.

1987   "The Jewish Collectivity." In *Women in the Middle East.* London: Zed Books.

Zacharia, Christian

1996   "Power in Numbers: A Call for a Census of the Palestinian People." *Arab Studies Quarterly* 18, no. 3: 37–52.

Zureik, Elia T.

1976   "Transformation of Class Structure among the Arabs in Israel: From Peasantry to Proletariat." *Journal of Palestine Studies* 6, no. 1: 39–66.

1979   *The Palestinians in Israel: A Study in Internal Colonialism.* Boston: Routledge and Kegan Paul.

1999   "Constructing Palestine: Population Count, Borders, and Surveillance." Unpublished paper, Queen's University, Kingston, Ont.

NEWSPAPER AND MAGAZINE ARTICLES

Chicago Tribune

Sept. 3, 1998   Clarence Lusane, "Invisible Nation; Millions on Society's Margins Are Overlooked in the Census Head Count," p. 25.

Fasl ul-Maqal (in Arabic)

Nov. 1, 1996a   "Plan to Judaize the Galilee Formally Revealed," pp. 1, 16.

Nov. 1, 1996b   "Whose Responsibility Is It to Change the Equation?!" p. 10.

Nov. 29, 1996   "Israeli Planning Map Deals with Arabs as a Stumbling Block Before Development and Uses Jews as a Tool in the Demographic War," pp. 8, 15.

Sept. 24, 1997 Afif Ibrahim, "Were the Children of Palestine Kidnapped? A Revisiting of the Children of Yemen," p. 3.

Focus: University of Haifa English Newsletter

Fall 1995   "Are Bedouins Changing, Modernizing? The Jury Is Still Out," p. 10.

Ha'aretz

Apr. 20, 1997   Amira Hass, "Violence in the Midst of Plenty." (In English.)

Feb. 11, 1998   Danny Rubinstein, "An Ironic Outcome in East Jerusalem." (In English.)

Mar. 4, 1998   Daniel Ben Simon, "Home on the Range?" (In English.)

Mar. 18, 1998   Joseph Algazy, "Battle in Bed Still Favors Arabs." (In English and Hebrew.)

July 8, 1998   Relly Sa'ar, "Pregnant Women Should Be Helped to Choose Life, Cabinet Told." (In English.)

July 9, 1998   "A Superfluous Demographic Initiative." Editorial. (In English.)

July 14, 1998   Joseph Algazy, "Containment, Mideast-Style." (In English.)

Aug. 17, 1998   Joseph Algazy, "Israeli Arabs Slam Memo Calling Them a 'Threat.'" (In English.)

Oct. 22, 1998   Sharon Gal, "Attorney General Looks into Disqualifying Likud Mayoral Hopeful in Karmiel." (In English.)

'Ittihad, al- (in Arabic)

May 25, 1994   "Every Month, 4 Thousand Newborns in Gaza," p. 1.
Sept. 5, 1994   "Victory for the Mind," p. 7.
Sept. 7, 1994   "Call for Investment in Humans Most Important Principle
                  in Existence," p. 3.
June 6, 1995   Dr. Fu'ad Khatib, "Commentary," p. 3.
June 9, 1995   "Danger of Judaization Again." Supplement, pp. 1–4.
June 20, 1995   "New Rumor: A Wall Cries in 'Ara," p. 9.
July 6, 1995   "Israeli Authorities Confiscate ID Cards of Palestinian
                  Women Forced to Move to the West Bank," p. 2.
July 28, 1995   Riad Baydas, "On the Latest Fashion," p. 22.
Aug. 4, 1995   Yusif Farah, "I Am Free and I Am Strong," p. 10.
Oct. 19, 1995   " 'Peace Bloc' Calls for Not Including Occupied Territories'
                  Settlements in Population Census," p. 16.
Nov. 1, 1995   "Rabin: The Red Line for Arabs Is 20% of the Population,"
                  p. 1.
Nov. 15, 1995   "Register that I Am Arab," p. 2.
Apr. 9, 1996   Asmahan Khalaili, "Aunt Hasibah and the Hospital," p. 12.
May 1996   Amal Shhadi, "16% of Women Have Unwanted Pregnan-
                  cies Because of Lack of Awareness."
Nov. 15, 1996   "We Are Not Asleep . . . !" p. 7.
Mar. 6, 1998   "Bourg-Sharon Plan." Supplement, p. 3.

Jerusalem Post

July 12, 1992   A. J. Ochert, "Israel's Demography." Letter to the editor.
July 14, 1992   David Rudge, "Arabs to Get Equal Child Benefits," p. 6.
May 26, 1994   "Ravitz Calls for Abolition of Law of Return," p. 3.

Jerusalem Report

June 15, 1995   Gershom Gorenberg, "A Holocaust? Not Quite," p. 54.
Aug. 26, 1999   Isabel Kershner, "The Population Bomb," pp. 28–29.

Jerusalem Times

Oct. 13, 1995   "Survey Won't Undermine the Rights of Jerusalemites,"
                  p. 6.

Kul ul-'Arab (in Arabic)

June 14, 1995a   "Citizen of Baqa El-Gharbiyyi Prevented from Buying
                  House in Katzir," p. 5.
June 14, 1995b   Wadi' 'Awawdi, "Yihya Rahim Could Not Tolerate Yihi'el
                  Rihamim Exposing Blatant Racist Treatment," p. 4.

Kul un-Nisa' (in Arabic)

Apr. 1996   Yusif Al-Qaz'a, "My Homeland in a Woman," pp. 35–36.

Ma'ariv (in Hebrew)

Aug. 16, 1998   "Israel's Arabs Have Basis to Demand Autonomy," pp. 2–3.

Manbar, al- (in Arabic)

1995 (issue 4)   Hasan Ghanayim, "Family Planning and Its Social Effects,"
                  p. 60.

Manchester Guardian Weekly

Feb. 21, 1988   Yossi Melman and Dan Raviv, "A Final Solution of the
                  Palestinian Problem?" p. 19.

New York
   July 14, 1997   Craig Horowitz, "Are American Jews Disappearing?"
                   pp. 30–37, 101, 108.
New Yorker
   June 23, 1997   Amitav Ghosh, "India's Untold War of Independence,"
                   pp. 104–121.
New York Times
   Dec. 11, 1997   "Palestinian Census Ignites Controversy over Jerusalem,"
                   p. A3.
   Mar. 1, 1998   "Israeli Learns Some Are More Israeli than Others,"
                   pp. A1, A6.
   Nov. 16, 1998   "To Bind the Faith, Free Trips to Israel for Diaspora
                   Youth," p. A8.
Sawt ul-Haq wal-Hurriyya (The Voice of Truth and Freedom) (in Arabic)
   June 16, 1995   Umm Mu'ath, "Great Women," back cover.
   June 30, 1995   Walid Abd-il-Latif, "Sunna with Suspended Sentence,"
                   back cover.
   May 1996   Khitam Mahmud Dahli, "Multiply and Reproduce."
Sinnara, as- (in Arabic)
   Oct. 20, 1995   "Palestinians Refuse to Include Jerusalem in Census," p. 1.
Washington Report on Middle East Affairs
   Sept./Oct. 1993 "Jews Now Majority in East Jerusalem," p. 4.
Yedi'ot Ahronot (in Hebrew)
   Oct. 31, 1996   "The Goal: 2.4 Million Jews in the Galilee," p. 6.

WEB SITE

Israel Ministry of Foreign Affairs
   1999   "Ministry of Labor and Social Affairs."
               http://www.israel-mfa.gov.il/mfa/go.asp?MFAH00hy0
Qatamish, Ahmad
   1998   "Making Hope: The Need to Build a New Movement for Pales-
               tinian Liberation." *Free Arab Voice*, Oct. 31. http://www.mind-
               spring.com/~fav

Index

Indexer: Ruth Elwell
Compositor: G&S Typesetters, Inc.
Text: 10/13 Sabon
Display: Sabon